Other Books By The Authors

The Colorado Angling Guide

The Wyoming Angling Guide

The
MONTANA
Angling Guide

The
MONTANA
Angling Guide

Chuck Fothergill and
Bob Sterling

Stream Stalker® Publishing
Woody Creek, Colorado

First Edition
                    8 9

Published by:
Stream Stalker® Publishing
Box 238
Woody Creek, Colorado 81656

ISBN: 0-9614704-2-9

Set in Optima type by Suzy Sterling of Word Works, Woody Creek, Colorado and printed by Walsworth Publishing Company, Marceline, Missouri, U.S.A.

Maps, illustrations and artwork by Robert Sterling, Jr.

Contents

INTRODUCTION

Let's imagine that someone conducts a survey of all trout fishermen and asks one pertinent question: "What state has the rivers that best match the trout rivers of your dreams, those ribbons of seduction that flow through your daydreams, splash the fount of your desire and excite your imagination of the perfect fishing opportunity, and is the <u>one</u> state that you would visit if it were your last ever?" A truly in-depth question such as this deserves only one answer—MONTANA!

This state is blessed with abundant water; water surging from the ground creating instant spring creeks, water from the mountains collecting in remote forests, water charging from glacially-carved mountain tops and flowing into fertile valleys to form the many rivers whose names conjure enticing images in the minds of anglers who wish to search their currents for native cutthroat, feisty rainbow and the elusive brown trout.

Montana is our nation's fourth largest state and is also one of the least populated. Its wide open spaces border no fewer than three Canadian provinces. Its land area is equal to the combined total of that in Connecticut, Delaware, Maine, Maryland, Massachusetts, New Jersey, Rhode Island, Vermont, Virginia and much of West Virginia. Montana is truly "Big Sky" country—flatlands of wheat in the east, rolling hills rising to rugged mountains in the west. Its largest cities would be no more than average-sized towns when compared to the metropolitan communities in the more heavily populated eastern areas of the country. Traffic delays are rare and traffic jams all but unknown. Occasionally a cattle drive will slow progress along the highway, but this event often proves to be more interesting than irritating. Besides, how many roundups does the average tourist witness back home?

The entree we call Montana has many smoothly blended ingredients, yet fortunately the recipe can still be modified to meet individual tastes. Montana isn't all any one thing. It is history, mountains, plains, fishing, hunting, hiking, golf, tennis, sightseeing and relaxing. It's Lewis and Clark, grizzly bears, caddis flies, caves, mines, wheat, power-generating dams and gourmet float trips down scenic, remote rivers. And Montana also has something else— more important than all of the above— friendly, helpful people. It's a state in which you feel at ease. If you wish to talk, you'll find someone to listen; if you

1

you want to learn, you'll find a knowledgeable voice to explain; if you need some help, it will be close at hand. There seems to be little paranoia here, just people who know who they are and what they're doing and no bravado or explanations are necessary. Visitors to Montana find that people tend to trust each other and this trait is felt wherever you go. Montanans make the visitor feel at home and when it's time to leave, it will be with reluctance. The best part of leaving is knowing that Montana isn't going anywhere; it will be there for a return trip—and who knows, the fishing could be even better next time!

It would require a small library to tell the whole story about Montana. Many volumes exist which cover specialized facets of the state's personality—past and present—from many points of view. This volume now becomes part of that collection.

The primary theme of this book is trout fishing and the primary focus is on the many productive streams and rivers in the state. A few lakes are included, but many excellent ones are not. We realize that a large number of fishermen come to Montana on family vacations and pursue activities other than casting to trout. That is why we address the needs of the entire family by highlighting the many towns and cities situated in close proximity to rivers we write about. To serve the non-fishing family members, we describe those recreational, cultural and community activities and events that all family members can enjoy. The community maps and business listings are included for convenient reference. These businesses particularly value patronage by fishing families who visit their community and trust their goods and services will add to the enjoyment of one's stay in their town.

The rivers, lakes and towns are presented as objectively as possible. They all have differing characteristics and their own unique personality. When using this book to assist in your vacation planning, it's best not to spread your time in various areas of Montana too thinly. Try to allow enough time on each water and in each town to at least gain a bit of the flavor each has to offer. This may require several return trips!

The folks in Montana know the importance of tourism and that high-quality fishing will continue to attract many visitors. Both individuals and angling organizations coordinate closely with the Montana Department of Fish, Wildlife and Parks (DFWP) to implement research projects that will enhance the fisheries. Trout Unlimited, the Federation of Fly Fishers and the Montana Trout Foundation are non-profit entities who work both independently and with federal and state agencies on projects to gather and amplify data concerning the state's fisheries. These and other volunteer groups work very hard to improve the quality of fishing for everyone and need all of us to support their efforts with ideas, time and monetary contributions. These organizations delve into the effects on fish and their food supply caused by stream channelization, de-watering, pollution, thermal shock, habitat destruction or creation, fishing pressure, fish harvesting and a raft of other problems that constantly seem to bedevil our favorite rivers. We support the goals of these organizations and suggest you contact a tackle shop for up-to-date addresses and phone numbers should you need more information concerning their activities.

Even though this is a book concerned with Montana fishing, we felt it necessary to include two areas of strong fishing interest outside the legal boundaries of the state. They are Island Park, Idaho and Yellowstone National Park in Wyoming. Both of these areas are fished extensively by visitors who "headquarter" in West Yellowstone, Bozeman, Gardiner or other nearby towns. Driving times from one area to another are relatively short and conceivably you could spend the morning on the Henry's Fork in Idaho, move to the Madison River in Montana for the afternoon, and finish the day in Yellowstone fishing the Firehole. We trust you'll find the inclusion of these two regions a valuable addition to your trip planning and eventually to your Montana fishing experience.

MONTANA—AND IN THE BEGINNING...

And in the beginning, Jefferson created Lewis and Clark. Not literally of course, but President Thomas Jefferson did create the "corps of discovery," an expedition to be led under the joint command of Captain Meriwether Lewis and Captain William Clark. Their mission was to commence with their assignment at St. Louis, proceed into the Montana Territory which had been acquired by the U. S. in 1804 as part of the Louisiana Purchase, follow the Missouri River to its headwaters, find a "Northwest Passage" to the Pacific and return to St. Louis when the mission was complete. They accomplished all of the above within twenty-seven months, seven months of which were spent in Montana. This journey was the beginning of what is known as "historic" Montana—that period of time in which a written record has been kept. The journals of Lewis and Clark are both fascinating and comprehensive and the landscape of Montana is abundant with landmarks and physical features that either bear their surnames or bear names designated by them and recorded in the diaries they maintained throughout their travels. In all, they traveled 1,900 miles throughout Montana, sometimes together, sometimes on separate trails. One thing is certain to the traveler today—their impact on the history of Montana cannot go unnoticed. It's easy to understand why their activities have been referred to as the most famous expedition in U. S. history.

This volume was not written as a history primer, but we sincerely believe that an angler who spends time fishing anywhere will leave a bit richer if he learns even a small amount about the history of the area he visits. We feel the significance of the Lewis and Clark expedition is worthy of a brief chronicle here to help enhance your enjoyment of traveling throughout the state.

After leaving St. Louis in the spring of 1804, the party followed the Missouri River up through North Dakota to the mouth of the Yellowstone River where they hired a French Canadian trapper to act as their guide and interpreter. At the same time, they hired his Shoshone wife, Sacajawea, who ultimately proved to be most valuable to the success of the expedition. They wintered in North Dakota that year and finally entered Montana in April of 1805.

By June the party had reached the Great Falls of the Missouri and were forced to portage. After eighteen days of transferring their equipment they

4

proceeded up the river and on July 27 arrived at the source of the Missouri River, the target of their journey, 2,500 miles from St. Louis. The expedition then proceeded up the Jefferson River, the Beaverhead River, then northwest to the Bitterroot Valley and finally to an August passage over Lolo Pass, into Idaho and on to the Pacific Ocean where the party remained through the winters of 1805 and 1806.

In June of 1806 the expedition once again entered Montana, over Lolo Pass, and decided to split forces in order to explore a greater area. Captain Lewis proceeded north down the Bitterroot River, then northeast along the Blackfoot, which the Indians referred to as "The River of the Road to the Buffalo." On July 11 his group had again arrived at Great Falls on their way to the Marias River country for further exploration there.

Meanwhile, Captain Clark, Sacajawea and ten men went south up the Bitterroot Valley, then down into the upper Big Hole, down to Grasshopper Gulch and finally northeast to Three Forks. They proceeded up the Gallatin River for a short distance, then east over Bozeman Pass to Livingston. They continued east down the Yellowstone River and on July 25 arrived at a solitary rock formation east of Billings that was used by the Indians as a signal tower. Here Clark climbed the rock, carved his name into its surface and named the landmark Pompey's Pillar, after young Pomp, Sacajawea's son.

On August 12 Lewis and Clark reunited at the confluence of the Missouri and Yellowstone Rivers to continue back to St. Louis where they were greeted on September 23.

This brief summary of the journey cannot, of course, portray the emotion of discovery that must have excited and stimulated the party on a daily basis as they rowed hand-built boats up uncharted rivers, walked paths historically known only to Indians and sighted thousands of buffalo churning the ground to dust. Out of view of any man-made object, the journey had to be an adventure of grit, tenacity, joy and hardship. To put that in terms of the modern man, just try to imagine what things will be like two hundred years hence!

After Lewis and Clark completed their expeditions, there was a modest influx of trappers and fur traders to this area who responded to a national demand for beaver pelts. The growth of this area, however, occurred rather sporadically until the 1850's, at which time the development of this territory accelerated in a hurry. In general, the period between 1850 and 1865 was the period of the prospector and miner, after which followed the cowboy, the homesteader, the railroader and the retail businessman. A short review of Montana's historical highlights looks like this.

1841—First settlement at Stevensville.

1862—Gold found on Grasshopper Creek; and the mining camp of Bannack was established.

1863—Gold found in Alder Gulch.

1864—Montana became a Territory with the capital at Bannack.

1865—The capital was moved to Virginia City. During the 1860's and 1870's the mountains were becoming settled, but the plains still were home to the Indians.

1875—The capital was moved again, this time to Helena, after gold was discovered there in Last Chance Gulch.

1876—June 25 and 26—Lt. Col. George Custer and a battalion of 260 men attached to the 7th Cavalry, were killed by a large force of Sioux and Cheyenne warriors at the Battle of the Little Bighorn.

1877—Nez Perce Indian War—two battles—the first at the Battle of the Big Hole and the last at Chief Joseph's Battleground of the Bear's Paw. Both are now State Monuments.

1876 through 1881—Buffalo hunters exterminated the bison herds. Estimates indicate up to thirteen million animals before the hunt and two hundred afterward! Indians were now starving and during this decade they were sent to the reservations.

1880's—The cattle boom; cattle brought into Montana from the east, from Texas and from the state's western valleys.

1881—The railroad came to Montana Territory. The first line was the Northern Pacific, followed in a few years by the Great Northern.

1885—Butte had now become the greatest mining town in the west.

1886-87—Winter cold and storms killed most of the over one million cattle in the state.

1889—November 8—Montana became the country's forty-first state.

1880-1890—The population grew from 38,000 to 132,000.

1910—Free land caused a land rush, the ground was plowed and fenced and life in the Twentieth Century began!

Montana Facts and Figures

Animal: Grizzly Bear
Bird: Western Meadowlark
Capital: Helena
Fish: Blackspotted Cutthroat Trout
Flower: Bitterroot (Lewisia rediviva)
Gemstones: Yogo Sapphire and Montana Agate
Grass: Bluebunch Wheatgrass
Tree: Ponderosa Pine
Derivation: Latin, meaning "mountainous"
Nicknames: "Treasure State," Big Sky Country," "Land of the Shining Mountains"
Fourth Largest State: 147,138 square miles; 93,157,952 acres; average 550 miles long, 275 miles wide
65 million acres in farms and ranches
Average farm/ranch size is 2,597 acres Elevations: from 1820 feet to 12,799 feet
56 Counties
126 incorporated towns and cities
Population: 1985 census—836,000—the sixth least populated state; averages 111 acres per person.
Home to 7 Indian Tribes
Home to 7 Indian Reservations
11 National Forests
12 Wilderness areas
7 State Forests
2 National Parks
11 State Parks
20 State Monuments
67 State Recreation areas
232 Fishing Access sites
Primary Industries: Agriculture, timber and lumber products, mining, energy and tourism. Tourism is the second largest employer in Montana.

MONTANA OUTDOORS

Camping

Thousands of visitors to Montana, whether fishermen or families, whether passing through or staying for awhile, enjoy spending their nights camping in the forest rather than staying in towns or at commercial accommodations. Whether in a pup tent, pop-up or recreational vehicle, camping in Montana is similar to camping anywhere else in the country. Rules will apply, permits and fees may be required, length of stay at any one site might be limited, or fires could be prohibited during severely dry conditions. Otherwise, a night in the woods is pretty much the same everywhere, particularly since most campgrounds are managed under the jurisdiction of the U. S. Forest Service. Other agencies such as the U. S. Bureau of Land Management, the National Park Service and state recreation commissions also maintain facilities for use by the public.

Some campgrounds remain open throughout the winter, but most are usable only during the warmer months from May through September, or even June through August in higher elevations where water valves must be shut off to avoid freezing. Length of stay in a given area is usually limited to ten or fourteen consecutive days, and fees vary from none to $10.00 per night depending upon facilities provided.

An inquiry at the local Forest Service office is always a good idea when planning to camp in an unfamiliar area as regulations do vary concerning road conditions, vehicle length restrictions, accommodation of pets, creature comforts available, fire, firearm and fireworks restrictions, firewood gathering, boat launching, and trash removal. Roads to some remote areas can be slippery and dangerous after periods of rain, so information on their condition should be acquired before using them.

Temperature variation, from nighttime lows to daytime highs can vary as much as fifty degrees. Combine this with elevation changes and wind chill factors and camping can become considerably more challenging than in states where such conditions are less dramatic. The interplay of mountain peaks and rain clouds can quickly cause a dry day to become wet and warm air to become cold. These stormy conditions can be dangerous if you are caught outside with no shelter nearby and without clothing to protect you from the cold and wet. Whenever you leave civilization to head for the high country, don't overlook the possibility of inclement weather, as afternoon showers commonly occur after the nicest morning sunshine you can imagine. The rain could turn to snow; your body temperature could drop allowing hypothermia to set in; disorientation could confuse your senses, and you might take the wrong trail. This is not a pleasant story, but well within the realm of possibility in a locale where weather conditions sometimes do change quickly and dramatically, even during the summer months.

Because much of today's camping is done in organized areas with some degree of developed facilities, it's important for our own comfort, and that of neighboring campers, to recognize what is available to us, what our responsibilities are and what we might do to enhance our experience. A few thoughts for consideration:

1. Be very careful with fires. Much of Montana receives little rainfall and fire danger can be very high at times.

2. Use a rock fire circle as protection from wind blowing hot embers to areas not within your control.

3. Firewood is not normally provided at campsites and deadfall should be used. In most areas it is easily obtainable outside the campground itself.

4. When leaving the campsite, be sure to drown fires thoroughly with water. Make sure the entire fire is soaked and all embers are extinguished.

5. Campgrounds in national forests usually contain tables, toilets, garbage receptacles, fire grates and individual parking spurs.. Attempt to leave the campground at least as clean as you found it.

6. If your camping site doesn't have piped, drinking water, be sure to treat or boil for at least ten minutes the water you drink from springs,, lakes or streams.

7. Most campgrounds have a maximum use limit of fourteen days.

8. Use biodegradable soap for dishwashing or bathing and dispose of grey water away from streams.

9. If you intend to use an organized campground, try to select a site by noon in areas of heavy use.

10. Fees are usually charged at campgrounds that provide drinking water. Such fees are normally deposited in envelopes found at the campground entrance.

We have indicated on the maps all those campgrounds that seem reasonable to be designated in a guide of this type. Many campgrounds have bulletin boards offering useful information on the local area and nearby attractions; forest offices can provide information, maps, and permits as might be required to enter protected, hazardous, or restricted areas.

Hiking

In some of the more remote regions of Montana, particularly in the wilderness areas, hikers and back packers are advised to carry U. S. Geological Survey 7.5 minute topographic maps. An index to these excellent maps is usually available at U. S. Forest Service offices in the district where you're hiking or from the U. S. Geological Survey; write to: U. S. Geological Survey, Denver Federal Center, Box 25286, Denver, Colorado 80225.

Use normal hiking precautions when going out for more than just a short stroll; take along some snacks, a flashlight, matches, a jacket or sweater, rain gear, proper shoes or boots, first aid kit, appropriate maps, sunscreen, sunglasses and drinking water. Be sure to tell someone where you plan to hike and when you expect to return.

Always be prepared for bad weather as mountain storms can, and do, strike with almost no warning and can cause serious problems. During electrical storms, stay inside your vehicle if possible; if not, find a dense stand of timber, crouch between rocks in a boulder field, or, if possible, take shelter in a cave.

If you become lost, try to remain calm and find a high point from which to get your bearings and plan a route to safety. If you find a trail, stay on it heading downhill. Follow a watercourse downstream. If no trail or watercourse is available, stay where you are, build a fire, relax and enjoy the scenery. It is by far wiser to save your energy and let others find you than to expend it and put yourself into a dangerous situation. If you have the proper equipment, make signal noises or light flashes; and remember that three of either indicate that you need help.

As a general rule during the summer, you can expect daytime temperatures to be between seventy and ninety degrees F. in all mountainous areas discussed in this book; you should expect nighttime temperatures to fall into the forties. A sweater or heavy shirt is usually needed in early morning and late evening and the time in between is generally shirt sleeve weather. With every 1,000 feet of rise in elevation, the temperature drops about 4 degrees F., which is the same as going approximately 350 miles to the north. Don't hesitate to throw another sweater into the suitcase!

Mountain Sickness

This problem occurs when the human body is subjected to an excessively rapid rise to a higher elevation, normally over a mile high. Symptoms of mountain sickness include nausea, diarrhea, shortness of breath, insomnia, fast heartbeat, headache, nasal congestion, cough, increased flatulence, fatigue and loss of appetite. To alleviate these symptoms, return to a lower elevation if possible. When first arriving at higher elevations, eat lightly, avoid alcohol, coffee and sugar drinks and keep physical exertion to a minimum. If you feel the effects of mountain sickness, stop and rest, breathe deeply, take nourishment from fruit juice or candy and drink plenty of liquids.

Hyperventilation

Lightheadedness and a chilled feeling are the symptoms of hyperventilation which is caused by excessively rapid breathing creating a decrease in the carbon dioxide levels in the blood. To treat this problem, relax and breathe into a bag or hat until normal breathing is restored.

Hypothermia

This is the number one killer of outdoor recreationists. It is caused by exposure to cold and is aggravated by wetness, wind, and exhaustion. Cold reaches the brain, reasoning power is lost, and you are not aware of what is happening. You lose control of your hands, your internal temperature drops, and this leads to stupor, collapse, and finally death.

It's very important to stay dry. Choose rain gear that covers the neck, head, body and legs. Most hypothermia cases occur between the temperatures of thirty and fifty degrees F.; sudden, summer storms in the mountains often produce these temperatures. In essence, you freeze to death even though the air temperature is above the freezing mark.

Symptoms: Slurred speech, uncontrollable shivering, incoherence, loss of memory, fumbling hands, problems with walking, drowsiness (to sleep is to die), exhaustion.

Treatment: Get the victim out of the wind and rain. Strip off all wet clothes and get the victim into warm, dry clothes and/or sleeping bag. Give the victim warm drinks but no alcohol. Keep the victim awake. Build a fire to keep the camp warm and get help as soon as possible.

Giardiasis

This serious disease is contracted by drinking untreated water containing the organism Giardia lamblia. The water can have a very good smell, look and taste, and animals may drink from it, but while they are immune to the effects of the disease, you are not. Fortunately, Giardia is curable when properly diagnosed and treated by a physician.

Symptoms: Diarrhea, little appetite, abdominal cramps, nausea, fever, increased gas and bloating. Signs are not necessarily immediate; they may show up several days or even weeks after ingestion and can last up to six weeks and recur over a period of many months.

Prevention: Boil water for at least ten minutes. Boiling is more effective than chlorine or iodine water treatments, although these work well against most bacteria in water.

Creatures

Although estimates place the number of grizzly bears in the U. S. at under one thousand (they're on the government "threatened" list), the population in the lower forty-eight states is primarily concentrated in Idaho, Montana and Wyoming with the highest concentrations in Yellowstone and Glacier National Parks. These majestic animals shouldn't be considered as "people eaters," and confrontations between them and humans can usually be prevented by following a few common-sense rules and procedures.

Bears do not like to be surprised! Therefore, it's recommended that when hiking in bear country, you make your presence known to them by noise-making; wear bells, rattle tin cans, sing a tune, talk a lot and do it loudly. Let the bear know you're in the neighborhood, but don't let your dog run free, as a bear may follow it back and surprise you.

Bears prefer the habitat of three major feeding areas: high meadows with their lush grasses, roots and small mammals; valleys that provide berries; and lake and stream areas where vegetation and fish are abundant. Grizzlies are omnivorous and will eat almost anything. A prime adult female may weigh 450 pounds, while the male could weigh 750 pounds. The prospect of confronting such an animal is not appealing and precautions need to be taken to prevent it.

In the winter bears hibernate in dens usually dug into north-facing slopes, but from March through November a single bear may roam an area of over three hundred square miles in search of food. To reduce the risk of meeting a bear, the following considerations are offered by the U. S. Forest Service:

1. Food and odor attract bears.

2. Keep a clean camp and store food and garbage properly at all times. Store food in your car trunk if possible, otherwise hang it from a tree fifteen feet from the ground and five feet out from the trunk. Do not store food in your tent.

3. Never bury garbage! Discard it in bear-proof containers when possible or pack it out

4. Sleep some distance uphill (at least one hundred yards) from your cooking area. Don't sleep in the clothes you wore while cooking. Keep sleeping gear clean and free from food odor. Avoid cooking greasy foods.

5. Don't use perfumes or deodorants.

Should you and a bear meet unexpectedly:

1. Remain calm, don't make any abrupt moves, leave the area quietly or look for a climbable tree while waiting for the bear to move away.

2. Don't run. The bear can run faster than you can (with bursts up to forty miles per hour)!

3. If the bear charges:
    a. Drop your pack or coat to distract him.
    b. Climb at least twelve feet up a stout tree.
    c. As a last resort, play dead by assuming a "cannonball" position on the ground while protecting your head and stomach.

If it makes you feel any better, a report of attacks in national parks reveals the following statistics: from the year 1899 to 1979, 2,450,000 people died in the U. S. in auto accidents; during that same period 36 people were killed by grizzlies!

In addition to grizzly bears, three more creatures of the wild need be of concern to those enjoying outdoor activities. The first is the rattlesnake. When fishing or hiking in rocky canyons or warm desert terrain, one should always be aware that snakes can be present and should therefore take proper precautions to avoid startling them. Make plenty of noise so they'll hear you coming!

Another creature that can cause us problems is the tick. This small (1/8 to 3/16 inch) parasite will gladly take advantage of your body as a place to bore in and spend some time; the warmer the place, the more he likes it. As a relative of spiders and scorpions rather than insects, the tick lives under leaves and in rotten wood; he usually finds his way to our tender epidermis as we walk through riverside alders and willows or rest on a log stump. Before modern antibiotics and cures were developed, the tick had given death-causing Rocky Mountain Spotted Fever to some of its unfortunate victims. Repellents used for chiggers will usually work against ticks.

Ticks usually don't make their presence immediately known and can dig into a tender spot on your body (folds of skin and hairlines are favorites) and not be discovered for a day or two when the skin swelling and irritation finally reveal their residency. Don't try to pull a tick from your skin as you will just break his neck and his head will remain in place causing infection. It's better to hold something hot (a match or cigarette) near it, apply alcohol, kerosene, gasoline, or a strong tobacco solution. Such techniques will usually force the critter to back out pronto! Ticks are particularly evident from April through July, and a body check after a day outdoors is a wise idea.

The moose is the last animal that deserves our respect and, although not often confronted by the sportsman, this creature can be very territorial and charge an intruder without warning. He is most likely to be encountered in swampy, marsh-like areas near lakes, river bottoms and in patches of dense vegetation such as a willow copse. When good judgment prevails, the fisherman or hiker will back off, go around and test neither the speed nor strength of this huge animal!

Photography

With clean air, rugged mountains, narrow canyons, sparkling streams, abundant wildlife, colorful geology, and signs of snow year-round, Montana offers even the most experienced photographer the opportunity and stimulus to take photographs. Particularly for visitors who spend most of their time in less spectacular surroundings, the mountainous areas of Montana will provide fuel for the fire in any shutterbug's eye. Because of the brightness of the sun's rays during midday, we'd suggest photos be shot in the morning and evening to take advantage of the dramatic effect of shadows, light and reflection. Don't leave home without your camera and be sure to bring along plenty of film!

MONTANA FISHING--
A GENERAL PERSPECTIVE

Guides and Outfitters

Montana has an impressive list of guides and outfitters who specialize in a variety of fishing excursions. Some guides conduct trips only to high-country lakes, others specialize in rivers, sometimes the one or two they know very well and sometimes rivers throughout the state, depending on which one is "hot" at a particular time. Some prefer to use drift boats, others prefer rafts. Some take fly-fishing clients only, others guide for both fly and spin fishing. Some have a good deal of expertise and some are just getting started. One thing is certain; most of them work hard at what they do in order to provide the client with the best possible fishing experience. Many visitors who wish to fish, but are new to the state or the river or to the sport itself, could do much worse than hiring a guide in order to get started on the right foot. Experienced guides know where the fish are located and they know the techniques most effectively used to catch them. Guides are also companions and teachers and are devoted to their sport and committed to preserving it. Many discourage the killing of trout in preference to taking a photo and returning the beautiful creature to the water to be available for another angler to enjoy.

You'll do yourself a favor by asking some questions before making a final commitment to hire a guide and here are a few you might want to consider:

1. Where will we fish?
2. How long will we be out?
3. What is the meal arrangement?
4. What are the costs and what do they include?
5. What does the guide provide, if anything, in the way of tackle, lures, meals, transportation, sun lotion, etc.?
6. What clothing/equipment should I bring?
7. Will we return all fish?
8. If I bring a camera, will it stay dry?
9. Will we wade, float or both?

There's one question you may be reluctant to ask, so we'll answer it for you right here! Yes, guides do appreciate a gratuity for a job well done—which doesn't mean a lot of fish caught. Some days the fish don't cooperate! But if the guide did his best, kept his word and provided good company, that constitutes a job well done as far as these authors are concerned!

Success, Failure--And In Between

Whether or not you hire a guide, whether or not you're an experienced fisherman and whether or not you use the "secret" fly or lure, sometimes the "catching" is far less than you expected it would be. Just because any or all of the above conditions are true, you aren't guaranteed to catch fish, even though you are in Montana! Yes, we know you're now at Mecca; yes, we know what the magazine articles said; and yes, we know it's the right time of day with the correct phase of the moon in the most desirable week of the most productive month of an outstanding year. But, let's face it, you're dealing with a wild, wet creature and as such his predictability level stands at about three on a scale of one to ten! Sometimes our energy and eagerness overpower our patience and judgment. Sometimes it pays to concentrate on one river or lake for more than just a few hours before moving on to the next. No matter where you fish—be it the Madison or the Mississippi—you owe it to yourself to give the area a fair shake. Some waters fish best in the morning, some the evening, and they all vary depending on water level, water temperature, vagaries of the insects present, barometric pressure and a few other variables we'll likely never understand. Rather than snacking briefly on the hors d'oeuvres to satisfy your appetite, take the time to feast on a complete dinner. Don't rush around, as some fishermen do, fishing all the water in sight just to be disappointed because you didn't spend enough time in one location to get acquainted with the fish.

This And That--

You'll find that a wide variety of regulations apply as you move from stream to stream, so be sure to read the official regulation brochure before you start casting. Some waters are open to year-round fishing, many are not. Some are restricted to the use of artificial lures and some are not. Slot limits and sport-fishing-only areas are becoming more numerous as time passes and float fishing is seeing some new restrictions, so be sure to take a few minutes to understand the rules that apply to the water you're fishing.

Throughout Montana there are a few fly patterns that are historically effective on many, if not most, of the rivers anglers frequent. Each river has its own unique character, of course, with specific insect activity at relatively predictable times. Often at these times only specific imitations work well, but at other times a larger variety of artificials is effective and can be counted on to attract more than the occasional fish. We list those patterns here with the qualification that this is only a general list. Colors, dressings and size vary from time to time and place to place, but with these patterns in your fly boxes, in two or three sizes each, you could fish anywhere in the state with strong confidence that one or more of them would take fish. This basic Montana selection would include the following:

DRY FLIES: Adams, Blue Winged Olive, Elk Hair Caddis, Hopper, Humpy, Pale Morning Dun and Royal Wulff.

NYMPHS AND WETS: Bitch Creek, Girdle Bug, Hare's Ear, Montana Nymph, Pheasant Tail, Prince, Woolly Worm, Yuk Bug and Zug Bug.

STREAMERS: Matuka, Muddler Minnow, Spruce Fly (light and dark) and Woolly Bugger.

The spin fisherman will be well equipped with a variety of sizes and colors in Mepps, Panther Martin, Thomas Cyclone and Rapala.

In addition to fly patterns, lures, the state fishing regulations and a basic understanding of trout behavior, you must also be aware of your responsibility pertaining to stream access. A stream access law passed by the Montana Legislature and signed by the governor in 1985, states that rivers and streams suitable for recreational use may be used by the public regardless of stream bed ownership. Some recreational activities require landowner permission and some do not. The law does not grant permission to cross private property to gain access to rivers, but does allow access at bridges and designated fishing access sites. Once in the stream bed the fisherman may wade the river or walk next to the water's edge, as long as he does not trespass beyond the ordinary high-water mark. Flood plains next to streams are considered to be above the ordinary high-water mark. Posting of land by the landowner to deny entry can be accomplished either by written notice (signs) or by the painting of fence posts and gates in locations as the law prescribes. Such structures or natural objects will be painted with at least fifty square inches of fluorescent orange paint.

We are not agents of the state nor interpreters of the law, but we respect the importance of good landowner/sportsman relations and urge everyone who plans to fish a stream or river, to read the summary of this House Bill 265 and be aware of its provisions when fishing. This summary is available from the Montana Department of Fish, Wildlife and Parks, Con. Ed. Division, 1420 E. 6th Ave., Helena, Montana 59620.

Part I:
Rivers and Towns
of Montana

BEAVERHEAD RIVER

Map Reference 1

After the Lewis and Clark expedition had completed one of its objectives during 1805, that of finding the source of the Missouri River, they proceeded up the Jefferson and Beaverhead Rivers to an area called Clark Canyon. At the junction of two streams named Red Rock River and Horse Prairie Creek they established an encampment named Camp Fortunate. Here they cached some of their expedition equipment before leaving for the Bitterroot country on horses obtained from Shoshone Indians. The junction of the two streams now lies under the clear water of Clark Canyon Reservoir, built in 1964. The tailrace of the concrete dam here is the beginning of the Beaverhead River, thought by many to be Montana's premier, trophy-trout river.

The natural setting of this river isn't exactly what the mind's eye would envision as the location for one of the nation's heralded, western rivers—no jagged, snow-capped peaks with the wind whistling through a verdant, pine forest. Quite to the contrary, the surrounding countryside is dry, with sage and boulder-studded hills flanking the willow- and cottonwood-lined river bank. The river immediately below the dam wiggles forcefully through a fairly narrow valley before reaching the broader, agricultural valley below. This is irrigated hay- and grain-growing country; five million years ago the flat East Bench cropland between Dillon and Twin Bridges was a desert.

The Ruby Range of mountains rises to the east of the river and in the distance to the west stands the Pioneer Range dividing the valleys of the Beaverhead and Big Hole Rivers. The mountains of this region were thoroughly picked and shoveled and dredged by miners in the last half of the nineteenth century and vivid evidence of their efforts is starkly visible along some of the creeks that were disemboweled in the process. Gold finds at nearby Bannack, twenty-two miles west of Dillon, started Montana's first, large-scale, gold rush and the activity here became so intense that Bannack was declared the first territorial capital of Montana in 1864. Silver and lead were also taken from nearby hills, but present-day mining is directed primarily toward the open pit extraction of some of the country's purest talc.

Although most stream fishermen are adamantly opposed to the construction of dams that will embrace a rushing stream into the clutches of a solemn impoundment, sometimes such construction does, in fact, create a downstream fishery that would otherwise not exist. Such is the case with Clark

20

Canyon Reservoir. Its irrigational intention is now served while providing flows and habitat that previously didn't exist in the river below. Prior to the construction of the dam most holding water would disappear by the end of August in very warm, very reduced water flows. The dam now captures water during run-off and doles it out as needed for irrigation use in the summer months, maintaining flows and water temperatures in which fish and other aquatic organisms can thrive.

The foregoing notwithstanding, the river, as planned, is affected by irrigation diversion at the Barrett's Diversion Dam. Water is taken from the Beaverhead at this facility twelve miles below the reservoir and diverted to the East Bench during July and August. This procedure translates into a healthy flow of water above Barrett's and a depleted flow below. By way of comparison, when the river above the diversion is running six hundred to seven hundred c.f.s., the river below is reduced to two hundred to three hundred c.f.s. This diversion, along with some natural causes, gives a different visage to the river below. Irrigation return and eroding banks cause considerable turbidity during low-water periods. The water temperature is raised, conditions for trout growth are not as favorable as in the water above, the bottom is more silted, almost no rainbow trout are found here and fishing is restricted more to morning and evening during the summer. On the upside of the scale is the fact that fishermen can wade the lower river much more easily than the upper, which is seldom wadeable. As a matter of fact, the locals refer to wading the upper part as "bobbing," a tongue-in-cheek description of the way an angler moves downstream while fighting a fish displaying broad shoulders and a fullback's tenacity! In these instances the gladiator with the rod tightens his wader belt and pushes to the shallow side of each bend as he bobs along in an effort to stay with the fish. The technique sounds cold, wet and somewhat perilous and we don't recommend it.

A profile of the upper river would include some characteristics not confronted by anglers on most rivers they frequent. The most obvious, and disconcerting, is the tight press put on the river's edge by bank vegetation. The tall willows bow to the water's surface and their roots tangle against the bank. The channel is serpentine and is so narrow you can cast a fly line across it. This thread of water from Clark Canyon Dam to its confluence with the Big Hole is about fifty miles long. If the thread were pulled out tight, it might measure sixty to seventy miles. The water moves swiftly, three to five miles an hour. The water is deep in places, up to ten feet in some holes. Does the logistical nightmare start to appear?

The upper river is a floater's river most of the time. There are, of course, places where bank fishing is feasible and times and places when wading is possible, but to cover the water in any reasonable fashion, a boat and oarsman is required. The oarsman should have not only rowing experience, but experience on this particular river. For this reason we strongly recommend to everyone planning to float the river in his own boat to first hire a guide and make at least one float to become acquainted with the ways of the river and its challenges. The boatman needs skills in maneuvering the boat, just as the angler needs skills in casting, particularly with a fly rod. The river bends, the boat moves, targets change, fish strike, anglers strike back and all at a fairly fast pace! The fly rodder should be adept not only with the overhead cast, but sidearm and backhand casts as well. One local guide told us he was hooked twenty-nine times in one day by a client. That's really beyond the call of duty, so when you float the Beaverhead with a guide, take pity and be very mindful of where your hook is at all times, both in front of you, as well as to your rear. Another guide expressed fishing here as the "black art" of fly fishing due to the difficulty and frustration that can bemuse you. He said floating here was like "going through the Everglades in a speed boat—" most likely an analogy for effect, but not without a hint of accuracy.

The water in the spring has a green, murky appearance that allows you to use a heavy tippet—twenty pound is standard. After the water clears in July you might want to drop back to fifteen pound test. This maxi-size material isn't used to maneuver monster-sized fish, but rather to allow you to recover your fly when an errant or overly aggressive cast has attached it to a greedy willow branch. Usually the fish here just react to the fly, not scrutinize it, particularly when presented with large patterns, so rather than surrendering half the contents of your fly box to the bushes, use a heavy tippet. You can also use a short leader; four to five feet in length is common.

Nymph fishing is a favorite method used on this river throughout the year, but dry flies are used starting in late March and continuing through April as Baetis appear on the water and size #16 to #18 Blue Winged Olives are used by fly anglers. This same hatch emerges in September as well. The water temperature through May and June remains cold; insect hatches are few and fishing is restricted primarily to nymphs.

The Fourth of July is the time of year when the water temperature has risen to over fifty degrees and insects mature and hatch in good numbers. Caddis are on the water starting in early July and are an important insect for both fish and fishermen through August. The salmonfly hatch that most anglers look forward to on many southwestern, Montana rivers does not occur here but a heavy cranefly hatch that takes place in August generates similar excitement among anglers.

The cranefly hatch is probably the most famous happening of the season on the Beaverhead. This big insect emerges from its even larger pupal case starting in mid-August and continuing until mid-September. The larvae of this insect (dirty olive in color and one- to three-inches long) will drift back into the soft water against the bank and under logs and roots to pupate. Not only do the trout observe this annual ritual, but magpies and skunks are also attracted and often frequent the river bank to feed on the pupae. Rises to adult craneflies are not timid gestures. The fish explode from the water and strike the large, but rather delicate, insects with at least the aggressiveness fish on other rivers display toward adult salmonflies. The artificial adult cranefly is usually a high-floating, hairwing dressing that is cast to the bank and then skittered across the surface. Many local anglers prefer to use a dropper fly in conjunction with a point fly. The dropper can be a nymph or a grasshopper imitation. The hopper pattern is also used with good success as a dropper in conjunction with a Girdle Bug point fly. The Girdle Bug on the Beaverhead is thought to be taken as a cranefly larvae and is a very good pattern throughout the year. Another dropper arrangement used here consists of a Brown Bear (similar to a Sandy Mite)/point fly with a caddis emerger dropper (a peacock soft hackle works well) about thirty inches up from the point. Cast to the willows and strip the flies upstream to imitate the naturals.

Also starting to emerge in July are Pale Morning Duns and Light Olives in #14 and #16, along with Yellow Sally and Golden Stone adults. Most of the specific hatches last about a month, so you can usually expect some form of insect and fish activity all summer. Terrestrial fishing in the upper river is not the important consideration it is on many rivers, although beetles and ants will take fish on occasion. Hoppers don't get to most areas on the upper river due to the dense willow growth, but they do interest fish off the grassy banks downstream.

Overcast days are always preferred during the bright, summer months as the fish are shy under a bright sun and hug tight to the banks, making pin-point, casting accuracy a necessity. Casts need to be made very close to the bank or to the overhanging willow branches for optimum success. Unless the boatman can hold the boat stationary in the current, the caster has but one float over a given location, so casting speed and accuracy plus good line control play an important part on this river. When the day is bright, you should consider fishing from six to ten in the morning and again in the evening from six to dark.

Throughout the summer a growth of grassy-type weeds clings to the bottom gravel preventing the angler from spotting fish, which can normally be done earlier in the year. Some of these weeds will extend downstream up to two feet, but much of the growth merely forms a carpet of stiff, hairlike strands one to twelve inches long on the rocks and doesn't create a problem when wading. Each stone has a "head of hair." In the fall after the first frost the weeds break loose and clearing one's hook becomes a constant maintenance chore. Coincident with the weed separation from the bottom gravel, snails are released that not only adhere to boat bottoms, but delight the hungry trout. Some fishermen feel snail-laden, trout bellies account for a decided reduction in catch rates during September, although it is also thought that this particular month is one of the very best for hooking the trophy-size fish of ten pounds or better.

The upper section of river (above Barrett's Diversion) is not only deeper than below, but also swifter. The lower river can be waded quite comfortably while the upper section cannot. The lower section contains more pools, gravel bars and silted bottom than the upper river. The upper river receives the vast majority of angling pressure. The lower river has less access, but permission from ranchers is usually granted to a polite request. There are two camping areas on the upper river (at Pipe Organ and Poindexter) but none below Dillon. Average fish size is larger in the upper river (eighteen to twenty-one inches) than in the lower river (fifteen to seventeen inches). The upper river contains a good population of rainbows where the lower section holds very few. Recent population studies conducted in the upper river by the Montana Department of Fish, Wildlife and Parks revealed counts as high as 1,900 fish per mile over 16 inches in length and a hard-to-believe 700 fish per mile over 20 inches. (That's one fish over 20 inches every 7-1/2 feet). Averages in the lower river are somewhat smaller than these. Anglers wishing to float should consider the use of prams and rafts on the upper river and canoes on the lower. The canoe allows you to move more quickly through unproductive water when it's low.

Lure fishermen will want to consider lures that are fairly large and heavy for the upper river with Thomas Cyclone or hammered brass and gold spoons being quite effective. Spoons are thought to produce better than spinners, although a #9 Panther Martin with a black body and red dots is recommended as are medium Mepps and Rapalas. Spin lines in the upper river can be as heavy as 12 pound test while lighter lines and smaller lures are used below.

A list of wet flies for the Beaverhead would include the following: Girdle Bug, Yuk Bug, Bitch Creek, Brown Bear Brown, Brown Bear Black, cranefly larvae imitations, smaller nymphs in size #12, such as Hare's Ear, Brown Hackle Peacock and wet Renegade, Kiwi Muddler, White and Yellow Marabou Muddler, Woolly Bugger and Zonker. Dry flies include Adams, Royal Wulff, Royal Trude, Pale Morning Dun, Blue Winged Olive, Cranefly, Elk Hair Caddis, Goddard Caddis and the local Flashback.

Some additional random thoughts include:

1. The river does stay clear except after prolonged or heavy rain showers when Grasshopper Creek silts badly due to erosion of bare ground along the creek left by mining operations many years ago.

2. You can't strip a streamer too fast. On the retrieve, give long, strong tugs; up to eighteen inch pulls can be very effective, especially when large browns are feeding.

3.   Because dropper flies are used here often, it's important when netting a fish that you get him into the bag on the first attempt to avoid hooking the free fly in the mesh while the fish thrashes for freedom outside the net.

4.   We wish to applaud all anglers who release the sizeable trout of this fishery after catching them. Montana, and the entire angling community, is fortunate to have public access to such a valuable resource. With thoughtful appreciation for the enjoyment these fish provide to all of us, the catch-and-release philosophy here, and on all Montana rivers, will ensure and enhance that enjoyment for many fishermen for many generations into the future.

CLARK CANYON RESERVOIR

There's no question among devotees of Montana lake fishing that Clark Canyon Reservoir ranks as one of the finest on which to pursue large trout. Rainbows predominate here with specimens to seven pounds; browns take second place for quantity but range a bit larger with sizes to ten pounds.

This reservoir is located twenty miles south of Dillon on Highway I-15 and rests at the head of the Beaverhead River. Two tributaries, the Red Rock River to the south and Horse Prairie Creek to the west of the reservoir, provide the water which fills this irrigation impoundment. The dam, which was built in 1964, is under the control of the East Bench Irrigation District and controls the flow of water to local crop lands, primarily during July and August. The landscape surrounding the reservoir is an austere, barren environment consisting of rolling hills of sage, rock and grass. The reservoir covers some six thousand acres, is triangular in shape and embraces two major islands. It is easily accessible from I-15 and there is a perimeter road on all sides of the reservoir. Picnic areas are plentiful and the state-controlled Lone Pine Campground sits on a point at the water's west shore.

In years past Clark Canyon was stocked with Montana's Arlee rainbow trout. Recently the policy has been changed and the DeSmet rainbow is now stocked with the goal of establishing a self-sustaining population that will move each spring into the Red Rock River to spawn. Fueled with a healthy supply of bait fish, leeches, scuds, damselflies, midges and Callibaetis mayflies, both rainbow and brown grow rapidly here.

The open-water fishing begins at ice-out during March and April. The fish are active then and trolling the eastern shoreline and the water around the islands is the most popular technique used. Effective lures include the Rapala, large Thomas Cyclone and large Daredevles. In the summer, as the fish head for deeper water, trolling continues to be popular but now the lures are attached to leaded lines to reach maximum depth. After runoff the water clears and fishing remains good through fall. Throughout the summer and fall, many fly fishermen use float tubes around the islands and at the southern end of the reservoir near the mouth of the Red Rock River. Popular wet flies include a Brown Mohair Leech in size #2 through #8, Woolly Worms and small nymphs such as Hare's Ear and Prince in sizes #12 to #16. Flies imitating scuds and damsel nymphs are effective. Popular dries include Callibaetis Flashback, Royal Wulff, Mosquito, Ant and Hopper.

Several other techniques are used to find fish in addition to tubing at the mouth of the Red Rock River. One is to drive the shoreline and spot working fish with binoculars. When fish are located, the fins and float tube are brought into action or boats are launched to use as a casting platform. There are many cold springs that feed fresh water into the reservoir, and float tubers will sometimes utilize fish finders to locate concentrations of fish near them when the water level is low and the water temperature is high. The technique here is to locate them, cast in front of their line of travel and retrieve with a hand twist. A favorite area for this approach is between the Lonetree Campground and the Red Rock River. Gulpers also work the surface in summer coming up to Callibaetis and midges. The midges here are large, about a #14 and are tied on a 2X long shank hook. At the south end of the reservoir there is an abandoned railroad track and a former roadway that were both drowned as the reservoir was being filled. Since the gradient here is quite gradual the fishermen can walk along them and cast into the shallows on either side.

Fall, of course, signals the movement of the brown trout toward the stream mouths in preparation for spawning and once again the Red Rock becomes an excellent location for the fisherman looking for the opportunity to hook large fish. At the end of the year float fishing goes out with a blast, usually of cold air that freezes the surface of the reservoir and those hearty folks who enjoy ice fishing take over. The emphasis during the winter is less on trout and more on burbot (also referred to as ling). These relatives of the ocean codfish average between two and four pounds and make excellent table fare. They are readily available to ice fishermen because they spawn under the ice in one to four feet of water.

If you like to fish for large trout in still water, Clark Canyon should definitely be one of your destinations.

POINDEXTER SLOUGH

It's ironic, but a great deal of the best fishing in Montana takes place along its well-developed interstate highway system. The Clark Fork, Beaverhead, Yellowstone and Missouri Rivers come to mind. It is, however, fairly rare to find exceptional fishing <u>under</u> an interstate highway, but when you fish Poindexter Slough, that is indeed the case.

This spring-fed creek is approximately twenty to thirty feet wide and is fairly "spooky" water. It runs crystal clear, is fairly shallow and has a flat surface. The banks are crowded with thistle, watercress and willows and the small bottom gravel is home to the root systems of long, trailing weeds. It is necessary in some areas to fish from the bank while keeping a low silhouette against the horizon. Other sections are suitable for wading.

Located just two miles south of Dillon, the stream twists and turns through a pastoral hay meadow and willow-brush environment and one of its best sections lies directly beneath an I-15 overpass. The resident rainbow and brown trout range from ten to fourteen inches in length. There are good numbers of fish here and they can be very selective. The noise from semi trucks passing overhead seems to not bother them at all. Long leaders, fine tippets and small flies are the order of the day.

Poindexter Slough

The main fishing access here is for day-use only, and all you need to do is park the car, walk to the right down the railroad tracks, go left under the fence and walk through the hay meadow toward the interstate. You will soon find the creek. At most times this is one place where you need to do a lot of things right in order to fool a few fish!

Poindexter Slough under I-15

DILLON

At an elevation of 5,100 feet, Dillon continues to function on the same business fuel, the railroad and the raising of livestock, that inspired its development in the late 1800's. Although much mining of precious metals took place nearby, Dillon was never a mining town as such. It is, and has been, a business and social center for the several fertile valleys that surround it and takes a place as one of Montana's largest wool shipping centers.

Dillon, with a population of nearly five thousand, is the county seat of Beaverhead County, which in total claims ten thousand residents and ten times that number of sheep and cattle. Dillon came into being when, during the winter of 1880-1881, its location happened to be a temporary end-of-the-track site as the Utah and Northern Railroad was being built across southwest

Montana toward the town of Butte. Business people took a liking to this site on the Beaverhead River and subsequently developed the community to support the agricultural activity already taking place. The town's name was derived from that of Sidney Dillon, president of the Northern Pacific Railroad.

Of substantial influence on the town is Western Montana College. When, as Montana's first teacher's college, its doors opened in 1897 the forty-two students paid an enrollment fee of $5.00 per semester. Today's one-thousand students, we assume, pay somewhat more than that to earn degrees in business, education and other liberal arts fields.

Visitors to Dillon can enjoy passing time in either of two city parks or take a self-guided, walking tour of the historic section of town using a map and brochure available at the Chamber of Commerce Office. Visitors enjoy viewing the nearly eighteen thousand artifacts that make up the Beaverhead County Museum which is in the same building with the Chamber. Included are Indian items, mining relics and photographs of county history. Golf enthusiasts may use the nine-hole course and clubhouse at the Beaverhead Country Club which is open to the public.

Another activity of historical interest is to drive about twenty-five miles west of town to the site of Bannack, former gold-mining community and first territorial capital of Montana. Gold was first found here in 1862 and a few of the old buildings still remain. The area offers sightseeing, picnicking and camping in what is now Bannack State Park.

Beaverhead County Chamber of Commerce: P.O. Box 830, Dillon, Montana 59725 - Phone: 683-5511

Beaverhead National Forest: P.O. Box 1258, Dillon, Montana 59725 - Phone: 683-3900

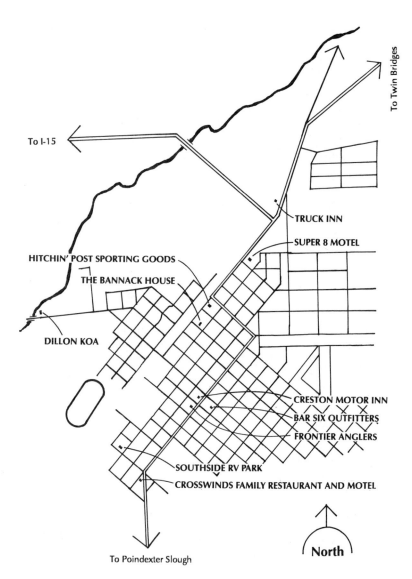

To Twin Bridges

To I-15

TRUCK INN

SUPER 8 MOTEL

HITCHIN' POST SPORTING GOODS

THE BANNACK HOUSE

DILLON KOA

CRESTON MOTOR INN

BAR SIX OUTFITTERS

FRONTIER ANGLERS

SOUTHSIDE RV PARK

CROSSWINDS FAMILY RESTAURANT AND MOTEL

To Poindexter Slough

North

Dillon

DILLON

FISHING SHOPS

FRONTIER ANGLERS
427 So. Atlantic, Box 11   683-5276

We offer a complete line of quality fly fishing gear. We can service everyone from the saltwater fishermen to bass fishermen to trout fishermen. Our catalog is filled with exotic fishing vacations with an extensive line of tackle to go with the trips. Toll free hotline for your convenience.

HITCHIN' POST SPORTING GOODS
124 No. Montana Ave.   683-4881

Serving southwest Montana with the finest in sporting goods. Professional guide service available.

GUIDES / OUTFITTERS

BAR SIX OUTFITTERS
325 So. Dakota St.   683-4005

We are a small and personal guide service with reasonable prices. Guided trips include floating the Beaverhead and Big Hole Rivers, and fishing local mountain lakes and streams. We try hard to make your trip the best ever.

DAVE WELLBORN, OUTFITTER
775 Medicine Lodge Road, 30 miles south of Dillon   681-3117

Moose, goat, elk, deer and antelope hunting. Combination antelope and fishing trips available. Accommodations, meals, cabin rentals to hunters and fishermen. Float trips arranged on Beaverhead with other guides. Family photo trips and sightseeing excursions.

RESTAURANTS / BARS

THE BANNACK HOUSE
33 E. Bannack   683-5088

Dillon's finest restaurant. Three star AAA rating. Specializing in locally grown beef, lamb, pork and veal and fresh seafood. All major credit cards accepted. We cater especially to fishermen. Largest selection of spirits in Montana and choice wine cellar.

CROSSWINDS FAMILY RESTAURANT AND MOTEL
1008 So. Atlantic   683-6370

Located across the street from Western Montana College in the heart of Beaverhead County. Serving daily specials and breakfast all day. Kids are welcome. Easy on and off access to I-15.

TRUCK INN
759 No. Montana Ave., Box 1064   683-4936

Serving breakfast all day. Lunch and dinner, also. Homemade pies and biscuits, salad bar. All homestyle cooking. Open at 6 AM and close at 10 PM. We make lunches to go for the fisherman.

MOTELS

CRESTON MOTOR INN
335 So. Atlantic   683-2341

Twenty-two clean, quiet, air conditioned, attractive units in the quiet end of town. Color cable TV, queen size beds, direct dial phones. Reasonable rates. Courtesy coffee. Bob and Linda Taylor, your hosts.

SUPER 8 MOTEL
550 No. Montana Ave, Box 226   683-4288

Dillon Super 8 is America's finest economy lodging. We have 46 rooms, all with queen size beds, direct dial telephones, color cable TV, HBO, tubs and showers and twenty-four hour front desk service. We serve a continental breakfast and furnish wake-up service. We are within walking distance of restaurants and shopping.

CAMPGROUNDS

DILLON KOA
735 W. Park St.   683-2749

Open all year. Quiet, country setting along the banks of the Beaverhead River. Superb fishing area. Day, or float trip planning. Come fish with us. Joe and Karla Roos welcome you.

SOUTHSIDE RV PARK
104 E. Poindexter   683-2244

Full service RV park. Forty-two pull-through spaces with shade, laundry, showers, cable TV. Quiet location on the south end of Dillon, but still close to all shopping and restaurants. Exit 62 off I-15, drive 2 blocks and turn right.

GUEST RANCHES

BEAVERHEAD ROCK RANCH
4325 Old Stage Rd., off I-15 at exit 56 at Barretts, 10 miles south of Dillon   683-2126

Weekly rental. Secluded old 2 bedroom farm home on the Beaverhead River at the base of Beaverhead Rock. Part of small active cattle ranch. Scenic, 9 mile drive from Clark Canyon Dam. Fishermen and hunters welcome.

GRANT

SERVICES

INDEPENDENT WELDING AND STORE
At Grant, 11820 Highway 324, Dillon MT 59725   681-3141

General store, gas, phone, auto, truck and RV repairs. Welding, propane tank and bottle refills. Hunting and fishing information. Groceries and supplies.

BIG HOLE RIVER

Map References 2, 3

How would you like to have five million gallons of liquid fish habitat pumped out of your favorite trout stream every day? Shocking as it may sound, it happens every twenty-four hours on the Big Hole River. At the community of Divide there is a 150-foot-high, steel smokestack standing like a sentry over the Big Hole Pump Station that is responsible for this alarming event. Fortunately the river survives. The facility, built in 1898, is a carry-over from the mining era and under the direction of the Butte Water Company it now pumps the water a distance of twenty-two miles over the Continental Divide to the city of Butte.

The Big Hole River was originally named the Wisdom River by Captain Meriwether Lewis of the Lewis and Clark Expedition but local sentiment dictated a change to its present name and the only Wisdom now in the valley has a main street and an active business center.

The Big Hole starts out flowing in a northerly direction near the border between southwest Montana and Idaho, continues north for some distance, bends to the east, then to the south, then back to the east and finally flows north once again to join the Beaverhead River at Twin Bridges. The upper river glides along through hay meadows in the Big Hole Valley and terminates in the hay meadows of the Beaverhead Valley many miles downstream. Between these two pastoral agricultural areas the current roars through a canyon at high water and plays the seductress to anglers at low water. The river is floatable and wadable. It has plenty of fish, plenty of insects, a variety of scenery, a variety of water types and access is fairly easy. We think that description fits the bill as an appealing prospect for angling ambitions.

To characterize the river, we'll consider three separate sections. The upper river is that section from Jackson down to Wise River. The middle reaches extend from Wise River to Glen and the lower portion begins at Glen and continues down to its confluence with the Beaverhead at which point the Jefferson River is created.

The upper portion of the river has its beginning in the southern expanses of the Big Hole Basin. The early mountain men and Indians called a large valley of this type a "hole" and this particular hole is the largest and highest in western Montana. It is also considered to be the "deepest" because it was found during oil and gas exploration in the 1980's that bedrock lies as much

30

Big Hole fifteen miles west of Wise River

as fourteen thousand feet below the surface. The oil and gas wells were not commercially viable, but the exercise did add a page to the geological knowledge of this area. The valley separates the southern Bitterroot Range on the west side from the Pioneer Mountains to the east. The Pioneer Mountains in turn have eastern and western sections which are similarly divided by a major tributary to the Big Hole, the Wise River.

The Big Hole valley is renowned for the high quality of the hay grown here and so vast and widespread is the production of this crop that the area has been named the "Valley of Ten Thousand Haystacks." It's also known for a battle that took place here in August of 1877 in which almost one hundred Nez Perce Indians were killed by U. S. Army troops whose assignment it was to stop the progress of the Indians as they fled from the Idaho Territory. This was but one battle fought in the Nez Perce War of 1877, but remains on record as one of the bloodiest. Many Indians managed to survive the battle and escaped to continue their journey, only to finally surrender two months later near Havre, Montana. Five years after the battle the first white settlers began farming here and the occupation continues to this day on large ranches spotted throughout the valley. This story, among many others, is recorded in the interesting exhibits at the Big Hole Battlefield National Monument located on Highway 43 about twelve miles west of Wisdom.

The site of the monument is in a transitional zone between a mountainous, evergreen forest to the west and a flat, agricultural environment to the east. The Big Hole River section below Jackson is small and remains so as it meanders downstream through willow bottoms. As it progresses it constantly adds water volume from tributary streams and by the time it reaches Wise River the stream has become a river and is about forty to sixty feet wide. These upper reaches are residence to brook and cutthroat trout, but more importantly, it holds one of the best remaining wild populations of stream-dwelling Arctic Grayling in the U.S., outside of Alaska. Whitefish are also found in good numbers in this section of river, as they are throughout the river system. As you progress downstream, increasing numbers of rainbow become evident. Most of the river in this entire area is on private ranch land and permission is required to fish it. There are a few locations where road and river meet and public access is available at these points.

Although the river picks up additional volume and speed below its confluence with Pintlar Creek, it is still relatively shallow and wading is the most practical way to fish the water. As you approach the Dickey Bridge, which crosses the river about two miles upstream from Wise River, floating becomes a more viable alternative.

The water between Wise River and Glen rushes at a much faster rate than above, flows over larger rocks, butts against midstream boulders and gathers less heat from the sun's rays as it wends its way between high canyon walls.

Big Hole at Wise River

The rocky, narrower portion of the canyon centers near Divide and gains even more dramatic proportions at Maidenrock Canyon. The narrow valley begins to open up somewhat above Dewey to the west and below Melrose to the south. Access is good throughout this middle section of the river with its deep runs, bouncing riffles and swirling pocket water. The river parallels Highway 43 between Wise River and Divide. At that point the river leaves the highway and from Divide to Melrose the water is best accessed by boat. This is a very popular floating area and is home to a large population of brown trout and smaller numbers of rainbow. Access in the area is essentially at six locations, the first of which is at the Divide Bridge off the Old Pumphouse Road. The second access is downstream at the Maidenrock Bridge which is reached from the frontage road that parallels the interstate. The third access is the Salmonfly Access at Melrose. There is also the Maiden Rock Fishing access Site on the west side of the river upstream from Melrose. It is reached by crossing the river at the community of Melrose and driving west 2-1/2 miles, then turning north for 3 miles on the county road that leads back to the river. The final two accesses are near I-15, upstream from Glen off the frontage road at Angler's Paradise Access, and Brown's Bridge Access.

The fish in this middle section average twelve to fifteen inches, with a good fish running seventeen inches and a big fish twenty-two inches. There is a slot limit regulation that applies here and it has greatly enhanced the quality of the fishery, but many fish are still taken from the river, interrupting the river's true potential to carry even larger fish.

The lower river below Glen pushes through ranchland and barren hill country on its last rush toward the Jefferson. This is brown-trout water and the prevailing braided channels and undercut banks provide important holding water for these reclusive fish. The area is constantly affected by busy beavers in the dark of night and the flood waters of spring, so channels change, trees fall into the water and the corridors floated one year might not exist the next. We suggest that a floater making his initial trip through this water might wish to be accompanied by someone familiar with the river.

Fisherman access to this part of the river is along the Burma Road which is an unpaved, country road, connecting the community of Glen to a point on Highway 41 south of Twin Bridges. It's a scenic drive, over a so-so gravel road, and in dry weather it's not a problem. If the weather is wet, it may be necessary to have a four-wheel drive vehicle. With the exception of one developed access site just east of Glen, there are no formal accesses along this road. There are, however, two casual access sites, Gunsight Pass and Pennington's Bridge, on the west side of the river. This narrow road does receive some local ranch vehicle traffic, so the prudent angler should take proper care to assure that his vehicle is parked a safe distance from the road's edge. There are two accesses in the Twin Bridges area, one at Seidensticker Bridge, and the First

River Access on the Beaverhead River right in town. Plan to acquire permission if you wish to fish here on foot at other than the access points mentioned above.

If you intend to fish the Big Hole from top to bottom, you'll need a broad selection of flies in the box and a couple of different rods in the car. The upper reaches are small and friendly to fish and require no more than a four-weight rod loaded with a floating line, a twelve foot leader and a 6X tippet. Evening caddis hatches here generate plenty of responses from the brooks, grayling, rainbows and whitefish, so you might try an Elk Hair Caddis or Adams in the evening and more colorful offerings during the day such as Royal Trudes, Humpies and Royal Wulffs. Nymphs, of course, will work well as long as they aren't weighted too heavily because the warm water temperatures promote an algae bloom on the bottom that will foul the hook of a deep-floated nymph. This algae bloom also affects bait fishing and anglers using this technique would best be served by using a bubble. Lure fishermen have few options and would have their best success with a bubble and fly combination used with the spinning rod. The higher water temperatures prevalent during the summer months would suggest that the most successful fishing will take place in the mornings and evenings An overcast day is always welcome when it comes along.

The middle section of the river is the one most frequented by fishermen.

Big Hole at Gunsight Pass

34

It has optimum water variety, challenge, plenty of nice fish and the insect life to support it. This is where the other outfit you should carry comes into play. It should be a six- to eight-weight rig with both floating and sinking lines balanced to the rod. Make sure the rod spools have plenty of backing. Caddis are dominant and a relatively small population of mayflies are present throughout the season. These mayflies vary in size with small species starting to emerge in June and large drake species appearing in July. The tiny Tricorythodes begin appearing in early morning clouds during August. The Adams in various sizes is a true workhorse fly on the Big Hole. Its subtle blending of grey and brown bespeaks of nourishment to the trout and they come to it as freely as any pattern used. Attractor dries—Wright's Royal, Royal Trude, Royal Wulff, Royal Humpy, Yellow Humpy and Hoppers, in fact the entire sovereign family—are also dependable. Size #14 is a good average size in all these patterns. A #16 Adams fished in the riffles on a warm August morning, when the Tricos are out and about, can be a wonderful angling experience.

Nymphs, as always, work throughout the summer and are particularly effective during the hot days of August when hatches are minimal and the fish have sought shelter in the cooler water of deep runs, protective undercut bank structure, or are out in the oxygenated riffles at the heads of pools and runs. The Hare's Ear Nymph is a favorite here as elsewhere and the Prince, Muskrat and Brown Hackle Peacock in sizes #10 to #16 are a close second. The larger nymphs also get good results because of the existence of the large stoneflies (salmonflies) in the river. Bitch Creek, Yuk Bug and Girdle Bug nymphs in size #2 through #6 cover the bases here.

Streamers usually find their acceptance greatest in the cool months of autumn, but they are used effectively here even during summer, particularly when fish are not rising. Casting to the bank with an olive bodied, Woolly Bugger with black hackle and tail or a white Marabou Muddler can produce very good results.

The water of the Big Hole has a high pH factor and the resultant algae and moss growth is evident throughout the river. This condition discourages spin fishing and keeps wading anglers on their toes, both literally and figuratively. The bottom is slick, the rocks are round and of large size and wading becomes a tricky, thoughtful endeavor. Felt soles are a must and, although somewhat noisy, cleats can be of great help as can a wading staff. Fortunately, for those fishermen without a boat, foot access along the river is quite good, even if it is slippery.

The lower river, with its long runs, slow pools and braided channels supports less insect life than the water above, but still fishes very well on large nymphs and streamer patterns. This is brown-trout water, shared with numerous whitefish and a few rainbows. Irrigation is a problem here in August and resultant high water temperatures depress the trout. The fish population seems to cope with the situation, however, and in the fall, when the water cools again, this is an area of the river worth fishing for browns that average fourteen inches. Attractor nymphs and streamers such as Flasha-Bugger, Marabou Muddler, Zonker and Matuka Sculpin size #2 to #6 work just dandy.

There are those who would argue that a fly accurately placed and properly controlled with a drag-free drift will be more readily taken by a fish here than a fly which exactly matches the hatch but floats farther from the fish than he is willing to move. These Big Hole trout seem reluctant to move very far to take a natural insect and are just as disinclined to move to an artificial. When casting to a riser put it over his nose! Most of your casting will be to the water rather than to specific fish, and line control is an important consideration because the fish are very sensitive to drag. Use a short line when possible.

The spring run-off on the river occurs in a double dosage. In May, depending on weather conditions, the river receives the snow melt from the upper valley. After a brief respite, the high-mountain melt commences sometime in June with final stabilization of water levels no later than mid-July.

During this high-water period the salmonfly hatch occurs. If the sight of a hundred boats a day bobbing along the river is your cup of tea, this is the time to see them. If on the other hand, you'd like to catch a trout of generous proportions, this is your chance to do it. The bigger fish lose their normal inhibitions when the three-inch long Pteronarcys californica stoneflies rise from the cobble, ease to the river bank and fly into the stream-side brush. The fish are on the feed and for approximately three weeks (in a normal year from June 10 to June 30) these clumsy insects emerge at various locations between Twin Bridges and the Dickey Bridge. The hatch moves upstream from three to five miles a day and the ability to pinpoint the location of maximum activity on any given day is the secret to success. Usually about three days out of the three weeks are rated as exceptional and if you can be at the proper place on those few select days, you'll probably ascend to angling heaven! Well maybe you won't ascend, but you may develop a case of extreme exhaustion from playing fish!

The traditional floating patterns will usually do the job when the adult insects are about, but the angler should never overlook the good fishing that can occur when using large, black salmonfly nymph imitations in the water immediately upstream from the actual "hatch" location. Many times this upstream water will be the most productive. This hatch is fairly predictable year to year, but the vagaries of nature can alter the schedule somewhat so before making a special trip to catch the hatch here, we'd recommend a phone call to someone in the area to obtain an up-to-the-minute status report on weather and water conditions and their effect on the insects.

Those anglers who fish the river on a regular basis are of the opinion that

Big Hole near Twin Bridges

the large numbers of boats on the water are making the fish more wary and are suppressing the free-wheeling, feeding activities of the trout during this important hatch. Fortunately the activity lasts but three weeks, at the end of which time the armada moves on to the Madison River to fish the salmonfly hatch there. But floating does, of course, continue on the Big Hole for the balance of the season, but at a much reduced intensity.

It is nearly impossible to fish this hatch by wading if the river is experiencing its normal June run-off volume. Not only is it life-threatening to be standing in the river in most places, but often access restrictions preclude your being in that particular location on the river where the insects are active. Fishing from a boat is by far the most effective and facile method available and that's the reason for the armada on the river at this time of year. When floating, the boatman must pay close attention to the river conditions. At times in the canyon section there are standing waves to six feet in height which can swamp even the most stable of boats or rafts.

Following the salmonfly hatch, fishermen see the emergence of golden stoneflies and caddis. The hatch of these smaller stoneflies overlaps the salmonfly emergence and lasts for a couple of weeks into the first part of July. The caddis continue to hatch throughout the summer and into fall. Once again, the most efficient manner in which to fish them and cover the river well is by floating.

Angling techniques here are not appreciably different from those used on other rivers. The floater here must contend with more inconvenient put-ins and take-outs than he'd experience on some other Montana rivers but it is obviously worth it as evidenced by the number of boats on the river during the salmonfly hatch. The boat of choice on this river is the raft because of its low profile. The high bow profile of some drift boats seems disarming to the fish, particularly when the angler stands above the bow while casting. Whichever craft you use, we strongly recommend that you carefully check the water and the access points before attempting a float and that the oarsman have river experience when floating the canyon area between Divide and Melrose.

Be sure to carry your mosquito repellent when on this river and keep a sharp lookout for nature's other creatures such as osprey, eagles, Cooper's hawks, blue herons, deer and the herd of mountain sheep that live at Maiden Rock.

As a friend of ours sagely stated, "It's difficult to become bored on the Big Hole. Just go to another section and it's like another river." We agree!

River Notes

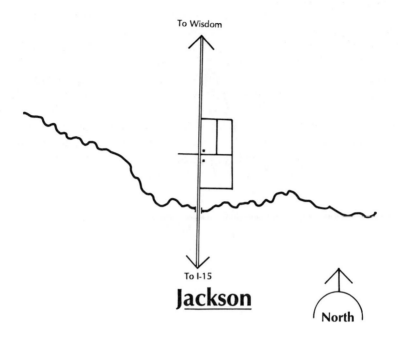

To Wisdom

To I-15

Jackson

North

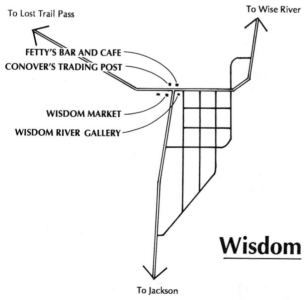

To Lost Trail Pass

To Wise River

FETTY'S BAR AND CAFE

CONOVER'S TRADING POST

WISDOM MARKET

WISDOM RIVER GALLERY

Wisdom

To Jackson

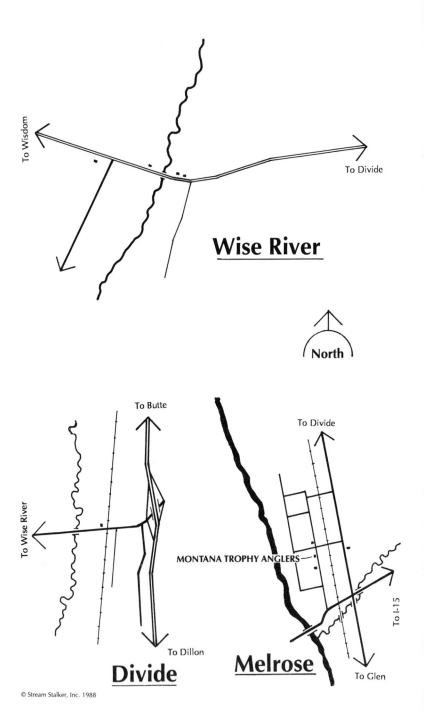

To Wisdom

To Divide

Wise River

North

To Butte

To Wise River

To Dillon

Divide

To Divide

MONTANA TROPHY ANGLERS

To I-15

Melrose

To Glen

© Stream Stalker, Inc. 1988

WISDOM

FISHING SHOPS

CONOVER'S TRADING POST
Highway 43, Box 84   689-3272
>Specializing in souvenirs, gifts, hunting and fishing supplies. Large stock of favorite local trout flies. Montana Fish and Gam licensing agent.

RESTAURANTS / BARS

FETTY'S BAR AND CAFE
Highway 43, Box 177   689-3260
>Sportsman's headquarters in the Big Hole. Try our famous hamburgers, homemade soup, chili pies and well drinks after a hard day on the river. Swap lies with your fishing buddies!

GROCERIES

WISDOM MARKET
Downtown Wisdom, Box 31   689-3271
>Wisdom Market. "If we don't have it, you don't need it!"

ART GALLERIES

WISDOM RIVER GALLERY
Main Street, Wisdom, Box 72   689-3400
>Visit our gallery in the beautiful land of 10,000 haystacks. Enjoy the luxury of selecting from our exclusive line of fine western art.

WISE RIVER

GUIDES / OUTFITTERS

CRAIG FELLIN'S BIG HOLE RIVER OUTFITTERS
Eight miles south of Wise River, Box 167   832-3252
>Float the scenic Big Hole River. Our lodge and new cabins are comfortable and modern amidst a wilderness setting. Superb dining, expert fly fishing instruction and guiding. Classic autumn river tours.

MELROSE

GUIDES / OUTFITTERS

MONTANA TROPHY ANGLERS
Main Street, Melrose, Box 127   835-3071
>Phil Smith, Outfitter. Full service fly shop. Float trips our specialty. Thirty years guiding experience on the Big Hole, Beaverhead, Jefferson, Madison, Missouri and Ruby Rivers.

BIGHORN RIVER

Map Reference 4

If you should happen to receive an invitation to fish the Bighorn River and if it should happen to be your very first fishing trip ever, you may want to decline the offer on the grounds that you will undoubtedly be spoiled on trout fishing before you barely get started! This river can be a spoiler for a variety of reasons, not the least of which is the quality of the fish, both in numbers and in size.

The river is basically an entity unto itself, flowing through its own, isolated portion of southern Montana. It is seldom visited for reasons other than angling and bird shooting and it does receive a great deal of fishing pressure due to its preeminently high rating among trout fisheries. The Bighorn is a destination river, not one where anglers happen to come along and feel the urge to pull the car over and set up their rods for a couple of hours of casual fishing. Rather, it is a place where intense, day-long floats take place, followed by a good meal and a long night's sleep with the same routine occurring the next day and the next...and the next! For the angler who wishes to come to Fort Smith via private aircraft, a paved four-thousand-foot landing strip is available nearby, from which shuttle service to the river can be arranged with local businesses. The commercial hub around which the fishing centers is at the settlement of Fort Smith, which is forty-two miles south of the town of Hardin. The road between these two communities dead-ends just beyond Fort Smith, so you can understand why the journey is one of purpose, not happenstance. Fort Smith is small, but it is geared to the needs of fishermen with several forms of lodging arrangements available, from tent spaces to motel rooms, and boat rentals, showers, guide service and boat shuttle service.

The Bighorn flows through a cottonwood and willow bottom land rather than a mountain environment and its flanks are planted in sugar beets, corn and hundreds of thousands of acres of wheat. At at one time the river cut through the rugged Bighorn Mountains, but it is now impounded behind the Yellowtail Dam. The river below the dam is cold and clear and fertile. It supports abundant plant, insect and fish life. It is open to fishing year-round and it is fished year-round; albeit there are many frozen days in mid-winter when the trout are totally and gratefully unmolested!

The river flows through the heart of the Crow Indian Reservation where tribal rules prevail, meaning a couple of things to visiting anglers. First of all, property rights must be respected, and whether wading or floating, anglers must stay in the river channel below the high water line except at designated public access points; secondly, should you wish to enjoy a cold libation during your stay here, you'll have to provide it yourself as no alcoholic beverages are sold on the reservation.

For the enjoyment of fishers and non-fishers alike, the immediate surrounding area does offer a couple of diversions. A visit to Yellowtail Dam can be an interesting experience and visitors can either view the displays at the visitor's center or take a guided trip through the dam's interior to witness some of the engineering accomplishments that make the dam perform its intended functions. This 525 foot high structure was completed in 1965 and now contains the water of seventy-one-mile long Bighorn Lake, created for power generation, irrigation and flood control. The lake itself is accessible for fishing from a boat ramp just south of the dam.

Another very interesting area to visit is the Custer Battlefield National Monument where the battle in June of 1876 between the forces of General George A. Custer and those of the Sioux and Northern Cheyenne Indian tribes proved to be disastrous to the army forces. On this rolling hillside overlooking the Little Bighorn River, just fifteen miles south of Hardin off highway I-90, Custer's entire command was lost in the battle. The attractive displays at the visitor center and the headstones on the grassy slope nearby bear witness to a dramatic era in our country's western history.

For our description of the fishing here, we'll categorize all the elements of interest into as succinct a narrative as possible. Some information will overlap from one category to another but will be repeated to maintain continuity or amplify important points.

THE WATER—Most of the river volume in Montana actually originates in Wyoming. By the time the water is expelled from the bottom of Yellowtail Dam, it is, with rare exception, very clear and very cold. During early spring it is not unusual to find the water temperature to be down in the high thirties and low forties. When fishing this time of year be sure to wear your snuggies! Long underwear should be considered a must, even when the air temperature is mild. As the summer season approaches the water warms and August temperatures have been recorded as high as sixty-five degrees in the most utilized section of river, the first thirteen miles of river below the dam. These warmer temperatures usually curb feeding activity of the fish, but this is normally a short-lived condition. Optimum fishing temperature is between fifty-four and sixty degrees.

The level of the water fluctuates throughout the year with flows through early spring generally at their lowest point, around 1,500 c.f.s. Near the first of June the water in the river comes up as the reservoir fills and water is released. Flows of four thousand to five thousand c.f.s. into late July are not

Bighorn Lake

uncommon. If the mountain snow pack is exceptionally high during a particular winter, the water can run as high as nine thousand c.f.s. The river is seldom affected directly by the run-off or heavy rain showers until it reaches the confluence of Soap Creek. This tributary often discolors the river below after heavy rain. The volume it contributes isn't enough to raise the level of the river, but the sediment load it carries can create some turbidity.

After July, water levels are usually maintained at about 2,500 to 3,000 c.f.s. which is ideal for fishing because enough water is in the channel to cover the banks, yet the water is low enough to allow some wading.

During abnormally warm summers, the lake may develop an algae bloom that permeates the water and in turn, discolors the river and adversely affects the fishing.

As one progresses down river, beyond the thirteen-mile access, the river becomes more susceptible to turbidity. Irrigation return begins to show its effect and small prairie streams influenced by rain storms will in turn color the river. Rotten Grass Creek, in particular, can carry a disturbing quantity of sedimentation. The water below Hardin experiences turbidity and temperature increases to a degree that discourage residency by trout, but these water conditions do support a population of ling, catfish and sauger.

The riparian environment of the river remains essentially constant because of regulated water flow. Spring run-off doesn't tear through the channel taking with it fragile gravel banks, willow thickets and cottonwood groves.

41

This is prairie country and the river bottoms are gently soft with vegetation, birds and animal life. From nearby promontories you can scan a panorama of wheat-covered landscapes to the very crown of the distant horizon.

Because of the nature of this watercourse ecosystem, it is a wonderful area in which to enjoy bird watching, particularly during springtime. Waterfowl abounds here and it's not unusual to sight curlew, heron, sand hill crane and good numbers of geese and raptors, particularly during the fall migration season. Another creature that thrives in this area and deserves your attention is the snake. There are rattlers in the area, but they usually reside away from the river in the more arid benchland. Bull snakes, however, do occasionally visit the river's edge, and have been known to swim out and pay a visit to unsuspecting anglers.

The first thirteen miles of river, from the afterbay to the Thirteen Mile Access, displays a good amount of flat water, spotted with plenty of traditional holding lies that are easy to read by experienced fishermen. The water here is well suited to all methods of fly fishing, whereas the water below is much flatter, slower and generally deeper and better suited to streamer fishing than to nymphs or dries. Because of its nature, there are smaller numbers of fish below but many people feel they average a bit larger than those above.

THE FISH—At one time rainbow trout of more-than-impressive proportions finned in the clear currents of the Bighorn. They populated the river in strong numbers and for several years were almost totally unmolested because the river was closed to fishing on the reservation. In 1981 after a long legal battle the river was opened to public fishing and fishermen responded with grateful, but lethal enthusiasm. Rainbow still inhabit the river, but they are now outnumbered by browns at an estimated eight to one ratio. The rainbow population was so decimated that special regulations were instituted several years ago to help increase their numbers and size.

Along with natural mortality and harvesting by fishermen through the years, another problem plagues the trout of the Bighorn—nitrogen supersaturation. The problem is created as the water plunges down through the various workings of the dam, and the fish living closest to the dam are most seriously affected. A good number of influenced fish are caught in the spring, which is the time of rainbow spawning activity, and the time when their strength and physiological defense systems are at a minimum. Should you catch fish afflicted with skin lesions, blisters or other deformities, they will most likely have been caused by this supersaturation problem. Not only are the adult fish affected, but the phenomenon is also killing their eggs. Fisheries biologists are currently conducting studies to help find remedial answers.

The numbers of trout in the Bighorn are as impressive as any river in the state. The number of fish per mile over thirteen inches is estimated to be two to three times greater than in other highly ranked rivers of Montana. The

42

average fish here is fourteen to eighteen inches in length with many to twenty-one inches. Beyond the twenty-one inch size, the number of browns seems to recede very rapidly, while the number of rainbows remains quite high. The old days, when anglers expected to hook fish up to twenty-four inches, continue to remain "the old days." Don't expect fish of that size now. Not only are the fish of the Bighorn larger than average but they're considered stronger than average—so hang onto your tackle when you hook one! The bows are more acrobatic than the browns and therefore rank as the preferred fish to catch, and you'll find them most often in the faster, deeper water. The fish here seem to pod into small, isolated areas of the river and will be found in large numbers in one spot and not at all in others. Experienced Bighorn anglers look for these concentrations of fish as they float.

In addition to browns and rainbows the river has a small population of whitefish, a very small population of sculpin, a few carp, a few suckers, very few walleye and very few northern pike. These species don't exist in numbers large enough to attract attention from the anglers.

THE INSECTS AND ARTIFICIALS—The Bighorn is a fly fisherman's river! The combination of factors valued by flingers-of-the-fraud are here in spades; rich water flowing from limestone formations in the Bighorns, plenty of trout that, in the considered opinion of Terry Ross, "are gentlemen—they do their part," a small-gravel river bottom facilitating easy wading, and lastly an

Bighorn River

abundant variety and quantity of insect life.

In general, the most prevalent insects are caddis, small mayflies, small stoneflies and midges. The river contains a few craneflies and a great number of scuds (fresh water shrimp). Late summer sometimes produces excellent grasshopper fishing, but it is unpredictable from year to year.

Later we'll review in detail the fishing through the various seasons of a typical year, but due to the wide variety of artificials that can be especially effective at certain times, we'll furnish here a comprehensive checklist of patterns. If your fly boxes contain these flies, you're totally prepared to head for the Bighorn at a moment's notice. DRIES: Midge #18-22, Griffith Gnat #14-18, Adams #14-18, Dark Blue Dun #18-20, Blue Winged Olive #16-20, Pale Morning Dun #14-18, Polywing Trico Spinner #18-22, Hopper #8-10, Elk Hair Caddis #12-18, Henryville Caddis #12-18, Black Caddis #16-18, Caddis Emerger #14-16, Golden Stonefly #10-14 and Yellow Sally #12-18. WETS: San Juan Worm #4-6, Scuds (orange, pink, tan and olive) #8-12, Gold Ribbed Hare's Ear #12-18, Pheasant Tail #14-18, Brassie #14-16, Miracle Nymph #14-18, Peeking Caddis #14-16, Soft Hackle #12-16, Cranefly larvae #2-6 and rubberleg patterns (Girdle Bug, Yuk Bug) #2-6. STREAMERS: All in size #2-8; Woolly Bugger (black/black, olive/black), Zonker, Marabou Muddler and Woolhead.

This is a long list, but they all have their moments! If your flybox looks like Mother Hubbard's Cupboard, worry not; local shops can help you out! You'll notice that one of Montana's very favorite patterns, the Royal Wulff, isn't included on our list. It really isn't very effective on the Bighorn because these fish require a somewhat higher degree of angling skill than seems to be required on many other rivers. Fishermen using lures prefer the Mepps, Blue Fox Vibrax, Rapala, Rooster Tail and Krocodile.

THE FLOATING—A wide variety of craft are put onto the water here and for the most part, they are taken from the water as planned, no worse for wear. Occasionally, however, and we stress "occasionally," a boat won't reach its destination as high and dry as when launched! Misfortune, for one reason or another, does strike from time to time; boats tip over (usually canoes) and passengers lose gear and learn little lessons. Certain deep holes on the river have become unplanned repositories for a variety of worldly goods—including favorite fly rods and cherished cameras! The Bighorn really has no white-water as such, but there is a spot or two that can unexpectedly tug and turn a boat, so boatmen shouldn't be lulled into a feeling of unwarranted complacency when floating.

The water from the afterbay down to the Thirteen Mile take-out receives approximately ninety percent of the floating pressure on the river. This is the area of most insects and most fish, the area of fly and lure fishing only, the area of greatest water variety and the area where no motors are allowed on boats.

This stretch of river is not difficult to negotiate from behind the oars, but the person in control would do well to have previous floating experience. River traffic includes both individual fishermen and licensed guides and at times— particularly weekends and holidays—a sizeable number of boats will be on the river, so it becomes imperative that everyone stay alert and operate in a considerate and courteous manner. Sometimes an angler's favorite run or pool will be occupied by other fishermen, so rather than being grievously dismayed and irate, one should wish them well and continue downstream to the next likely looking water.

There are several access sites for boats. Most boats are put in at the afterbay access. A short float of one to two hours brings the angler to the Three Mile Access, also referred to as the Lind Access, where you can either put-in or take-out. The next access is the Thirteen Mile or Bighorn Access. This site is the downstream boundary of what we call the Upper River. The middle river starts here and continues to the Two Leggins Access twenty-four miles downstream—a long, slow float. A new access has been established at the half-way point of the middle river, making this section a more feasible area to float. The new site is called the Mallard Access, and trips may be reasonably started or terminated at this location.

GENERAL FISHING TECHNIQUE—Sometimes in our impatience to realize immediate gratification or unqualified success at a given venture, we fail to give fair attention to the object of our efforts. This shortcoming is particularly true when success has been touted as being automatic by merely expending a little effort. The Bighorn certainly has a wonderful reputation throughout the entire country: "Come one, come all. Throw thy fly upon the silvery surface of this unrivaled river and realize instant fulfillment of your fishiest fantasies!" Well, it doesn't usually work out quite that way. As a matter of fact, the fish here usually insist that you do a few things rather properly before they'll play your game. Fortunately they will play it!

To be fair to the river and fair to yourself, plan to spend more than just one day here. Stick around for three or four days and try to learn the vagaries of the river. It can often be a capricious adversary, but can also be a predictable accomplice. Don't set your expectations too high, be willing to try a variety of angling techniques, find the fish and make accurate casts, particularly when fishing dry flies. The fish here are fairly selective, and don't often move far to take an insect, or fly, from the surface. Exact imitation is less important than putting the fly right over the fish's nose.

Nymph fishing is the preferred method used on the Bighorn and it prevails throughout the year. Dry fly fishing spans from early spring to late fall and streamers are most productive during the fall months. When circumstances favor it, wading is the most productive way to fish, using the boat for transportation and to locate working fish. Spin fishermen are in a minority here, but find the most rewarding fishing from June through August. Floating, slimy moss on the water before June and a bottom-weed break-up in September and October that fouls most casts prevent much success with spinning gear.

Holding and feeding lies change as water volume changes and fish will move into or out of a particular area in response to the river's water level and their own "comfort" level. As water moves away from the banks, so do the fish. As water temperature rises, fish seek cooler currents and more oxygen. Where you fished successfully on a previous trip, may not fish as well on a subsequent trip. Staying flexible and having a willingness to experiment are important on the Bighorn. Regardless of the water level, promising water types include fast riffles, drop-offs, heads of pools where water falls from a riffle lip into the pool head, the slack water of a riffle corner, deep water against a bank and any type of structure in the river. The upper river contains several islands and they provide very good fishing potential, particularly where channels meet forming a riffle immediately downstream.

The Bighorn can be fished like a big river or a small one. The former approach would best be accomplished with a fly rod from seven to nine weight, while the latter requires no more than a six weight. Floating lines are used predominantly, but fall fishing with streamers sometimes requires a sink tip, or Hi Speed, Hi-D shooting head. Each reel should be loaded with at least fifty yards of backing. Chest waders are most essential and felt soles are preferred by most anglers.

THE SEASONS—Winter in Montana is hardly lawn chairs by the pool and Sunday afternoon barbeques, but a few intrepid anglers still throw flies into pools on an afternoon when the weather is on the mild side. The fishing season is open year-round, but most fishermen will wait until March to seriously get the season underway. During late March the weather begins to temper, and insects start to appear on the river's surface. Dry fly fishing from March through May can be excellent, with midges appearing first, followed by Baetis hatches. The midges are imitated either as individual insects, or as clusters and to the delight of anglers and fish, the appearance of the insects is fairly consistent day in and day out. This is a time of year when the Adams in small sizes is an effective pattern to imitate the midge cluster. For the Baetis imitation a Dark Blue Dun works very well. The water level is at its lowest point of the year now, so wading is fairly easy. The water is also extremely cold, which puts the fish into the softer, deeper water, out of the current, during the day and into the quiet shallows as evening approaches.

The Baetis and midges work well now because, except for nymphs, no other insects are on the water. But the fish aren't always heads-up; they also respond very well to small nymph patterns such as Hare's Ears, Pheasant Tails, Brassie and Miracle Nymphs in sizes #16 and #18. Along with these insect imitations, the shrimp patterns also do well and will continue to be effective throughout the year. As crustaceans, these arthropods remain underwater throughout their entire life cycle and are a favorite food source for the trout. June is not a particularly active month for surface fishing, so weighted flies fished near the bottom is normally the most productive technique.

You'll soon be aware of a few things that take place in the spring that are not apparent the rest of the year. First, you'll be contending with a slimy moss that hangs in suspension in the water. It is certainly aggravating, but inescapable, and more of a problem when fishing wet than dry. Second, you'll notice the fish are more slender than they will be later in the season. The browns in particular show the effects of their reduced metabolism in the cold, winter water, particularly after having expended a large amount of energy during the previous fall spawning ritual. In addition they have had to endure the rigors imposed by the water's high nitrogen load.

The summer hatches on the Bighorn get underway in later July. The midge and Baetis activity has subsided by the end of June and July will see the onset of different hatches.

The little golden stoneflies (Isoperla marmona) start to appear about the third week of July and the fish move well to both the nymphs and the adults. This hatch is particularly strong during mid-day, from Noon until 2:00 p.m. These insects show themselves through August and sometimes into September. A Mormon Girl tied with a red tag and trimmed to present a low profile seems to work very well to imitate this insect.

Another insect that can occur starting in July is the Pale Morning Dun in sizes #16 and #18. This isn't a hatch that does well each and every year, but when it appears it lasts a long time and fish will come to a variety of pale cream adult patterns as well as to the spinner fall.

The insect providing the most excitement during summer is the caddis— in several sizes and colors. Through the months of August and September fishermen can expect to find fish feeding on all of the stages of this ubiquitous insect's life cycles—larval, emerger and adult. Fishermen have success with many patterns including Peeking Caddis nymphs, soft hackles, standard Elk Hair and Henryville patterns and emerger dressings as well as the adult imitations. A small Black Caddis is very effective. The evening hours produce the greatest numbers of insects and the greatest response from the fish; the problem of selectivity sets in concurrently as your imitation becomes one of thousands of choices to the fish and very difficult for you to differentiate from the naturals. You, as well as the trout, might better distinguish the fly if it were larger than the naturals. Emerging patterns work well at this time as do soft hackles barely submerged under dancing riffles.

One would think that this river, being a prairie stream, would see abundant grasshopper activity during August as afternoon breezes brush across the dry, grassy banks. And indeed, sometimes it does—but not every year. Like the Pale Morning Dun, the appearance of this chunky terrestrial isn't necessarily a given. When this fishing is good, it can be great—starting in late July and continuing on through August. Later during this period the fish have seen every fraud ever contrived by human cunning and respond to them infrequently and with care! The first two or three weeks of the hopper's appearance can provide very good fishing, particularly when you wade fish and toss the fly against the bank in water having at least a small amount of chop on its surface. The flat, quiet stretches are considerably less forgiving and, consequently, less productive. The hopper's terrestrial cousins, the ant and beetle, can be considered of little consequence here.

One other insect of importance during late summer and into fall is the tiny mayfly, Tricorythodes. These delicate creatures will swarm above the water during the morning hours providing a minute, but multitudinous quarry to the trout below. Spinner patterns seem to be especially effective during this hatch.

If the water is at a level where it pushes up against the sloping banks with enough depth to hold fish, you can throw large rubberleg nymph patterns with fair success. Cast in as close as possible to the bank and pull the fly out with some force. Make it look worth chasing! This technique isn't particularly effective during spring, but in summer and fall it can be deadly.

One last observation on summer fishing here; the combination of fertile water and abundant sunshine stimulate the growth of trailing weeds on the river bottom. This vegetation provides living quarters for many of the aquatic creatures of the river and yet is not slippery, a valued consolation to the wading angler.

Fall is a time of mixed emotion to serious trout anglers everywhere as it announces the beginning of the end of another fishing season. On the Bighorn this means not only the anticipation of hooking a big brown trout in spawning colors, but to some sportsmen, the anticipation of shooting under late fall flights of waterfowl.

Many of the hatches of summer have waned, or totally ceased for the year, while others continue, and still others renew to provide prolonged dry fly fishing through November. Although the caddis of summer are but a memory, the Baetis of spring once again return and allow you to fool fish using those small Blue Winged Olives in your fly box. Late September will see a continuation of Trico, nymph, shrimp and midge fishing, and the anticipated fall streamer fishing. Those breathable patterns such as the Woolly Buggers and Marabous work especially well now. Cast them into the banks, but don't overlook the tails of runs and pools in mid-river as well. Often you can fish streamers on a floating line, but water depth and holding lies will dictate whether or not to use your sink-tip or fast sinking head. This is the time of year to get out of the boat and wade the river. Cover the water well with consecutively longer casts and if you need to add some lead to your leader to speed up the sink rate, go ahead and do it! The Three Mile Access offers good potential for wading because the islands create smaller sized channels as well as the important structure of the islands themselves.

There is a debit column to be aware of during fall and it reflects two items that are somewhat disconcerting. First of all, there is one day in the life of the Yellowtail Dam when it receives an annual safety inspection. This procedure takes place sometime in October, lasts but a half day, but unfortunately disturbs the river below. The water flow is shut back to four hundred—yes, four hundred c.f.s. This happens in the morning and later in the day the water is brought back to its normal volume. This action sounds innocuous enough, but it can discolor the river for up to three weeks thereafter. You can imagine what that does to the fishing! The second problem has to do with those weeds that grew on the river bottom during the summer. During late September and October they begin to break free and float downstream. The fishing remains good, but wet fly fishermen will be clearing hooks regularly, while dry fly anglers will experience less of an inconvenience.

There you have the Bighorn. We've told it like it is, as accurately as possible, and you can understand why the Bighorn is the destination of many fishermen. It has its periodic problems, it's out of the way, it flows through a more desert than alpine environment, but it offers challenge and reward enough to keep fishermen coming back year after year for the great fishing it offers.

HARDIN

Hardin lies at the northern edge of the Crow Indian Reservation in southern Montana. The area surrounding the town is known primarily for its agricultural products and for coal mining; a good deal of wheat is harvested from nearby fields and large strip mines yield millions of tons of coal each year. It's an interesting perspective on the vast extent of trout fishing in Montana to realize that the distance between Hardin, which is located on the easternmost edge of the trout fishing area, and Libby, which is on the westernmost edge, is 555 miles! Montana is, indeed, the Big Sky state!

Visitors to Hardin may enjoy a visit to the Big Horn County Historical Museum. This progressive museum features rotating exhibits which reflect not only the social and cultural aspects of early Big Horn County, but also the involvement of the military in settling this region of the Montana Territory. In addition to the indoor exhibits, the museum features restored buildings including a log cabin, a farmhouse and a church. In the main museum building you'll find a gift shop as well as the Chamber and Visitor Center for south central/southeastern Montana where you can obtain more information on the area.

Hardin provides the visitor a swimming pool in which to splash or dash, as well as a place to hook and slice on the attractive Fort Custer Golf Club nine. Family-oriented activities include rodeos, fairs and festivals. One of the most significant is Little Bighorn Days held the last weekend of June. During this event participants and spectators dress in early western clothes to enjoy the rodeo events, athletic contests, dancing, barbeque, kid's-day parade and community theater. When the fish of the Bighorn River wear you out, you can relax in Hardin.

Hardin Area Chamber of Commerce: Box 1206A, Hardin, Montana 59034 Phone: 665-1672

River Notes

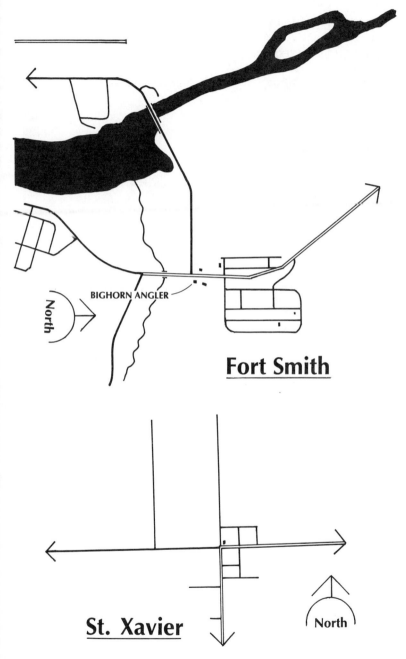

BIGHORN ANGLER

North

Fort Smith

St. Xavier

North

© Stream Stalker, Inc. 1988

FORT SMITH

GUIDES / OUTFITTERS

BIGHORN RIVER OUTFITTERS
Fort Smith, Box 483 YRS   666-2351
> Come fish the world famous Bighorn River with us. We offer complete guide services, motel accommodations, trophy trout fishing and waterfowl and upland bird hunting.

MOTELS

BIGHORN ANGLER
Rt. 313, Fort Smith, Box 577   666-2233
> The Bighorn's most comfortable lodging offers private baths, air conditioning, cooking and laundry facilities. Also, a complete fly fishing shop, experienced guides and boat rental. Your hosts are Mike Craig and Holly Brooks.

BIG SPRING CREEK

Map Reference 5

We imagine most people like a good surprise in their lives once in a while; finding out the operation won't be necessary, winning a fly rod on a raffle ticket or hooking a twenty inch trout when you thought by the subtle rise form that he was only ten inches long. Well, we think you'll be similarly surprised when you first see Big Spring Creek at Lewistown.

The environs surrounding Big Spring give little indication that at this geographical center of Montana is a gin-clear trout stream flowing unobtrusively through the agricultural landscape. The creek is twenty to thirty feet wide, quite small when compared to Montana's more famous trout waters. It is easy to wade because the bed gravel of limestone and sandstone is small and not slippery. It's also easy to fish from the banks where they open up enough to permit casting. Fishing is not always easy, however, as there are thick growths of alder and willow with branches hanging down into the water in many areas.

Big Spring Creek above Lewistown

The creek originates at the Big Spring Fish Hatchery five miles southeast of Lewistown where the water gushes from the ground at a constant fifty-six degrees. Some of the water is diverted for domestic use as the Lewistown water supply, some is diverted for use at the hatchery and the balance provides the wellspring for the creek. The bottom gravel is covered with weed beds for its entire length, offering good cover for the trout and a home to good numbers of caddis, mayflies, snails and small stoneflies.

The community of Lewistown divides the river into its upper and lower segments. The upper section is more "residential" with many private homes built along the stream. This part of the creek has more dense growth along the banks than below town where stone rip-rap has been placed along the banks to prevent erosion. Although the rip-rap looks "manufactured," it does provide good holding water for the trout. The lower river has more insect life, plus more and larger trout, while the cemented gravel of the upper reaches restricts development of large insect populations.

The fish throughout the river include rainbow, brown, cutthroat, a few brook trout and a few whitefish. The average size upstream is ten to twelve inches and below, more on the order of twelve to fourteen inches. The creek is too small to float, so permission to wade is necessary throughout its length, except at the Hatchery and a few places where the road meets the water. The creek flows down a gradient that keeps the current moving at about four to six feet per second, so the fishing is much like that on a mountain freestone river.

Caddisflies, mayflies and a few stoneflies make up the aquatic food source for the fish here, with hoppers becoming available at the end of July and continuing through August. A variety of hopper patterns with either tan or yellow bodies will work. Local tiers prefer to dress them with a spun deer hair head. For most of the year the caddis is the most important insect to the fish and anglers will see it come off the water from March through November. In addition to the standard Elk Hair Caddis and Goddard Caddis, also try a #14 Brown Bivisible on the surface. Under the surface the Carey Special, Pittman Special and Hare's Ear Nymph prove effective. Mayflies are generally small, with Blue Winged Olives the most used pattern, but you should have some small Red Quills, Lt. Cahills, Pale Morning Duns and Adams in your fly box as well.

The insects, fish and fishermen aren't severely affected by the spring run-off because it's not only short, but most of the tributary streams have been dammed and upstream reservoirs collect much of the turbid water before it can reach the creek. Likewise, the creek is fortunately spared the negative effects from irrigation practices. Significant dewatering doesn't take place, and the heavy sediment loads usually found in return water have little impact on the stream.

Big Spring Creek is also referred to as Cold Spring Creek and it's the cold,

Big Spring Creek below Lewistown

fertile water pouring from the ground at the spring that makes the area so well suited to the hatching and raising of trout. We recommend you visit the hatchery to witness the effort that goes into supplying one-half of Montana's stocked trout. Five strains of rainbow are raised here and a good deal of research takes place in order to stock the proper strain to satisfy certain conditions and fulfill management goals. The mainstay of the different varieties is the Arlee rainbow, which has an excellent growth rate, resists disease and takes flies and lures well. The Eagle Lake strain is more predatory and is used more where a strong forage fish population exists.

There are special regulations limiting fishing on Big Spring, but there is no limit on the number of mosquitoes that come off the hay meadows to hover over the water, particularly on the lower river. Be sure your repellent is handy! Also be alert for rattlers, as they are sometimes seen on the lower river section.

Mention should be made here of another spring creek in the Lewistown area called Warm Spring Creek. It is located fifteen miles north of Lewistown and flows out among the barley and wheat fields after coming out of the ground at 58,000 gallons per minute at a temperature of 68 degrees. It empties into the Judith River about twenty miles from its source and, because of its warmer water temperature, has been stocked with bass to supplement its trout population. The stream is about twenty to twenty-five feet wide, moves along quite rapidly at about six feet per second, and is rarely fished, maybe because of the lack of access, maybe because of the rattlesnakes.

LEWISTOWN

With so many places and entities in Montana having been named after the two protagonists of the Lewis and Clark Expedition, either because they were the first white men to discover them or because they traveled nearby, one would think that Lewistown was likewise so named. Not this time, even though their party did pass through here. Prior to the town's designation as Lewistown there was established here a military outpost called Camp Lewis after Major William H. Lewis who commanded the camp during the mid-1870's. By 1879 families settled here; in 1882 the townsite was formally laid out; and in 1889 the city was incorporated and became the social and economic center of the region, a distinction it holds today.

Lewistown (not pronounced "Lewis-ton") is the agricultural support community for a broad area within the Judith Basin and, in addition to being the seat of Fergus County government, it is also located on the precise geographic center point of the state. Lewistown is a contemporary city involved not only in activities which center around the agricultural economy of the region, but in meeting the needs of visitors who come here on business, to enjoy the fishing and hunting, or just to do a bit of sightseeing. Although the Judith Mountains lie to the north and the Big Snowy Mountains stretch out to the south, Lewistown itself lies in an area of rolling countryside with a landscape of grain and hay fields, dotted occasionally with grazing cattle.

For anyone arriving by vehicle or renting a car at the Lewistown Municipal Airport, which does accommodate small jets, several attractions are within relatively short driving distance. A popular site near town is, of course, the Montana State Fish Hatchery at Big Spring where ninety million gallons of water per day surge from the recesses of the earth in the third-largest, fresh-water spring in the world. The water from the spring forms Big Spring Creek and supplies the city with all of its domestic water needs, without treatment of any kind, a benefit greatly appreciated by the 10,000 residents here. In the Judith Mountains you can visit the ghost towns of Gilt Edge, Kendall and Maiden, or if you enjoy rock hounding, search out the several minerals available here. Crystals may be found in the Moccasin Mountains situated north of town. You'll also find many fossils in the Snowy Mountains and in the gullies entering the Missouri River about sixty miles north of here. Local inquiry should be made to pinpoint some of the better locations at which you'll be most successful.

In town you can play golf and tennis and swim in a pool or picnic at one of several city parks. The Lewistown Art Center exhibits works of local, regional and national artists and the Central Montana Museum features items of historical interest including firearms, minerals and western and Indian artifacts. Another activity of interest to history/architecture buffs is a self-guided walking tour of the "Silk Stocking District," an area of town in which seven stately homes stand as elegant examples of design and workmanship from the period 1905 to 1919. A descriptive brochure offering historical information on each home is available. Many other buildings in town are worth perusal also including the railroad depot and the county courthouse.

Lewistown isn't located on one of the more famous rivers in the southwestern section of the state, but it is home to many friendly sportsmen who enjoy fishing the fine stream that does enhance their city.

Lewistown Area Chamber of Commerce: P.O. Box 818, Lewistown, Montana 5945 - Phone: 538-5436

River Notes

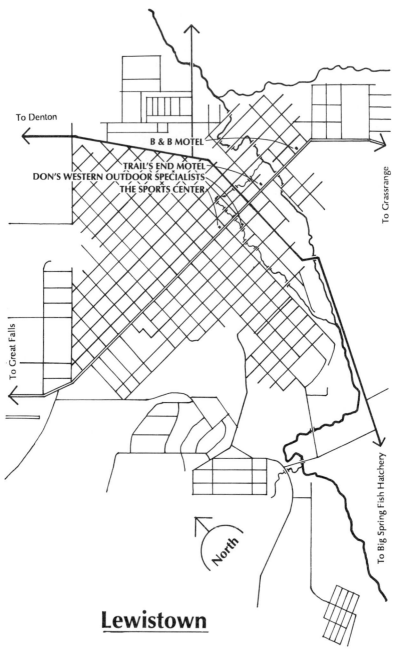

To Denton

B & B MOTEL

TRAIL'S END MOTEL
DON'S WESTERN OUTDOOR SPECIALISTS
THE SPORTS CENTER

To Grassrange

To Great Falls

To Big Spring Fish Hatchery

North

Lewistown

SPORTING GOODS

DON'S WESTERN OUTDOOR SPECIALISTS
120 2nd Ave. South, Box 780   538-9408

Lewistown's store for everyone. Complete sporting goods, diamonds to denims, boots to books, sports to sapphires!

THE SPORTS CENTER
320 West Main   538-9308

Complete sporting goods store. Come see our most interesting display of trout and game from the local area and shop for all of your fishing, hunting and sporting needs. We also have a large selection of toys and models.

MOTELS

B & B MOTEL
520 E. Main St.   538-5496

Thirty-eight units, some with kitchenettes. One, two bedroom kitchenette suite. Color cable TV, air conditioned. Owner is an excellent fly fisherman and can give you good advice about finding the best spots for local fishing and hunting.

TRAIL'S END MOTEL
216 N.E. Main St.   538-5468

Eighteen rooms, including kitchenettes. Phones in rooms. Heated swimming pool. Close to town park and convenient to golf course. Weekly rates available.

SPAS

GIGANTIC WARM SPRINGS
15 miles north of Lewistown, Rte. 3, Box 46   538-9825

Sunbathe, soak, picnic and swim at this one of a kind natural warm spring. 50,000 gallons per minute flow of 68 degree water in a beautiful natural setting. This is one attraction in the Lewistown area that everyone should visit.

BITTERROOT RIVER

Map References 6, 7

A root by any other name would be just another tuber—but this root, the Bitterroot, is much, much more. It's not only the Montana State flower, Lewisia rediviva as so designated in 1895, but it's also eighty-five miles of attractive, fishable, productive trout river that parallels Highway 93 from its beginning at the community of Conner to its terminus at the city of Missoula in western Montana. In its upper reaches anglers enjoy fishing for brook trout while in its lowest sections anglers throw lures to largemouth bass and northern pike. Within these two areas and all the water in between, fishermen also pursue cutthroat, rainbow, brown and Dolly Varden trout, as well as occasionally encounter the Rocky Mountain whitefish, sculpin and sucker.

To the west of the river is the glacier-cut Bitterroot Range and to the east rises the smoother-sloped Sapphire Mountains. Just west of the Bitterroot Range lies the Selway Bitterroot Wilderness which extends into Idaho, covers 2.15 million acres and is the largest wilderness in the lower, forty-eight states. It is veined with hiking trails and small streams, dotted with lakes and is home to a wide variety of wildlife, making it a popular area for back packers and hikers. The river valley is home to ospreys, blue heron, eagles, hawks, beaver, moose and white tail deer.

The river was referred to by its present name back in the 1830's after having several other designations through the time of the Indians, explorers and settlers. In 1806 Captain Lewis referred to it as "a handsome stream," and now over 180 years later, we feel the compliment is still deserved.

The upper river includes that stretch from below Conner at the Upper Darby Bridge (also called the West Fork Bridge) by the Hannon Memorial Access down to Hamilton. As you travel north on Highway 93 from Lost Trail Pass and approach the very upper reaches of this portion of river, the first river sighting is that of the East Fork at Sula. It's a pretty stream ranging from twenty feet to forty feet in width, with evidence of stream improvement work in the slack areas to provide rock cover for the trout. The valley here is narrow and covered with willow, evergreen and cottonwood. Within this wooded canyon the road winds to within fifteen feet of the river in many places.

The West Fork enters at Conner (elevation 4,000 feet). South of Darby the high peaks of the Bitterroots come into view and the valley floor widens to show small ranches, grazing cattle and horses as well as occasional lumber mills. This area is very well known for excellent log home construction. The homes are assembled here, then disassembled and shipped throughout the country. Between Darby and Hamilton the highway continues to follow the river, while residences and lumber mills continue to show their presence as the valley broadens as you approach Hamilton.

The middle reaches of the river extend from Hamilton to Victor. This is an area of islands and braiding and periodic channel alteration that took place during years of heavy run-off when unstable banks fell to the driving force of a charging current; this problem continues to occur during high-water months.

The lower river extends from Victor down to its mouth at the Clark Fork River in Missoula (elevation 3,210 feet). In this section of the river the current slows appreciably but stays clear as it enters the Clark Fork. Upstream between Stevensville and Florence the river skirts the Lee Metcalf National Wildlife Refuge. Named for a former Montana congressman of twenty-five years, who was active in the field of wilderness preservation, this 2,700 acre refuge hugs the river bank for over 4 miles offering the floating angler in particular a great opportunity to sight many species of migrant birds and waterfowl, plus a large population of whitetail deer. This slower water is more like a large, meadow-type stream. During low-water years and/or when irrigation draw-downs severely deplete water levels, the water temperature can rise appreciably as the river nears Hamilton, but fortunately Blodgett Creek brings new water to the channel and, with it, lower water temperatures.

During its eighty-five mile journey from its headwaters to its confluence with the Clark Fork River this shining ribbon of blue has dropped only eight hundred feet. This average descent of approximately ten feet per mile results in a very comfortable current speed in which to wade, float and fish. This is not an intimidating river; it has a well-defined character of riffles, pools, log jams, deep, dark holes cut under the bank, pockets, eddies and all the other traditional holding water the angler enjoys on a trout river. Some of the holes are as much as ten feet deep, but the river is relatively easy to wade in most places over a bottom of small granite, quartzites and mudstone from one to six inches in diameter.

The Bitterroot is blessed with a good population of insects including caddis, mayflies, stoneflies, damsels and dragons. As is common on so many Montana rivers, the salmonfly hatch on the Bitterroot is an anxiously awaited event each year and, as on other rivers, corresponds somewhat, depending on weather and snow pack, with the spring run-off. It usually commences near the first of June and lasts through mid-June having advanced upstream from its start near Stevensville. Prior to this hatch and the high water, fishing is good in the lower river. In this region the river produces a small olive stonefly that comes off in March and is represented with a #10 dark olive stonefly nymph.

Bitterroot River

At this time of year local anglers also fish this stretch with large streamers.

After the run-off of late May and early June recedes, which happens earlier than on most rivers in the state, the lower river will start to feel the effects of irrigation demands, but the upper river will fish well throughout the summer. During the hot days of August, anglers prefer to be on the river in the evening and particularly on a day that is overcast.

During the summer caddis are important insects to both fish and fishermen, with Colorado King and olive-bodied Elk Hair Caddis being good imitations. Two excellent caddis patterns that have been developed locally are curiously called Ugly Rudamus and Madam X. The most popular fly on the river is a Royal Wulff and we imagine this is the most-recommended and most-used dry fly throughout the entire summer. Size #10 and #12 are most popular, but #8's and #14's should be in your fly box as well. Other summer patterns include Adams, Lt. Hendrickson and March Brown. Let's not forget the use of nymphs; the Gold Ribbed Hare's Ear is excellent here in both olive and in brown, from size #12 to #16. The Prince nymph is good as is the Red Squirrel and, of course, those patterns that imitate the salmonfly larvae.

Beginning in August and continuing into September, grasshoppers will be evident along the river and their imitations will be effective, particularly next to the bank. You can expect to see golden stoneflies and green drakes during the latter half of June when size #10 fly imitations will work well. During the summer, particularly as the water drops to lower levels, the spin fisherman's chances of taking fish are diminished some and the fly fisherman's chances increase. Spin anglers enjoy using Mepps, Panther Martin and Thomas Cyclone throughout the season. The Panther Martin in all gold and gold blade with black body and yellow spots works well.

Starting in early September the Tricos become numerous over the water from late morning until early afternoon. Autumn also sees a large, orange October Caddis emerge and an emerging Sparkle Caddis works well fished subsurface. Fish it quartering downstream and don't worry about letting it drag across the river as this can be an effective technique. Another special hatch this time of year is a brown drake, when imitations in size #10 and #12 are commonly used.

The approach to fishing the Bitterroot involves concentrating on those areas of the river that provide good protection for the fish. That sounds like an obvious observation, but it seems to make even more sense on this river because there are great numbers of such places. The river contains many snags and log jams; eddying water is frequent and, because of the unstable gravel in the banks, deep holes are created and fish find them to be secure places in which to hold.

Trout behavior is affected by many influences during the course of the year and as we all know the fish sometimes act differently from day to day. Water temperature is certainly an influential factor to consider and the general rule-of-thumb on the Bitterroot is to fish the heads of pools when the water is warm and expect more fish at the tails when the temperature cools.

Normally the trout prefer to position themselves in holding lies against the bank, where overhead trees and brush offer protection. The middle of the river is not their favorite place to be unless insect activity draws them into riffle feeding lanes or the water is low and the fish move out into the channel to take advantage of the greater dissolved oxygen levels and greater protection of the broken surface in the riffles. A cast placed close into the bank and a drag-free float produces most fish on dries during the summer, but a moving streamer in the fall will consistently get the trout's attention!

Upon reviewing your day's success on the river, you'll probably remember hooking more rainbow than other species, with browns running a close second along with cutthroat. Of course, you must add a fair number of whitefish into the total tally, particularly if you're using flies. The Dolly Varden will be caught primarily by spin fishermen using lures, although a few are taken with flies. These fish run larger in size and smaller in number than the trout. They are slender fish here, with a thirty incher weighing only about five pounds.

The trout fisherman looking for a change of pace should investigate the potential in fishing for largemouth bass and northern pike in the slow pools and back water sloughs of the lower river, particularly between Florence and Lolo, although they have been sighted as far upstream as Corvallis. The spin fisherman will enjoy some action using Daredevles and similar spoons, while the fly fisherman can generate strikes by offering big, leech patterns and Marabou Muddlers. Crayfish are a part of the food chain in this area and their imitations can produce for fishermen who try them. The pike have very sharp teeth so don't be reluctant to use a short, steel leader behind the flies and lures.

Floating is something you can do on the entire river, from the West Fork to Missoula, and if you do the entire float it will take up to six days. This isn't a river for only guides, outfitters and other experts; the river can easily accommodate beginners in the lower reaches and intermediate-level boatmen on the balance of the river. Everyone not familiar with the river should, however, make local inquiries about current conditions before setting out.

Floats usually average ten to twelve miles and take all day—seven to eight hours on the water. The boat is generally used as a taxi to reach areas anglers prefer to wade and when this is done, the boat is beached above the hole and the fishermen walk down to it. Several access points allow a variety of trips and local inquiry should be made for up-to-the-minute information on where fishing might be most productive.

The preferred craft on the Bitterroot is an inflatable raft as, in low water periods, it can be walked over gravel bars if necessary and is easier to portage around water diversions in the river. Such diversions include one immediately below Hamilton, just upstream of the sewage treatment plant, and two more on the right side channel after the river splits about three miles below Corvallis. These can be avoided by choosing the left channel. Two other diversions are located just below the confluence of the river and Lost Horse Creek which enters from the west and just below Sleeping Child Creek which enters from the east. Both of these are between Darby and Hamilton.

Miscellaneous observations of significance include:

1. Check the regulations before fishing the Bitterroot because special rules have been instituted to enhance the quality of fishing.

2. Just as it's essential to keep your eye on a dry fly as it floats along on the river's surface, it is also prudent to keep your eyes open as you walk the river's edge. Each year rattlesnakes are sighted and killed on the east side of the river, particularly from Sleeping Child Creek upstream to past Darby. This is the area where the Urage Hills come right down to the river. Downstream from this area the agricultural activity seems to reduce the snake's numbers. Supposedly the west bank of the river is free of snakes, but we won't bet our best fly rod on it!

3. The Bitterroot has traditionally been closed to trout fishing from late November through late May, although whitefish have been sought all year. Recent changes allow trout fishing in the winter with artificials only on a catch-and-release basis. Check the regulations for specific dates and current rules.

4. Access sites to the Bitterroot for camping, boat launching and wading are available throughout the river's length and they are clearly marked.

EAST FORK BITTERROOT RIVER

Somewhat smaller than the West Fork, the East Fork flows around the south edge of the Sapphire Mountains, past the settlement of Sula, then joins the West Fork to proceed north in the main channel of the Bitterroot. This fork winds through private ranch land and is followed for almost forty miles by a good, gravel road. The stream has had it's problems with channel alterations from highway construction and agricultural practices, but does offer some fishing. The trout in the twenty- to forty-foot wide stream are predominantly ten- to twelve-inch cutthroat and rainbows, with a few brook, brown and bull trout.

Two small campgrounds are located upstream ten and fifteen miles respectively from Highway 93. This is a good area in which to sight big horn sheep.

WEST FORK BITTERROOT RIVER

Leaving Highway 93 at Conner and proceeding southwest on County Road 493, you follow the West Fork through a tight valley lush with pine and cottonwood, affording a pleasant environment in which to fish or drive. The road moves to and from the river, but generally access is good. The river here is about forty to fifty feet wide and has a riffle/pool character with an occasional three-foot-diameter boulder offering special cover for the trout. Most of the cobble, however, is from four to six inches in diameter. The bottom is fairly flat throughout the channel, but the occasional deep runs are very inviting. The upper and lower portions of the river—which contain cutthroat, rainbow, brook and bull trout—are separated by the Painted Rocks Reservoir. The lower

West Fork Bitterroot River

section is floated in the spring when water levels are up and fish to twenty inches are occasionally taken.

LAKE COMO

One of the first white settlers in the area of Hamilton and Stevensville, along the Bitterroot River, is reported to have been Father Anthony Ravalli who built a church in Stevensville in 1866 and is credited for naming Lake Como because it reminded him of Lake Como in Italy. His name is also used to identify Ravalli County in which the lake is located, about fifteen miles southwest of Hamilton. This originally natural lake has been enlarged by an irrigation dam constructed at its east end and as a result the lake level now fluctuates severely during the summer months when most folks have the greatest desire to fish and water ski here. When at its fullest the lake covers up to one thousand surface acres and is considered to be one of Montana's most attractive impoundments. Summer draw-downs drop the water level as much as fifty feet and, coincidentally, decrease its attractiveness a substantial amount. The lake is approximately three miles long and one mile wide. There is a hiking trail along the north shore which leads to the inlet stream, an attractive five-foot waterfall and a primitive camping area. A more formal campground, which is accessible by vehicle, lies on the north side of the lake's east end. There is a boat ramp on the south side of the east end.

A few cutthroat trout reside here, but the fishing is directed primarily at the rainbow population which averages twelve to fifteen inches in length. Each year the state stocks cutthroat/rainbow hybrids up to eight pounds, but these fish spread out and aren't caught in large numbers. The best open-water fishing occurs during spring just after ice-out and again in the fall when the water is low and the fish are concentrated. A boat isn't necessary because fishing from shore can be good especially in the areas around protruding tree stumps. At times you'll spot cruising fish and have an opportunity to cast to them, or you can take to the water with a float tube and search for fish using standard lake flies and lures. Ice fishing is popular in the winter.

BITTERROOT VALLEY

The valley through which the beautiful Bitterroot River flows has as much historic interest as any area in the state. It is a region of "firsts" for Montana including the first recognized water right, Catholic church, white settlement, school, doctor, saw mill and grist mill. With a current population of approximately 25,000 the valley relies heavily on agriculture, log-home manufacturing and tourism for its economic base.

Because each community is relatively small, the information and promotion responsibility rests with a valley-wide Chamber of Commerce located in Hamilton which, with approximately 3,000 residents, is the largest town. We list appropriate addresses here one time rather than after the write-up on each individual community.

Bitterroot Valley Chamber of Commerce: 105 E. Main St., Hamilton, Montana 59840 - Phone: 363-2400

DARBY

If you enjoy ice cream with your country and western music, you should try to be in Darby in late July when the Darby Strawberry Days celebration continues a tradition of over thirty years. This community-wide, ice-cream social is enjoyed by resident and visiting families alike—there are never any leftovers!

Darby lies along Highway 93 at the south end of the Bitterroot Valley, not far from Lake Como, and very close to fine trout fishing in the river. It's a major logging center in the valley and has been involved in that industry since 1890. It is also a center for the manufacture of log homes and evidence of this special field of enterprise is seen along the highway nearby.

An early-day example of local initiative took place in 1888 when James Darby took it upon himself to give a legal name to the new community. He called it Darby in deference to the local postmaster—himself!

HAMILTON

Of all the communities in the Bitterroot Valley, Hamilton has emerged as the largest as well as the most active, particularly since it is the Ravalli County seat. This is a town that didn't just casually happen for one reason or another; it's a community that was conceived in the mind of a local citizen who had the desire and means to make it come about. During the late 1880's a gentleman named Marcus Daly wanted to develop a town which would be the social, economic and cultural center supporting the needs of the people employed in his growing enterprises in the valley. He was the owner of area sawmills and a large stock ranch as well as having been one of the "Copper Kings" with the Anaconda Company in Butte. He hired a man by the name of James Hamilton to lay out the town which, in 1890, would take on his name. Hamilton was incorporated in 1894 and designated the county seat in 1898. Much information on the history of the town and the Bitterroot Valley can be obtained at the Bitterroot Heritage Center in Hamilton where regional archives are available for public perusal.

Hamilton was a bustling community at the turn of the century, and it continues to be so today. It's an upbeat town with facilities for the tourist as well as appeal for the locals. As a matter of fact, the town, as well as the entire valley, is appealing enough to have been designated as the country's eighteenth most desirable location in which to retire. Just outside of town, east of the county fairgrounds, a paved 4,200 foot airstrip allows small planes to land; we wouldn't be surprised to hear that even a fisherman or two has arrived in this manner! We know a good number of people arrive here for the festivities of the July Fourth celebration. This is the time set aside annually for the Daly Days Festival of the Arts, when folks dress in turn-of-the-century clothing and dance in the streets. There's plenty of music, food and entertainment including contests, a golf tournament, theater presentations, art exhibits and an art market. Hamilton is also the center of activity during the annual Ravalli County Fair, with its horse races, rodeo and other traditional fair activities.

For the athletic-minded, this is the home of the Hamilton Golf Course, with an eighteen hole layout. A public swimming pool is available to help you cool off on a summer day and city tennis courts provide a place to warm up on a summer day. The Chamber here acts on behalf of the entire valley and can provide information concerning all activities and events of interest to the public. See their address under the "Bitterroot Valley" section.

Bitterroot National Forest: 316 N. Third St., Hamilton, Montana 59840 - Phone: 363-3131.

CORVALLIS

Corvallis is the home of the Western Agricultural Research Center where a wide variety of research is conducted in the fields of horticulture, agronomy and biology. The subjects of soil fertilization, weed control, new-crop adaptability and the effects of cold on fruit buds represent only a few of the many research topics pursued.

Visitors can tour the Bitterroot Stock Farm which is located two miles north of Corvallis. The estate originally belonged to Marcus Daly, was acquired by the state in 1986 and opened to the public the following year. This 20,000-acre, race-horse farm includes gardens, a greenhouse and a forty-two-room residence, the Daly Mansion, which is considered to be Montana's most beautiful mansion.

A series of special events held in the valley each summer begins with the annual Corvallis Memorial Day Street Fair. Participants enjoy a flea market, bake sales, marching bands and a parade.

The earliest white settlement in Montana was established in 1841 in the Bitterroot Valley, near what is now the community of Stevensville, when Father Pierre Jean DeSmet and his friends, the Flathead Indians, built St. Mary's Mission. This, the first Catholic mission in the northwest, was constructed from cottonwood logs cut from the banks of the Bitterroot River. It's interesting to note that the Flathead Indians were always on amicable terms with the white man and have never been known to engage in hostile acts with whites. The mission was abandoned in 1850 and the site was purchased that year by Major John Owen, who, between the years 1857 and 1860, built a trading post called Fort Owen. In 1866 Father Anthony Ravalli, who is thought to be the first medical doctor in Montana, built a church and pharmacy nearby using the logs from the original St. Mary's church. In 1937 the land and ruins of Fort Owen were donated to the state and in 1971 the Fort Owen State Monument was entered on the roster of National Historic Sites. The church and a portion of the fort can still be seen today. Throughout the 1860's missionaries and farmers settled in the area and in 1864 the townsite was named Stevensville in honor of Isaac Stevens, first territorial governor of the Washington Territory.

This town, with a current population of approximately 1,400 residents, is located thirty miles south of Missoula and is reached by vehicle from Highway 269. Small aircraft can land at the Stevensville Airport which has a paved 3,800 foot runway. Golfers and tennis players will find a course and courts here on which to pursue the improvement of their skills and the entire family can enjoy the annual Creamery Picnic held in August. This local celebration includes band music, dancing, a "Mountain Man Trailthalon," fiddling performances and an event with the intriguing appellation of "Spotted Ass Race." Could this contest involve donkeys with freckles?

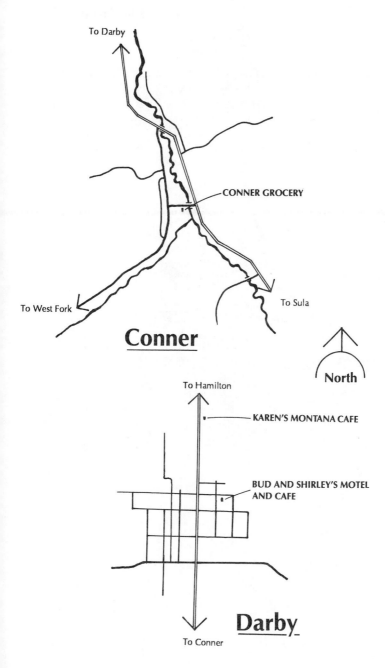

To Darby

CONNER GROCERY

To West Fork

To Sula

Conner

North

To Hamilton

KAREN'S MONTANA CAFE

BUD AND SHIRLEY'S MOTEL
AND CAFE

Darby

To Conner

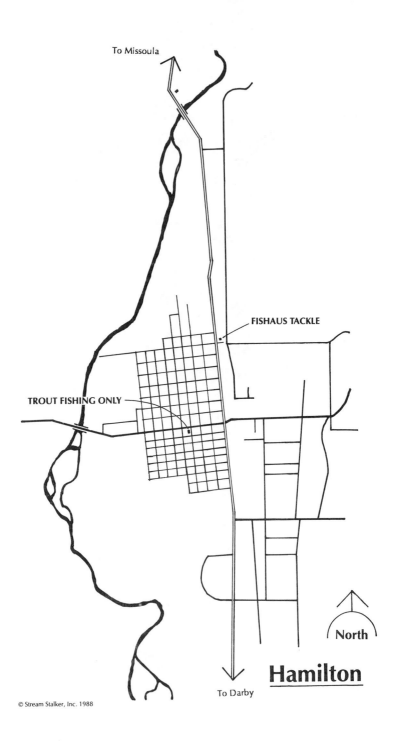

To Missoula

FISHAUS TACKLE

TROUT FISHING ONLY

North

Hamilton

To Darby

© Stream Stalker, Inc. 1988

SULA

LODGES

BROAD AXE LODGE
1151 East Fork Road   821-3878
> Watch Bighorn mountain sheep graze on the nearby ridges as you graze on charbroiled steaks, chicken Kiev, seafood and prime rib. Then relax in one of our exceptionally clean and comfortable cabins.

CONNER

GENERAL STORE

CONNER GROCERY
Conner Cutoff, Box 121   821-9909
> We offer the public groceries, beer, wine, fresh produce, fishing supplies and information. Located at the junction of th east and west forks of the Bitterroot River. We are open seven days a week to serve you.

DARBY

RESTAURANTS / BARS

KAREN'S MONTANA CAFE
Darby, Box 363   821-3322
> Open seven days a week. A full service restaurant with excellent salad bar. Breakfast any time. Specializing in ethnic Montana food for the entire family.

MOTELS

BUD AND SHIRLEY'S MOTEL AND CAFE
One block east of Main St. on Missoula St., Box 362   821-3401
> Thirteen clean, reasonably priced motel units. Cable color TV, phones available. Full service restaurant catering to the fisherman, right next door to the motel.

GUEST RANCHES

ALTA RANCH
2 Miles south of Painted Rocks Lake, West Fork Route   349-2363
> Remotely located in the Bitterroot Range. We offer excellent fly fishing and unparalleled mountain scenery. Relax in our comfortable, fully furnished log cottages.

HAMILTON

FISHING SHOPS

ANGLER'S ROOST
2255 So. First St.   363-1268

> Angler's Roost is located on the Bitterroot River, 3 miles south of Hamilton. We offer the Angler's lodges, RV park, camping , Orvis fly shop, guided fishing trips, sporting goods, gift shop, gas, groceries and genuine Montana hospitality.

FISHAUS TACKLE
702 No. First, Box 583   363-6158

> Fully equipped fishing shop, with the largest selection of fly tying products in western Montana. All flies locally tied. Home of "The Ugly Rudamus" and "Baler Hopper." The coffee pot is always on for you!

GUIDES / OUTFITTERS

TROUT FISHING ONLY
415 Main St., Box 1332   363-2408

> Located at the City Center Motel in Hamilton, Montana!

RESTAURANTS / BARS

WANDA'S WAGON WHEEL RESTAURANT
2370 Old Highway 93   303-1434

> Welcome to one of Montana's oldest and finest dining establishments. Marvelous cocktails and delightful dinners. Reasonable prices. Master Card and Visa.

BLACKFOOT RIVER

Map References 8, 9

The countryside in the region near Missoula is abundant with forested hillsides, tumbling streams and impressive rivers. The people here love outdoor activities and during the warm days of summer one of their favorite pastimes is floating the Blackfoot River. The river provides a wide variety of floating challenges from silent flats and whispering riffles to white-water rapids; all levels of personal boating expertise, or lack thereof, can be accommodated. The Blackfoot is referred to as a "family river" as well it might. Its pristine environment and recreational potential is just minutes away from the urban surroundings of the bustling city of Missoula. So kindred is this stream that local groups have banded together to form local alliances to protect the river. Businesses, the Nature Conservancy, private landowners, the forest service, Montana Department of Fish, Wildlife and Parks, individuals and political groups have all agreed on the establishment of the Blackfoot River Recreation Corridor. This thirty-mile ribbon of land along the river provides fishing access, campsites, launch areas for boats and public picnic areas. It's a model program that works for everyone, not only locals, but out-of-town visitors as well.

The gravel road through the corridor begins at the Johnsrud Park Access at its lower end and follows the river upstream to its eastern terminus at the Missoula County line near the Scotty Brown Bridge. For most of its length it follows the river, sometimes at river level and at times high above it providing dramatic views of the river canyon and the pine and larch forest through which it travels. On the other hand, Highway 200, which roughly parallels the river road, passes through forest as well as an agricultural environment with cattle and crops evident along its route. You might be interested in taking a short, thirteen-mile side trip from the highway to the ghost town of Garnet. The turnoff is about ten miles south of the intersection of Highway 200 and Highway 83. This well-preserved site of fifty buildings shows what mining life was like at the turn of the century when a thousand residents made their homes here. Gold mining was started nearby in 1865 and the town survived until World War II when expenses became too high to realize a profit. Fortunately today, neither mining nor ranching has an effect on the river. But recreationists do!

During the summer the river is used intensively by boaters. Many floating

67

craft are on the river including rafts, canoes, kayaks and inner tubes. The river itself is about sixty to eighty feet wide in most places and there is much interesting water to float as well as fish. The water above the Scotty Brown Bridge is fairly slow and uninteresting; but it does hold browns and cutthroats in limited numbers along with a few brook trout and bull trout. This is a narrow, brushy section of river and not well suited to floating.

The desire to float and fish really gains more fervor below Scotty Brown Bridge, where insect and fish populations increase dramatically as does the water's speed. Slightly downstream from the bridge lies the Box Canyon, an area of rapids and white water. Montana law requires that you wear a life vest when floating a river and this is an area where you'll be happy to do so! The entire distance between this point and Johnsrud is marked with long, deep runs, willow banks, boulders, pocket water, standing waves and dark pools. Floating is not always easy, nor is the wading; the grey and black river rocks average four to twelve inches in diameter. They're angular in shape and usually covered with algae, particularly in the quieter sections. One advantage to the wader is that the rocks are "cemented" together with bottom silt and the river is referred to as "solid" because the rocks don't rock and roll as they do on most streams. This doesn't, however, dismiss the need for careful placement of your feet. You should always watch where you're going and you should frequently watch the river upstream. Wading fishermen have been known to be knocked over by boaters, but we've heard of no instances of the opposite occurring. If you fish on the weekend, an even keener level of alertness is required because the river is considerably more congested with boat traffic.

Blackfoot River at Scotty Brown Bridge

Spring run-off usually starts sometime in late April and continues to the first part of July, making the Blackfoot one of the last rivers in the area to return to normal. Because run-off traditionally peaks in late May, the emergence of the salmonfly and Golden Stonefly hatches can occur when the water is clear and dropping. These hatches proceed upstream as far as the river's confluence with the North Fork and the fish throughout this fifty miles of river take advantage of this annual feast which continues into July.

The Blackfoot is considered to be better for dry fly fishing than for nymph or streamer fishing; the dry fly activity actually gets underway in April, prior to run-off, when Blue Winged Olives in size #12 works well from twilight to dark. Throughout the summer the evening fishing is considered to be best with significant numbers of caddis often on the water. Standard imitations work well as do attractor dries and small muddler minnows thrown in close to the bank. Whether using wet or dry patterns, they will normally prove most effective when fished in the pockets around boulders where the water is at least two feet deep.

On many summer evenings there are small insects on the water which anglers will attempt to imitate until dusk, at which time they change to large attractor dries, a stratagem that seems to stimulate the larger fish into coming to the surface.

The Blackfoot is a good river for novice fishermen because the fish are aggressive and will come fairly readily to flies that are well presented, whether they be imitative patterns or the more forgiving attractors. Hatches here aren't as dense as they are on many rivers, but the fish do rise boldly when they're feeding actively on surface insects.

The weeks of autumn are considered the best times to fish here since many of the floating craft of summer have been stored in the garage, the grasshoppers are floating tight to the banks offering their broad profiles to watchful trout, and the browns are nervously preparing for their annual procreative rites. The big fall caddis are winging over the river and fishermen are casting large #10 and #12 Fluttering Orange Caddis imitations. Sink tip lines are dusted off and attached to backing for use with large streamer patterns.

Throughout the season the fish caught are predominately rainbow with a few cutthroat and occasional browns coming to the net. If you throw a large streamer or lure into the water and suddenly feel a resistance that will surely put your name in the record book alongside those of the titans of the sport, you've most likely hooked into a bull trout. He might not be a record, and your dreams of angling fame may be shattered, but you'll enjoy the experience and will have caught a fish not frequently caught in these waters.

The Blackfoot is not a river on which fishing records will be set, but it is a river that offers recreational tonic to good numbers of people in several different ways. It's a pretty place to be.

Blackfoot River

BOULDER RIVER

Map Reference 10

If ever a person were attempting to locate the rockiest river in the Rockies, he'd have to look no farther than the Boulder River above Big Timber. This river sets the "industry standard" in wading difficulty not only because of the lack of gravel and small cobblestones typical of most rivers, but also because the rocks and boulders under foot are large, round and very slippery. Be sure to wear a boot with a good stiff sole, cleats if you have them, use a wading staff when needed and take your time!

The Boulder heads in the Absaroka-Beartooth Wilderness about fifty miles south of Big Timber, after which it pushes relentlessly north to spill into the Yellowstone at Big Timber. It averages forty to fifty feet in width, is not a deep river, but moves right along over a fairly good gradient. It's a floatable river, but isn't floated extensively because it takes an experienced boatman on the oars to avoid the mid-stream rocks.

Although it separates two mountain ranges, the Beartooth to the east and the Absaroka to the west, and drains over 550 square miles of private and public land, the Boulder has all the characteristics of a small river and is easy to fish. We can divide the river into three sections for our purpose here including the forest section from the headwaters down to the Natural Bridge and Falls, the section between the falls and McLeod where the East Boulder and West Boulder enter the main river and, finally, the lower section between McLeod and the Yellowstone River.

The Natural Bridge State Monument is located thirty miles south of Big Timber. This area contains a spectacular gorge, jagged rock formations, a waterfall and, yes, a genuine arch of rock forming a natural bridge over the river. Even if you don't plan to fish this high on the river, we recommend you slip into your sightseeing shoes and spend a few minutes here—it's worth the time! Below the bridge browns and rainbow comprise the majority of fish with cutthroat and brook trout only in limited numbers. Above the bridge rainbow and cutthroat predominate with no brown trout known to have leaped the seventy foot falls! The land above the monument is public and therefore access is very good. Below the falls the river borders on private property for almost its entire length to the Yellowstone. Accesses are few here, but permission is sometimes granted by landowners—more so below McLeod than above, it seems.

Boulder River

The nature of the river makes it very well suited to nymph fishing and anyone who enjoys throwing these weighted, larval imitations will enjoy the Boulder. Pocket water, rocks, short runs, deep holes, fast chutes and plenty of broken water provide holding lies galore; the potential reward of a twelve- to twenty-inch trout makes the effort worthwhile. The water here is almost always clear, making it an appealing destination when the Yellowstone still runs high and dirty. The run-off on the Boulder is usually down and clear by the first week of July and remains so throughout the summer with little noticeable effect from irrigation withdrawals.

Prior to run-off, as the warm days of springtime give birth to uncontrollable urges to be on the river, it wouldn't be at all unusual to see anglers on the Boulder fishing small nymphs in the slower, deeper areas of the river. During March and April imitations of caddis, mayfly and stonefly larvae can be very effective. Caddis are the predominant insect of the Boulder and first sightings of the adults will take place in May after which they'll continue to hatch throughout the summer and into early September.

The salmonfly hatch gets underway here in mid-June and continues until the first week of July. In spite of the fact that run-off conditions may still exist during some or all of the hatch, the water should have good clarity and results can be very rewarding when nymphs and dries are fished up close to the bank. Nymphs with dark brown bodies work well as does the Bird's Stone for an adult imitation.

72

Hoppers become an important part of the trout's diet in August and the strong population of sculpin become prey to larger trout at all times. A good selection of flies for use below the Natural Bridge would include Elk Hair Caddis, Adams, sculpin imitations, hoppers, Humpy, attractor dries, small stonefly nymphs in a variety of colors, Matukas and Woolly Buggers in both black and olive. For fishing this area a five- or six-weight rod will do nicely. In the upper reaches of the river the fish are smaller and your flies should be smaller also; #16 and #18 are common. Mayfly patterns like Red Quill, Lt. Hendrickson and Quill Gordon are favorites. Pheasant Tail, Hare's Ear and Prince nymphs in #14 and #16 also work well in this water.

Do to the extremely rocky nature of the Boulder, it is less suited to lure fishing than fly fishing, however when lures are used, the favorites are Panther Martins, Thomas Cyclones, Mepps and Kastmasters. Black and brass seems to be a preferred combination.

The East Boulder and West Boulder Rivers are small tributaries entering the main river near McLeod. They have the characteristic slippery bottom of the Boulder and a similar access situation. They flow through ranch land and, for the most part, permission to fish is difficult to obtain. They are rainbow and cutthroat fisheries having channels from fifteen to twenty feet wide and serving as spawning streams to fish from the main Boulder.

River Notes

McLEOD

CAMPGROUND / CABINS

McLEOD RESORT CAMPGROUND
Downtown McLEOD, Box 27   932-6167
> Rustic fishing cabins, furnished apartments and campground on the banks of the West Boulder River. The only accommodations in McLeod!

GUEST RANCHES

THE HAWLEY MOUNTAIN GUEST RANCH
On the Boulder River, south of McLeod, Box 4   932-5791
> Enjoy superb trout fishing on Montana's finest wild trout waters in the Absaroka-Beartooth Wilderness, while non-anglers of the family enjoy the many diverse activities of our all-inclusive vacation ranch.

CLARK FORK RIVER

Map References 11, 12, 13, 14, 15

The Clark Fork of the Columbia was given that name prior to the First World War, having been referred to by several other names prior to this official government designation. This is a major river in Montana for many reasons, not the least of which is its size. When it leaves the western border of the state its channel contains more water than any other Montana river and as it pushes into Idaho it becomes the source of ninety percent of the water in Lake Pend Oreille. It is also the easternmost headwater of the Columbia River.

The Clark Fork isn't Montana's most heavily fished river, but it seems to be gaining favor among more and more anglers, and it means a good deal to many other folks as well. To farmers, it's a source of irrigation water; to power companies it turns the turbines; to mining firms and a pulp mill, it's been a conduit to carry away waste products; to cities along the river, it's had the same value, to recreationists, it is a surface on which to float a boat, to fishery biologists, it's a challenging environment in which to grow and maintain aquatic life forms; to conservationists, it's a living entity with a life worthy of saving and preserving in a healthy condition; to the folks in Idaho it's a testimonial to the conscience of their neighbors and to politicians it has to be a subject involving difficult decision making.

The river begins near Anaconda at the confluence of Warm Springs Creek and Silver Bow Creek. The river then flows in a northwesterly direction to nudge over the Idaho border 273 miles from its beginning. It is paralleled by an Interstate Highway for 167 of those miles.

For over a hundred years the earth close to this river has been the source of thousands of tons of extractive resources. Traditionally the ground nearby has been punctured and scraped in the search for gold, silver, lead, zinc, copper, barite, phosphate and manganese. The products which resulted from these terrestrial extractions have, in one way or another, affected the lives of all of us. Their removal has also left scars on the landscape and contamination in the soil and in the river. After a severe rainstorm in the river's headwater area in 1984 heavy metals were washed down Silver Bow Creek causing the death of an estimated ten thousand fish. That tragedy obviously reflected a serious environmental problem. What's to prevent another flash flood this year and the next and the one after that? State agencies have classified Silver Bow as a class "E" stream, suitable for industrial and agricultural use only, but not food processing. A pristine stream rates a classification of A-1. The lower Clark Fork is classified B-1. This gives you an idea of the effect of Silver Bow on the river. Local industries have made progress toward helping to revive the stream and insect populations are starting to take hold, but as yet the stream will not support a viable fish population. This is but one example of the abuse the Clark Fork must withstand.

In addition to the heavy metals, poisonous arsenic also finds its way into the Clark Fork because it is a metallic by-product of certain mining procedures. The river is sometimes de-watered to dangerously low levels for irrigation purposes, is the recipient of industrial and municipal waste and is silted from irrigation return. It's been channelized for road construction and its high nutrient load causes an extreme growth of algae in the form of trailing moss in the summer months, which promotes oxygen supersaturation. Water temperatures rise as high as seventy-five degrees in certain areas and bank degradation takes place because of cattle over-grazing.

Wow! That's an impressive list of problems! One person we talked to has lived along the river for many years and his feeling was expressed like this, "There are enough chemicals in that river that in the near future you'll be able to catch a fish already cooked." Well, we feel this may be an over-reaction to the situation, but he made his point. All of these conditions exist on given stretches of the river, but fortunately tributary streams enter the Clark Fork at irregular intervals to add a shot of sweet water and a spark of life. Where fish populations start to seriously diminish, tributaries come in and the river below these feeders again holds trout for a short distance downstream.

It's not our intent here to dwell upon, analyze or offer remedial advice on the ecological problems of the river, but you may be assured there are areas along its course that offer fine trout fishing, and there are people who are committed to the river's healthy well-being. For more information on what has been, is being and will be done in the future to preserve the river, you may write to the Clark Fork Coalition, P.O. Box 7593, Missoula, Mt. 59807. This dedicated group of citizens, businesses and organizations has been established to act as watchdog and protector of the Clark Fork River as well as Lake Pend Oreille.

From a fishing standpoint, we're dealing with a river of almost three hundred miles in length, but because the water below the community of Thompson Falls offers little appeal to the trout fisherman, we'll concentrate on the water down to Thompson Falls. The river's beginning commences on a very optimistic note; special protective regulations immediately below Warm Springs have been instituted to protect a strong population of brown trout, estimated to be approximately two thousand fish per mile. The river here is narrow, the water fairly thin during summer, the channel is edged with willows and brush reaches over the bank to splash the current. Its shallow riffles empty into deep pools that sometimes stand guardian to impressive undercut banks. The trout habitat between Warm Springs and Deer Lodge is considered to be some of the finest on the river. So tight are the quarters in some areas of this reach, that fly fishermen must restrain the distance of their casts, both back and forward. The fish here average about twelve inches, but a good percentage will run to fifteen. Spin fishermen do well with Gold Mepps and fly casters do well with a variety of nymphs early and late in the season. Warm summer temperatures produce a strong adversary in the form of trailing moss that causes the angler to keep his offerings on the surface. Some caddis hatches come off the river here and the use of small brown imitations can be very effective, particularly in the evening.

Trout populations and size start to decline above Deer Lodge and continue to do so below town. Counts of browns are estimated at only about three hundred per mile, far short of resident counts upstream. Specific reasons for this condition aren't clear, but the river does take on a new character below Deer Lodge. It broadens somewhat here, the banks are more eroded and the water becomes quite shallow in summer. The riparian character is that of a brushy river bottom flanked by adjacent farmlands. The banks are replete with undercuts, brush piles and a fair amount of tumbled debris offering good cover to the fish that do reside here.

At Garrison the Little Blackfoot River joins the Clark Fork and this rush of new water improves fishing quality below the confluence. The wider, less congested character here makes casting easier for fly fishermen, but the summer moss plague still precludes nymph and lure fishing. As the river approaches Drummond the valley opens up even more to cattle grazing and agriculture. The river is from thirty to fifty feet wide here and trout numbers drop considerably once again. From this point to the confluence of Rock Creek, the river is fished little because insect hatches are marginal and trout are few. Caddis is the predominant insect here, as it is throughout the entire river, and fly patterns such as Elk Hair Caddis, Henryville Caddis and Bucktail Caddis are favorites. Above Rock Creek the river also suffers from channelization and high water temperatures, plus a murky appearance probably due to irrigation return and algae growth.

From Rock Creek to Milltown Dam the river takes on new life and new character. The infusion of water from Rock Creek drops the water temperature, the fish population rises and the scenery improves, with high cliffs overlooking a river with deep runs and periodic rapids. Fishing improves and river usage increases both by anglers and pleasure floaters. Many more insects are present here and they receive the attention of not only brown trout, but a fair number of rainbows as well, the latter making up about a thirty percent share of the total population. This stretch is considered one of the best on the river for fishing, and it proves to be best early and late, with summer fishing

76

somewhat slower.

The flow at least doubles, when the Blackfoot River enters at Bonner because the total flows of the Blackfoot actually exceed those of the Clark Fork here. This is where the environment starts to lose its green riparian personality in favor of rocks and boulders. The river itself becomes more flat and there is less riffle water. The Milltown Dam is located about four miles downstream from the confluence and this point marks the end of the upper river.

Between the dam and Plains, the river takes on a different personality. It is broad, flows more slowly, has less surface and bank character, pushes against high, steep banks in several areas, smashes recklessly through a canyon at one point, and gives up its fish more reluctantly. The fish are dispersed here more than above and the water is harder to read. This is one of the few rivers we know about with plentiful erroneous zones, places where you shouldn't be fishing! The fish of the lower river gather in pods and will be in one spot and nowhere else within a relatively long distance.

It's only natural to look for greener pastures when considering a place to fish, but don't be deceived into thinking you must leave town to catch a fish as you peer at the river from one of the bridges in downtown Missoula. Plenty of fish are caught here right amidst the morning traffic and evening rush hour. There's even what locals refer to as an "urban float," where you float fish your way through the heart of town, catching primarily rainbows, the occasional brown and rare cutthroat. From Missoula downstream the most common fish caught will be the rainbow, strong and feisty ones at that. These fish seem to be from a strain developed to run and jump and be delightfully pugnacious after being deceived by our fraudulent offerings. One gentleman in Missoula calls them "firecrackers." 'Nuff said!

From Missoula to Superior the fish average a respectable fifteen inches in length, but the numbers of fish are low, estimated at about three hundred per mile. Fortunately their habit of gathering into pods, as discussed earlier, makes them easier to locate, although at times you think you've located trout and they are, in fact, whitefish.

The entire river is best fished by floating, but this is particularly true on the lower river where a boat helps you locate the fish and avoid casting to sterile water. If a boat isn't available, there are many pullouts along I-90 where you can stop and search the river with binoculars to locate feeding fish. Pods of fish often congregate around foam lines where insects become trapped and easily available. Because the fish stick together in bunches rather than finning off on their own in search of any food that moves, it's quite necessary to place your cast accurately in their feeding lane. They generally will not move out of their way to take a fly. The fish aren't hyper-selective, but they do expect good service. Put your fly in front of their nose!

At Alberton the river turns on the horsepower and cuts its way through the sedimentary rock layers of the Alberton Gorge, also called Cyr Canyon. This is an area of heavy rapids and boiling white-water; it's not a place you want to take your canoe or Sunday-afternoon raft. This is serious white-water and should be left to professional rafters who want a white-water thrill, not a place for the contemplative angler to forget his troubles. This is a twelve-mile stretch of water where most of the tragic accidents on the river take place.

Safe floating begins again at Tarkio. And yes friends, it's only two days to Paradise from here! Fish still continue to be present in limited numbers, but their size tends to increase as you progress downstream. During the spring run-off the bull trout of this region will gather at the mouths of feeder streams before ascending to spawn. This is a time when fishermen casting large spoons or using bait can catch large fish. Even though there's a dam at Missoula, the lower river remains as a free-flowing stream. Run-off begins in May and June, followed by dropping water throughout the summer.

From Superior to Plains fishing is considered best during the spring, especially when using stone flies along the banks. Even in this area of the river, algae growth proliferates during the summer and stifles lure and wet fly fishing. Fortunately good hatches of caddis come off and fish can be taken on dry flies, particularly in the evening. The summer fishing is most productive starting around July 4th when the water is dropping and clearing.

Because of its size, very little wading is done on the lower river. Fishing

Clark Fork River below Missoula

from the bank or from a boat are the preferred methods and, for the inexperienced angler, this is definitely an area in which you can benefit by hiring an experienced professional guide. Guides not only handle the boat, they know where the fish traditionally feed and can save the fishermen many hours of searching for targets to cast to. Not only that, but the river here is up to 150 feet wide so the fish have plenty of room in which to find feeding areas and often they are against the far bank.

Rafts and drift boats are probably the most commonly-used craft here. During high water, motor boats and jet boats are used, but exposed river rocks discourage their use during late summer and fall when the water level drops.

There is a variety of regulations governing fishing on the lower river some of which encourage fishing only for sport. One sagacious angler we talked to thought such practices were good for the trout. He says that, "A guy that fishes catch-and-release only is great for growing fish because you'd be surprised how fast that fish grows from the time he hooks it to the time he gets home and describes it!" An astute observation, we think!

A short distance above Paradise, the size of the Clark Fork doubles once again as it receives the warmer, turbid water of the Flathead River. We now witness the flow of a huge river. It is slow moving and rather featureless except for a few islands and its quality as a trout fishery diminishes quickly. Fishermen on the water from here downstream to the Idaho border are usually casting bait and lures to either northern pike or large mouth bass, both of which prefer the sloughs and backwaters instead of the main current Whereas the river upstream is home to tiny aquatic insects, the river here is home to six inch long crayfish. A last viable option for the trout fisherman in this region is on the beautiful Thompson River which flows into the Clark Fork from the north just east of Thompson Falls and is written about elsewhere in this volume.

Below the town of Thompson Falls, the big river is stopped in its tracks by three successive dams which, for all practical purposes, form one continuous reservoir. Traveling downstream west from town the structures include Thompson Falls Dam, Noxon Rapids Dam and then only a short distance into Idaho, the Cabinet Gorge Reservoir Dam.

There you have a description of the Clark Fork, from its unsettled beginning to its subdued departure toward the Columbia River and finally to the Pacific Ocean. We've looked at the favorable as well as the unfavorable aspects of the river, so now it's up to you to put a fly on the water and try to fool a few fish. This is a long river so be sure to check the current regulations regarding seasons, methods and limits.

The salmonfly hatch starts near Missoula within the first ten days of June, but prior to that fly fishing can be good in April and May using big nymphs such as the Montana Nymph, any of the rubberleg patterns including George's Brown Stone and Brooks Stone. In the parlance of some of the local anglers these immense flies are called "quarter pounders," and you readily get the idea they should be not only big but be weighted substantially! Of course the use of flies of grand proportion doesn't exclude using smaller nymphs, so don't overlook those caddis, mayfly and small stonefly imitations. Throughout the season the two most effective flies on the river are considered to be the Elk Hair Caddis and the Royal Wulff and the month of May isn't too early to give them a try in the smaller sizes. Caddis are the most numerous of insects on the river and it's difficult to beat the Royal Wulff as an attractor pattern.

The salmonfly hatch will migrate from Missoula to the Rock Creek confluence and then continue up Rock Creek. The total "hatch" will continue for about a month, with the Clark Fork itself seeing these heavyweights over the water for about a week. Standard nymph and adult patterns, including the Fluttering Stonefly, will work well throughout the hatch but keep in mind the water will probably be high. Run-off here normally begins in early May and continues through June. Early- to mid-June usually signals the peak of the high water. In the stretch from Missoula to Rock Creek you'll also experience a hatch of golden stones concurrent with the salmonflies. Caddis will also continue to emerge, so if you're on the water at this time you should see plenty of insect activity.

July and August are dry fly months, and a good number of patterns are effective. Caddis patterns will rank number one in usage, but also carry Humpies, Grey Wulff, Grizzly Wulff, Adams, Lt. Cahill, Blue Duns and Pale Morning Duns, along with the Royal family of attractors. It goes without saying that nymphs will be effective now, as they are throughout the season, and small Muddlers in size #8 and #10 are always worth trying. From late July to early September grasshopper patterns work well and one of the preferred local patterns is tied with a low-riding profile, and dressed with a fluorescent pink yarn head. The reach just below the Rock Creek mouth is particularly good for hopper fishing as are other areas with a meadow environment. The rocky banks are less productive with hoppers. Starting in late August and continuing into September a large fall caddis comes off and is well represented with a #10 or #12 Orange Bucktail Caddis pattern.

Fall provides Clark Fork anglers with some truly good dry fly fishing. In September anglers see swarms of Tricorythodes over the water in the morning with spinner falls taking place between 6:00 and 11:00 a.m. In the afternoon you might see grey drakes on the water to be followed in the evening by a hatch of Baetis, when your small Blue Winged Olives will be the appropriate artificial. October seems to be just as good as, if not better than, September for dry fly fishing; local anglers look forward to this time of year for consistently rewarding hours spent on the water. It pays to let the water warm a bit this time of year, so plan to start the fishing day at noon and fish until dark.

Streamer fishing is the other dimension to the fall bag of tricks so don't overlook throwing the Muddler, Matukas, Spruce Flies and Woolly Buggers with sink tip lines. The river has populations of sculpin, longnose dace and shiners in addition to small whitefish, so the larger fish, particularly browns, are accustomed to feeding on bait fish and using streamers in late fall can be effective. Spin fishermen will find most success when their spinners are equipped with gold blades. Most successful of lures seem to include Mepps, Panther Martin, Thomas Cyclone, Rooster Tail and Rapala.

Fishing the Clark Fork does not require highly technical equipment or complete mastery of stream entomology. What seems to be more important here is finding the fish and putting your fly in front of them. In the upper river you'll usually fish to the snags and undercut banks; in the lower river locate the pods of fish or cast to eddies, bank protrusions, seams between fast and slow water and foam lines.

Most of the river is floatable, but normal caution is necessary to avoid snags, log jams and occasional, barbed wire fences. Several of the take-outs require the boat be pulled up over rip-rap which makes the lighter, inflatable rafts a common choice of boat here. We recommend that boaters with no experience on the river check with local fishing tackle shops to gain as much knowledge as possible about diversion dams, rough water, hazardous areas and access problems. When leaving Missoula, for example, it's good to know to take the south channel of the river to avoid a portage around a dam on the north channel. Floating above Garrison in summer might require dragging the boat over gravel bars due to low water. It pays to scout the area to be floated before the float begins.

As with all the fishing centers in Montana, the folks who operate the tackle shops are very knowledgeable about local waters, and other waters as well, so it's always wise to check with them on current conditions.

BUTTE

There's a district in Silver Bow County that has surrendered to the world as much of its countenance and sinew as any area on earth. Placer gold was discovered here in 1864 and was taken by prospectors for a few years, but never on a "boom-town" basis. In the mid-1870's, silver was discovered and it was mined until the 1880's when the discovery of copper coincided with a new, world-wide demand for this metal. This combination of events triggered the production that made Butte a world leader in supplying copper to the electrical industry for use in power lines across the country, motors and home wiring. Through the ingenuity and tenacity of the people of Butte, Montana, approximately 20 billion pounds of copper, 5 billion pounds of zinc, 37 billion pounds of manganese, 850 million pounds of lead, 700 million ounces of silver and 3 million ounces of gold was extracted from the local milieu for world-wide use. It wasn't wistful optimism that inspired people to call Butte Hill the "richest hill on earth," it was production. The residual benefits to man from this surrender of ore and mineral wealth over the past one hundred years is incalculable.

For years the Anaconda Company reigned supreme in the mining and smelting industry in this region until, in 1976, it was sold to Atlantic Richfield. Then in 1983 the mines closed. Demand for copper was severely reduced because copper wire was being replaced by aluminum and inflation, plus the cost of extraction, made mining unprofitable. In 1985 Atlantic Richfield sold its interests here to a firm called Montana Resources, which is again mining in the East Continental open-pit mine on a relatively small scale with small crews and improved techniques. The Berkeley Pit is the most famous open-pit mine at Butte. This copper mine opened in 1955 and was operated until 1983. It is one of the largest truck-operated, open-pit copper mines in the world. Located on Butte Hill, it measures 1 mile wide, about 1-1/4 miles long and 1,800 feet deep. In the 28 years of its operation over 300 million tons of copper ore was extracted along with three times that amount of waste rock. The pit can be seen at close range from a viewing stand at the lip of the mine.

Butte is the county seat of Silver Bow County and, with a population of 38,000, the third largest city in Montana. The economy is based on mining, medicine, research, education and tourism. Entities that play a part in these diverse areas include the Montana Energy Research Development Institute, the National Center of Appropriate Technology, the Mineral Research Center and the regional medical center which employs over one-thousand people. Also important are the Montana College of Mineral Science and Technology and the High Altitude Sports Center. A new business in Butte that continues to develop is the Port of Montana, a storage warehouse and distribution firm utilizing the railroad and interstate highways to ship goods such as grain, forest products, bulk minerals, etc. to national and international locations.

Visitors to Butte can find plenty to do when not enjoying the rewards of the many lakes and rivers within a thirty- to fifty-mile drive. Rock hounding, as might be expected, is outstanding. Collectors digging in nearby areas will find quartz, fluorite crystals, amethysts and sapphires. The city offers two nine-hole golf courses, two swimming pools and plenty of tennis courts, picnic areas and playgrounds. Special events including concerts, community theater, fairs and festivals occur throughout the season. The Butte Symphony Orchestra and rodeos are particularly popular. Visitors may take walking/driving tours in both the historic uptown business district and the west side mansion district. Two commercial firms will take you on tours via bus or train to view the city or the underground mine area.

Four cultural facilities are open to the public and well worth visiting. The Copper King Mansion was built as a residence in the 1880's by mining magnate William Clark. This thirty-two-room structure is filled with original furnishings, antiques, sculpture, woodwork hand carved by German craftsmen, imported French bathrooms and an antique pipe organ, made in Vermont in 1910, replete with 825 pipes. The Arts Chateau Community Arts Center is housed in the 1898 Victorian mansion of C. W. Clark, son of William Clark. This center features a museum and changing exhibits of local, regional and international art; in addition, performing-arts' events are sponsored. The World Museum of Mining and Hellroarin' Gulch features both indoor and outdoor exhibits centered around the history of mining. Of particular interest is the reconstructed, turn-of-the-century mining camp which has more than thirty buildings set along cobblestone streets on a thirty-three-acre site. Visitors can pan for gold at the "U-Betcha" mine here.

Montana Technical College is one of the country's most highly respected mining and petroleum engineering schools and their mineral collection is one of the most comprehensive in the world. The Mineral Museum at Montana Tech has over 15,000 mineral specimens in its collection and up to 1,500 of them are shown at a time. Of particular interest to visitors is the display of fluorescent specimens. Butte is a very interesting city with a remarkable past that can be studied and enjoyed by visitors today.

Butte-Silver Bow Chamber of Commerce: 2950 Harrison Ave., Butte, Montana 59701 - Phone: 494-5595

Deerlodge National Forest: P.O. Box 400, Butte, Montana 59703 - Phone: 496-3400

ANACONDA

Envision, if you will, sitting in front of a cozy fire with flames dancing from pine logs and smoke curling up the chimney into the cold night air. Now, if you can, picture a chimney seventy-five feet in diameter at its base, sixty feet in diameter at its top, rising 585 feet straight up toward the clouds. If you can't quite imagine such a sight, you can visit Anaconda, view the real thing, and photograph it for future reference. This is the stack which, for over eighty years, carried away the smoke and gases produced in smelting the copper ore from the mining operations conducted at nearby Butte. When the mining there ceased, so did the smelting at Anaconda and today all that remains as mute testament to a great, bygone era in Montana history is this cylindrical intrusion into the skyline.

The benefits to the economic prosperity of the town provided by the smelter are sorely missed, we're certain, but the toxic effluvium rolling from the tip of the stack must be an unwelcome memory. In the early years, all in its noxious path suffered in some way; cattle died, trees perished, and crops wouldn't grow. The company bought out the affected farmers and traded good land for bad with the U. S. Forest Service as recompense for the damage done. Today Anaconda's reliance upon mining for economic viability has, out of necessity, converted to agriculture, retail sales, government and tourism.

The more than ten thousand residents of the city encourage us to visit their town and soak up some history as well as some sunshine. At just over a mile high in elevation, the air here will allow your golf ball to travel a bit farther whether on the nine-hole Anaconda Country Club course which is open to the public or on the eighteen-hole course at a nearby resort. With Washoe Park right in town on the banks of Warm Springs Creek, you can swim, play tennis, picnic and watch the kids fish in the stream. Also at the park is the state's oldest fish hatchery which opened in 1908 and still produces fish to be stocked in Montana's waters. The Copper Village Museum and Art Center is a good place at which to brush up on the history of the area as well as enjoy art works produced by local and regional artists.

When you're ready to see the natural sights in the nearby countryside, a drive along the Pintler Route anywhere between Butte and Drummond on Highway 10A will offer an exposure to regional history as well as scenic terrain. Allow about two to three hours for the round trip from Anaconda to Drummond.

Ananconda also invites you back during the winter months to enjoy skiing at Wraith Hill and Discovery Basin ski areas near Georgetown Lake.

Anaconda Chamber of Commerce: 306 East Park, Anaconda, Montana 59711 - Phone: 563-2400

DEER LODGE

The Indians called it "Lodge of the White Tailed Deer," early trappers no doubt referred to it as a good place to find game and miners and settlers found it a place to stop and shop because it was, after all, a trade center and stage stop for folks traveling west. With 4,500 residents, Deer Lodge is now the seat of Powell County and is considered to be the second-oldest town in Montana. Its economy is based on agriculture, the timber industry and the Montana State Prison.

Deer Lodge has traditionally been the site of the state prison. The Old Montana Territorial Prison, a twelve-building facility which was entirely constructed by inmates, accepted its first prisoners in 1871. That complex is now operated as an historical attraction by the Powell County Museum and Arts Foundation. Tours, both guided and self-guided are now conducted behind the high sandstone walls. If you want to experience a bit of claustrophobia, spend a few minutes in the maximum security area! The current prison facility was opened in 1979.

Another project of the Museum Foundation is the Towe Antique Ford Collection located in a building at the south end of the Old Prison, next to the parking lot. The collection was started in 1952 when Mr. Edward Towe restored a 1923 Model T Roadster. These vehicles which have either been restored to near-original condition, or are originals obtained in nearly perfect condition, make up the most complete such collection in the world. The approximately 150 cars on display include a Lincoln collection and some of Mr. Ford's personal vehicles.

For insights into the history of the area, the Powell County Museum offers exhibits of historical artifacts from mining, ranching, trapping, Indian life and the Territorial Prison. For the kids, don't overlook the Doll and Toy Museum. Visitors can take a hike'n'bike tour of the historic buildings in town with the aid of a descriptive guide pamphlet which can be obtained at the Chamber office.

At the north edge of Deer Lodge lies the Grant-Kohrs Ranch which is listed in the register of National Historical Sites. When the ranch house was built in 1862 it was considered the finest home in Montana Territory. The original owner of the ranch, John Grant, became wealthy selling goods and cattle to miners. In 1866 he sold the ranch to Conrad Kohrs, also a cattleman, and by 1890 the ranch covered 25,000 acres. It is still a working ranch, but is under the management of the National Park Service. Guided tours are regularly conducted at the house. On the grounds nearby are the bunkhouse, out-buildings and antique machinery which can be viewed at any time.

Deer Lodge has three parks, a nine-hole golf course with clubhouse and equipment rentals, local tennis courts and an olympic-sized, indoor swimming pool which is free to the public. Pilots can bring their small planes into the 3,800 foot paved, lighted airstrip 3 miles west of town. Each summer the Tri-County Fair with music, parades and rodeo is held here; the annual Native American Pow Wow features dances, food and entertainment; and in July the

Old Car Days is an event at which one can take a look at the past. The Chamber office can fill you in on the details.

Deer Lodge Chamber of Commerce: 300 Main St., Deer Lodge, Montana 49722 - Phone: 846-2094

MISSOULA

The townsite of Missoula no longer experiences the floods which were common in years past, but the evidence of these geologic baths can be seen on the hillsides overlooking the city. No, the floods weren't caused by sudden thunderstorms, they were, in fact, the result of a glacier that lodged in the valley of the Clark Fork River some fifteen thousand years ago at the present location of Pend Oreille Lake in Idaho. The glacier impounded the Clark Fork River to form a lake at least two thousand feet deep which covered a surface area approximately the size of Lake Ontario. Finally the glacier began to float, broke up, and allowed the lake, called Glacial Lake Missoula, to rush across Idaho, eastern Washington and finally into the Columbia River drainage and to the Pacific Ocean. Boulders from Montana can be seen as far west as Salem, Oregon.

Estimates made by geologists indicate that the glacial block formed and subsequently floated away, under the pressure of successive lakes, a total of forty-one times over a period of one thousand years. The lakes lasted for periods as long as fifty-eight years to as short as nine years. Each time the lake filled, wave action cut lines into hillsides; these shorelines are particularly evident on the oblique face of Mount Sentinel overlooking Missoula. Because some of the lake fillings weren't deep enough to allow the shoreline to reach back into the Missoula area, only about thirty-five shorelines have been counted here. Another phenomenon evident from the ice age is the angular boulders spotting the campus at the University of Montana. These boulders were dropped from icebergs floating on Glacial Lake Missoula.

Today the city is not under siege by the forces of glacier or flood, but water is a familiar fluid to all who live here near the banks of the Clark Fork and its tributaries. The city was supposedly named from a Flathead Indian word "Im-i-su-la," meaning "by or near the cold, chilling waters." If, in fact, this interpretation of history is correct, the name seems perfectly appropriate. In the year 1864 Missoula was but a small settlement containing one store and a very few lumber and flour mills. The area began to prosper and in 1866 the town became the county seat of Missoula County. The Northern Pacific Railroad arrived in 1883 and the city incorporated that same year. In 1908 the U. S. Forest Service established a regional office here and the first pulp mill opened in 1956.

Missoula, by Montana standards, is a fairly large city—the fourth largest in the state—with a metropolitan population of nearly 75,000 people. It is the industrial, educational, commercial, medical and transportation hub of western Montana, with the economic base centered primarily around wood products, the federal government, motor carriers (air, rail and bus) and retail endeavors. A good deal of this activity takes place in the area surrounding the downtown core. The core remains a comfortable, easy-to-circulate place in which to do business. It doesn't have a "big city" feel whatever.

Missoula is a university town and as such has an overtone of academic and cultural influence somewhat greater than communities without advanced education facilities. The University of Montana opened in 1895 with fifty students and today has an enrollment of nearly nine thousand. It is located one and one-half miles east of downtown. A broad range of events and activities are available to the public throughout the year—certainly too many to enumerate here—but amplification can be obtained from the Missoula Area Chamber of Commerce. The summer calendar reflects several events such as fairs, trade shows, festivals and rodeos. Special events are performed by the Children's Theater, the Blues and Jazz Society, City Band, Youth Symphony, Missoula Symphony, Mendelssohn Club Chorale, Repertory Theater, the String Orchestra of the Rockies, as well as several others.

In addition to the diverse fishing possibilities found nearby, there are numerous trails for the hiking enthusiast in the Rattlesnake Wilderness area which is only five miles north of town. Golfers can enjoy any of three public courses and tennis players can volley at several tennis courts. You can stretch out at three public swimming pools or soak in several hot springs in the area. The city library or university library will allow you to catch up on reading or research and many city parks offer relaxing surroundings in which to read, loaf or picnic. At McCormick Park a pond is available at which youngsters may pursue their angling interests and at the Memorial Rose Garden 2,500 plants push from the ground to please the olfactory responses of all who visit there.

Out of town, at Bonner, the public can take advantage of guided tours conducted at the Champion International Plywood Mill, one of the nation's largest. Johnson-Bell Field is the site of the Missoula County Airport, which services the commercial flights to and from here. It is also the home base of the Smokejumper Center, the largest fire-fighting-training school in the country. The center is open to the public and has exhibits showing the interesting and unusual aspects of forest fire detection and control. Forty miles north of Missoula lies the National Bison Range which provides an interesting half-day trip of sightseeing.

For art and history buffs, two sites in town are of interest. Art works in all media by artists of regional to international stature are on display in two levels of the Missoula Museum of the Arts. The Historical Museum at Fort Missoula is located at the original fort established in 1877 to protect early settlers. The museum has 11,000 artifacts in addition to twelve of the original fort structures that served the troops stationed here. The indoor galleries feature items from the fields of agriculture, forestry, military history, mining and transportation. The museum operates year-round and provides a map and descriptive brochure to facilitate a self-guided tour of the buildings and outdoor exhibits.

Missoula offers plenty of water to fish, many friendly folks with whom to do business and numerous activities to keep you busy when you're not on the river!

Missoula Area Chamber of Commerce: 825 E. Front St., P.O. Box 7577, Missoula, Montana 59808 - Phone: 543-6623

Lolo National Forest: Building 24, Fort Missoula, Missoula, Montana 59801 Phone: 329-3750

Missoula Ranger District: 5115 Highway 93 South, Missoula, Montana 59803

U. S. Forest Service: 340 Pattee, Missoula, Montana 59802

Northern Region Headquarters, U. S. Forest Service: Box 7669, Missoula, Montana 59807 - Phone: 329-3511

THOMPSON FALLS

Except for the influence of David Thompson, the town of Thompson Falls might be called Larchwood or Goat Mountain Falls, but the events that took place in the early 1800's determined at least a portion of this town's destiny. Mr. Thompson was an explorer, geographer, cartographer and fur trader. He was born in London in 1770 and emigrated to Canada with the Hudson's Bay Company when he was fourteen years old. He learned to speak the French language along with dialects of several Indian tribes and in 1809 he built a fur-trading post, called "Salish House," considered to have been the first building in Montana. The word "Salish" is the term the Flathead Indians used to refer to themselves—it means "the people." The post was built about three miles downstream from the confluence of the Thompson River and the Clark Fork, but no evidence now exists of the three log structures built there. Thompson traded with the Kootenai, Kalispell and Flathead Indians until the 1820's when the post was abandoned in favor of another location about ten miles upstream on the Clark Fork. Thompson has been referred to as the "greatest land geographer that ever lived!" When you consider his awesome accomplishments, you can understand the high praise. He mapped over one million square miles of Canada, a half million square miles of the U. S. and, in the process, wrote a diary of over four million words. A memorial cairn has been constructed in his honor along Highway 200 just east of town.

The 1,400 residents of Thompson Falls are involved mostly in the logging and lumber industries. Several mills produce dimension lumber and logs for homes. Other important economic influences are hay farming and cattle ranching.

Visitors to the area can gain a glimpse of the past at the Sanders County Historical Museum in the old county jail building. Other sights include the Thompson Falls Dam with its park and picnic area and the Noxon Rapids Dam northwest of town on Highway 200. Golfers can play at the Thompson Falls Golf Course, swimmers will enjoy the large pool, and tennis players can use local courts. Two annual events of interest to all who partake are the Vinson Ranch Rodeo and the "Huckleberry Festival" at Trout Creek twenty miles west of town. The latter is a three-day, mid-August celebration held at the town referred to as the "Huckleberry Capital of Montana." If you're dying for a taste of homemade huckleberry jam, set your plane down on the surfaced runway at Thompson Falls and head down river to the festival!

Thompson Falls Chamber of Commerce: P.O. Box 493, Thompson Falls, Montana 59873 - Phone: 827-485

Lolo National Forest: North of Thompson Falls, Thompson Falls, Motana 59873

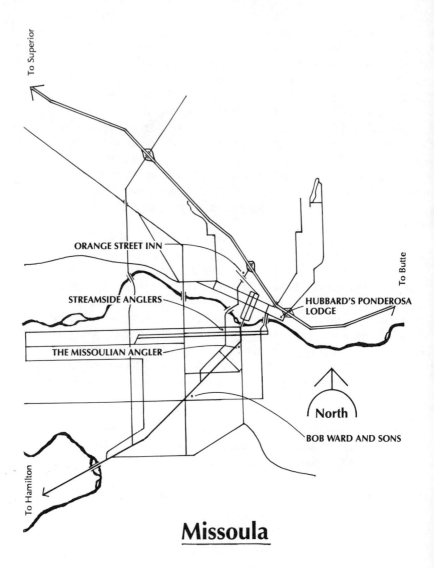

To Superior

To Butte

To Hamilton

ORANGE STREET INN

STREAMSIDE ANGLERS

THE MISSOULIAN ANGLER

HUBBARD'S PONDEROSA
LODGE

North

BOB WARD AND SONS

Missoula

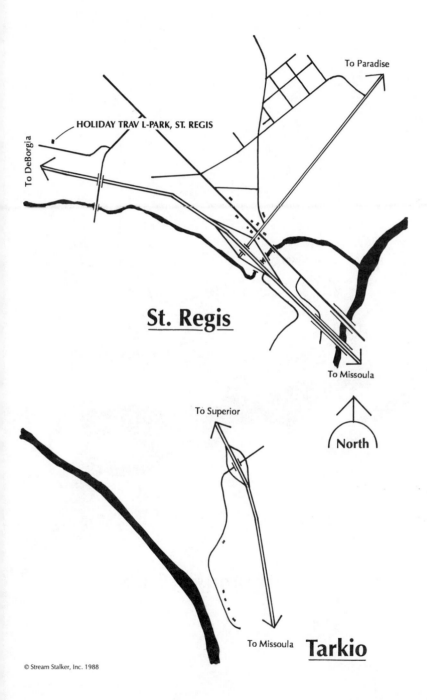

HOLIDAY TRAV L-PARK, ST. REGIS

To Paradise

To DeBorgia

St. Regis

To Missoula

To Superior

North

To Missoula Tarkio

© Stream Stalker, Inc. 1988

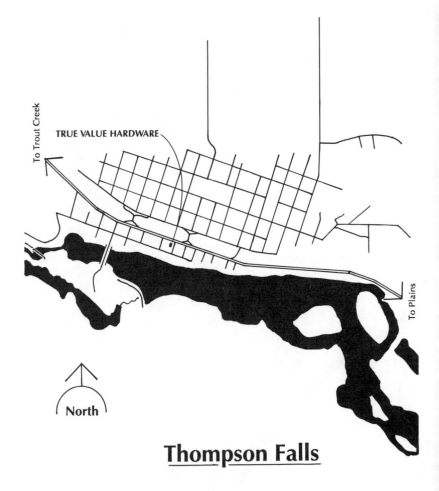

To Trout Creek

TRUE VALUE HARDWARE

To Plains

North

Thompson Falls

CLINTON

MOTEL / GENERAL STORE

ROCK CREEK LODGE
Exit 126 at I-90, Box 835   825-4868

> Your one stop headquarters for fishing Rock Creek and the Clark Fork River. Bar, casino, cafe, deli, mini-mart, convenience store, gift shop, Conoco service station and camping. Stop by and visit when you're in the area!

MISSOULA

FISHING SHOPS

THE MISSOULIAN ANGLER
901A So. Higgins, Corner of Higgins and Brooks   7287766

> Complete outfitting and guide services serving the Bitterroot, Clark Fork, Blackfoot Rivers and Rock Creek in western Montana. Complete, authorized, full service Orvis shop on the premises.

STREAMSIDE ANGLERS
501 So. Orange, Box 2158   728-1085 or 1-800-533-4741

> Western Montana's fly fishing headquarters. We have absolutely everything necessary to outfit the fisherman, from equipment to fly tying materials, instruction and guided fishing trips. For a good time, call 1-800-53FISH1 for recorded information about fishing.

GUIDES / OUTFITTERS

THE MISSOULIAN ANGLER
901A So. Higgins, Corner of Higgins and Brooks   728-7766

> Complete outfitting and guide services, serving the Bitterroot, Clark Fork, Blackfoot Rivers and Rock Creek in western Montana. Complete, authorized, full-service Orvis shop on the premises assures your every need for top quality equipment.

SPORTING GOODS

BOB WARD AND SONS
Highway 93 and South Ave.   728-3221

> Nestled in the hub of five mountain valleys. Streams and lakes in the vicinity offer fishing enjoyment the year around. We are open seven days a week to serve you.

MOTELS

HUBBARD'S PONDEROSA LODGE
800 E. Broadway   543-3107 or 1-800-341-8000

> Just off Interstate 90, near the University of Montana. Clean, comfortable, reasonably priced units. Queen beds, color cable TV, direct dial phones, group rates. Member of Independent Motels of America. All major credit cards accepted.

ORANGE STREET INN
801 No. Orange St.   721-3610 or 1-800-328-0801 in state only
> 10% DISCOUNT TO ANGLERS! Free continental breakfast, oversized rooms. Easy access to I-90. Twenty-four hour desk. Cable color TV with Showtime and sports channel. Our rates are reasonable and the friendliness is free.

VACATION CONSULTANT

VENTURE WEST VACATIONS
4217 Timberlane   728-1673 or 1-800-348-2729 ext. 12, 24 hr. answer
> VENTURE WEST VACATIONS. Cathy Ream, Ph.D. Representing quality outfitters and guest ranches for undiscovered trout streams in Montana and Idaho. Guides, float trips, stream fishing and horse pack trips to wilderness streams and lakes.

ST. REGIS

CAMPGROUNDS

HOLIDAY TRAV L-PARK, ST. REGIS
One mile west on frontage road,St. Regis, Drawer A   649-2470 or 1-800-323-8899
> This deluxe, full service park with swimming pool and top national ratings is internationally known for nearby fishing, spotless rest rooms, showers and roomy, shady sites.

THOMPSON FALLS

HARDWARE / FISHING SUPPLIES

TRUE VALUE HARDWARE
902 Main St., Box 1028   827-3251
> Thompson Falls' full service hardware store. Sporting goods, fishing tackle, pharmacy, shoes, automotive goods, gifts, greeting cards. We have everything the vacationer needs.

CLEARWATER RIVER

Map Reference 16

A discussion of the Clearwater River would be incomplete without the inclusion of the chain of lakes through which the river flows for approximately forty miles. They are not only individual fisheries in their own right, but they are responsible in part for providing the clear water that gave the river its fitting name. The river heads at Clearwater Lake, which is located near HIghway 83 between the village of Condon to the north and the town of Seeley Lake to the south. From this lake the river seeks its meeting with the Blackfoot River by passing through seven glacial lakes that nestle in the woods between the southern reaches of the Mission Range to the west and the Swan Range to the east. It is really a small ribbon of water that would best be classified as a creek. In succession from north to south the lakes include Rainy Lake, Lake Alva, Lake Inez, Seeley Lake, Salmon Lake, Elbow Lake and Blanchard Lake. One other body of water, Placid Lake, is part of the region's fishery because it lies close by but isn't associated directly with the flow of the Clearwater River.

The river between any two lakes may measure but a mile in length, or it might be as much as five miles. The lakes themselves have long, narrow configurations, and they too measure from one to five miles in length. In general, the lakes are fair fisheries that contain rainbow, cutthroat, kokanee salmon, some largemouth bass and a regrettably large population of yellow perch. Even though water quality is high and conditions are otherwise conducive to the trout's well being, the perch have depressed the capability of the trout to reach their normal potential in size and numbers. The most recent efforts of the Montana Department of Fish, Wildlife and Parks to remedy this problem consist of stocking two of the lakes with McBride cutthroat to determine whether they'll grow well in these waters. To date they are adjusting very well. Another test program involves the planting of McConaughy rainbows in nearby Upsata Lake. These fish are noted for their predatory nature, and the expectation that they will control the proliferation of the perch in this lake.

Lake Alva and Lake Inez are similar in size at approximately three hundred acres. Seeley Lake covers slightly over one thousand acres, and Blanchard Lake is but ten acres. Along with size variations the lakes also present a variety of habitats. Some have shoreline shallows preferred by the bass, some contain bull trout and some have greater or lesser problems with the perch populations. Clearwater Lake is rarely stocked and does contain some good-sized cutthroats. It is a quarter-mile away from the forest access road and is situated in a travel corridor for black and grizzly bears that range between the mountain ranges on either side of the valley. Their movement is normally restricted to the spring and autumn months.

Rainy Lake has an established elk calving area on its southwestern shore and, for that reason, the fewer motor boats used on the lake the less disturbed these animals will be. Lake Alva offers several areas for camping, but it isn't considered a good fishery because of its extreme population of perch. Seeley Lake is stocked each spring with McBride cutthroat and kokanee salmon. Hundreds of thousands of rainbows have been planted in Seeley Lake over the past few years but their return to fishermen has been negligible. It was eventually determined that the instinctive nature of this Jocko strain of rainbow was closely akin to that of steelhead trout, and these fish therefore sought the running water of the river below the lake. In addition to having a population of good-sized bull trout, the lake also receives periodic plants of trout brood stock with fish ranging in size to ten pounds. Seeley's largest attraction, however, is the bass fishing. The spring and fall periods are best for bass, and anglers tend to congregate at the backwater areas of both inlet and outlet ends of the lake. The fish fortunately don't leave the lake and knowledgeable bass fishermen do quite well at this sport. Prior to June 15 these fishermen should be aware of, and sensitive to, the fact that loons nest here, and the birds shouldn't be disturbed at their shoreline, nesting grounds. Seeley Lake, as with all the lakes in the chain, offers good conditions for float tubing for both bass and trout. Placid Lake is considered fairly good for cutthroat fishing and has an abundant population of kokanee salmon.

Whether tubing, bank fishing or casting from a boat, bass anglers use plastic worms, Jitterbugs, Rebels, Bass Orenos and Rapalas. Favorite spin lures are Mepps and Triple Teasers. Trollers also like the Triple Teaser when fished behind a leaded line and long leader. Bull trout are often taken when a hammered brass spoon is cast across an inlet stream, allowed to sink and then retrieved.

For the more adventuresome anglers, particularly those who enjoy combining their fishing with some mountain hiking, the Seeley Lake region offers close to fifty high-country lakes in the Mission and Swan Ranges. The back-country fisherman will find most of the lakes to be populated with cutthroat and a few are stocked with golden trout. The majority of the lakes is situated within five miles of the trail heads, and those within the Bob Marshall Wilderness fall under special regulations that should be reviewed prior to fishing this area.

The Clearwater River is a relatively small stream that flows through a very dense riparian environment of willow and alder. Its upper reaches measure only about fifteen feet across. For these reasons, the river is considered to be less popular to fish than the lakes. Four spots do stand out, however, and fishermen concentrate at them to enjoy their sport. The first is near the bridge two miles downstream from Seeley Lake. Bait fishermen in particular gather here from March to May to fish for brood trout released by the Montana Department of Fish, Wildlife and Parks. After May the river bottom becomes too overgrown with moss to allow good fishing. The next popular area is the marshy water at the head of Salmon Lake, where fishing can be productive before run-off. After run-off the fish fall back into the deeper, colder water of the lake. The third area includes the water from the Salmon Lake outlet to the river mouth at the Blackfoot. Lastly, anglers with canoes will float the water from the bottom of Seeley Lake to the top of Salmon Lake.

Overall, the river can be rated as an average quality fishery for fish of medium size. The nature of the water is such that it does not support a trophy fishery, but the combination of river and lakes does attract a good number of people who enjoy recreational fishing.

River Notes

FLATHEAD LAKE

Map Reference 18

Geologic theory asserts that during the Pinedale Ice Age some ten thousand to fifteen thousand years ago a huge block of glacial ice rested at the present site of Flathead Lake. During the course of many hundreds of years the ice surrounding this block melted more quickly and, while melting, deposited glacial till and out-wash rock in the areas both to the east and west sides of the lake. This deposition also formed the Polson Moraine to the south, which today is the terminal moraine that contains the lake. When the block of ice finally melted, the resultant hole in the ground filled with water and has been a lake for the past ten thousand years. Modern man has given it the formal name of Flathead Lake. It also has the informal designation of "Jewel of the Northwest," and rightly so, for the crystal clear water of this lake is not only a beautiful gem secured in a setting of nearby low mountains, but it offers recreation to people with many diverse interests.

The Flathead River which flows from the north is the main source of water to the lake. This water is gathered from springs, lakes and streams in the wilderness areas to the east of the lake as well as from the snow covered peaks of Glacier Park to the north. Water exits the lake through the power-generating Kerr Dam five miles below the town of Polson, to flow west, then south, then west again, finally entering the Clark Fork River near Paradise. This lowest section of the Flathead River runs almost entirely through the Flathead Indian Reservation and anglers fishing in the river here or on other waters within the reservation boundaries, must have a tribal fishing permit which can be obtained at several stores in the area or at the Tribal Administration Offices in Pablo. This reservation was established in 1855 as a place of residence for the Kootenai, Upper Pend d'Oreille, and Flathead Indian tribes. In 1936 chieftain-ships were discontinued and a tribal council was established as the elected governing board of the reservation. Today's population on the reservation numbers nearly twenty thousand persons, approximately three thousand of whom are Native Americans.

As you drive toward the lake from the south, the Mission Range rises dramatically from the valley floor to the east showing mountains whose bases are covered with evergreens while their peaks show through as barren rock points. It appears as if each mountain was compressed tightly against its neighbor, flattening its sides but retaining its individual jagged peaks. Subsequent erosion has opened up a large draws that drain into the broad, flat valley of ranch land below. To the west low hills rise along the entire distance from the National Bison Range to Flathead Lake. Your first sight of the lake from the highway is at the crest of a hill and you are greeted with a dramatic view of Polson Bay, several islands offshore and a golf course at water's edge.

Highway 93 continues north along the western edge of the lake, passing through several small communities. There are several campgrounds and lake accesses along this route. Wildhorse Island sits as guardian to Big Arm Bay and is accessible only by boat. The island is a state park of over 2,100 acres which offers picnic areas and hiking trails for day use but offers no facilities for overnight camping.

Highway 35 parallels the lake's lesser developed eastern shore and when not adjacent to the water, the road passes through stands of timber, many fruit orchards and past an occasional home. This area is heavily forested with evergreen trees and you can expect to see logging trucks on the highway. There are no communities along this highway until it reaches the modern resort town of Bigfork where the Swan River enters the lake at Bigfork Bay.

At Yellow Bay, the University of Montana has established the Flathead Lake Biological Station. This attractive facility, tucked between the trees on the lake's shore, was established as an education and research center and emphasizes studies of aquatic biology, botany, zoology and the limnology of the entire Flathead River/Lake ecosystem. To say the least, the effect of man's presence in the scheme of things is not always beneficial and his influence here at present is adversely disrupting the ecological balance of the lake. This disruption is but one of the projects the station studies and attempts to determine what change is taking place, to what degree, if and why it's a problem and devise the necessary steps toward a solution.

The lake is approximately twenty-eight miles long, seven to eight miles wide, with the exception of the expanses between Elmo and Blue Bay where the width reaches nearly sixteen miles. This 120,000-acre lake is home to a variety of fish species including its two main attractions, the cutthroat and the lake trout. There are also plenty of both mountain and lake whitefish, plus some rainbow, bull trout, kokanee salmon, and isolated populations of bass and perch.

The state record lake trout (forty-two pounds) came from this lake as did the record bull trout (twenty-six pounds). With incentives like these, the lake stays very busy in the summer, but it's not only fishermen who take advantage of the lake's beauty and clear water; it also acts as host to boaters, water skiers, swimmers and sailing enthusiasts.

Fishing here takes place year-round. In winter both ice fishing and trolling are popular, with trolling and jigging done for lake trout and bull trout wherever they can be located. The fish receiving the greatest attention during the winter months is the whitefish which is best fished near the lake bottom with bait, either by trolling or ice fishing. The perch are also an extremely popular catch in winter.

Spring is a time when trollers drop their lures to about the twenty-foot depth and shore fishermen cast small spinners in the protected bays for cutthroat. Bull- and lake-trout fishermen prefer to troll deeper, closer to the one-hundred-foot level, using leaded line, flasher blades and large lures and spoons.

Summer isn't considered the best time to pursue cutthroat, but lake trout continue to be caught when they can be located. South of Wildhorse Island is a popular lake trout area in the summer and fall when these large fish seek the shallower bays in which to spawn. Summer is also the time of year when bass and perch fishing come into their own; the lower lake, particularly in the Polson Bay area, is considered the most popular region for these fish. You can expect to catch bass up to fifteen inches and perch to twelve inches, using bait for the perch and plugs and spinners for the bass. Fall is again a time for pursuing the cutthroat, either by trolling or by casting from shore with small Mepps or Panther Martins.

We haven't written much about the kokanee salmon, which in years past have been an important resource in Flathead Lake. The tremendous populations of this species that were prevalent during the 1930's, 1940's and 1950's have now dwindled to rather insignificant numbers, and we don't feel justified in writing about them at this time because they seem to be virtually gone from the lake and those that do remain should be allowed to live and reproduce.

This body of water carries the name "lake" and, with a surface area of close to two hundred square miles, it is considered the largest natural lake west of the Mississippi. However, when you look at a map or read literature about the lake, you get the impression that this lake is really a reservoir because of the power-producing Kerr Dam which is situated at the lake's lower extremity. In a way, it's both. In 1938 the Kerr Dam was built for power generation and its construction raised the natural lake level by ten feet. Now, although water level fluctuations do occur, the level remains fairly constant during the summer and boat docks remain in the water. In the winter, however, the water might drop as much as fifteen feet, leaving some docks several feet removed from a wet spot! It's unlikely the fifteen foot drop will endanger fish populations though, for the lake is over three hundred feet deep!

BIGFORK

When Bigfork was first platted at the turn of the century and began its metamorphosis from an Indian camp, named "Half-Breed Village," to a more formally structured community, with planned streets and an established post office, its founders likely had no idea the community would become one of the state's more tourist-oriented and culturally-directed, small towns. Its tourist roots really began after 1914, the year Highway 35 was completed and area visitors had available a more convenient route to Glacier Park. Bigfork became a logical rest stop along the way and thereby commenced its changeover from a logging town to a tourist town.

The charm of small-town convenience combined with Montana friendliness and a more-than-usual inclination toward artistic and cultural pursuits has helped the town evolve into somewhat of a destination resort. At an elevation of almost three thousand feet, this community of two thousand residents wraps itself around Bigfork Bay at the mouth of the Swan River on the northern shore of Flathead Lake. The ambiance of the area and the town has enticed many artists to reside here and the amplification of artistic endeavors is manifested in the community events conducted each year. The annual Cherry Blossom Festival gets the summer started on an enthusiastic note, followed throughout the summer by sailboat regattas, the Festival of the Arts, musical presentations and repertory theater. In addition to water sports and fishing on Flathead Lake, visitors can now enjoy a beautiful and challenging eighteen-hole golf course which was recently built at the west side of town.

Bigfork, which is but forty miles from Glacier National Park, is well known in the region for having fine restaurants, plenty of accommodations and close access to the Jewel Basin Hiking Area.

Bigfork Chamber of Commerce: P.O. Box 237, Bigfork, Montana 59911 - Phone: 837-5888

POLSON

In the year 1898 a rancher named David Polson and a fellow resident of the south shore of Flathead Lake were selected by their neighbors to choose a name for the new community developing there. The area was referred to originally by the Salish Indians as "Foot of the Lake." After local merchant

Harry Lambert settled there in 1880 it was called "Lambert's Landing." Mr. Polson's fellow committeeman suggested Polson's name be used and we can only assume that, after a brief moment of modest reluctance, he did indeed allow it to be painted over the post office door. Today, in addition to its legal name, Polson is referred to locally as "Port City on Flathead Lake."

With a population of 3,000 residents and situated at an elevation of 3000 feet, Polson draws heavily on wood production, agriculture, light manufacturing, government contracts and summer tourism for its economic base. It's the largest town on the Flathead Indian Reservation and is the seat of Lake County. About twelve thousand years ago, during the Pinedale Ice Age, the Flathead Valley Glacier terminated at Polson and deposited the moraine that slopes up to the south from the lake and on which the town rests.

In May a celebration called the Cherry Blossom Festival takes place and by August those blossoms have ripened into mature cherries and owners of nearby orchards take to the task of their harvest. In addition to activities centering around the fruit orchards prevalent in the area, regattas and tours along with many water sports take place on Flathead Lake. Visits can be made to Kerr Dam where the water tumbles over the spillway in a drop greater than that at Niagara Falls. Below the dam rafting is popular on the Flathead River.

Golfers will enjoy playing the Polson Golf Course. This nine-hole course, located on the shores of Flathead Lake, is open to the public and features eighteen tee boxes. There are several local parks available for camping and picnicking, while more cultural activities include summer theater and the Miracle of America Museum which features Indian and military artifacts. The Flathead Historical Museum contains items of regional interest. Two musical events which take place here each year are the Mission Mountain Music Fest, held the first Saturday in August and featuring several bands, and the Montana State Fiddler's Contest which is a two-day event taking place in late July.

Commercial air transportation is available at Kalispell and Missoula, while small aircraft can come into the Polson Airport which offers a 4,500-foot, lighted, surfaced runway, plus services and maintenance facilities.

Polson Chamber of Commerce: P.O. Box 677, Polson, Montana 59860 - Phone: 883-5969

Flathead National Forest: 1935 Third Ave. E., Box 147, Kalispell, Montana 59901

For Flathead Reservation information and tribal permits: Consolidated Salish and Kootenai Tribal Headquarters - P.O. Box 278, Pablo, Montana 59855

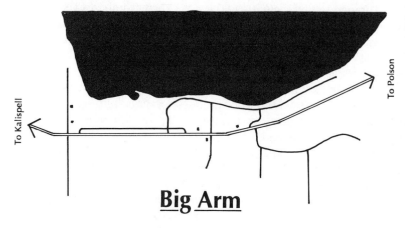

<u>Big</u> <u>Arm</u>

To Kalispell

To Polson

To Glacier National Park

North

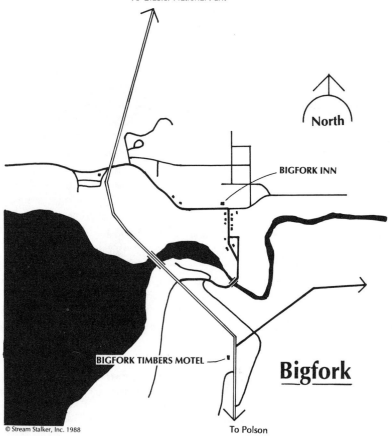

BIGFORK INN

BIGFORK TIMBERS MOTEL

<u>Bigfork</u>

To Polson

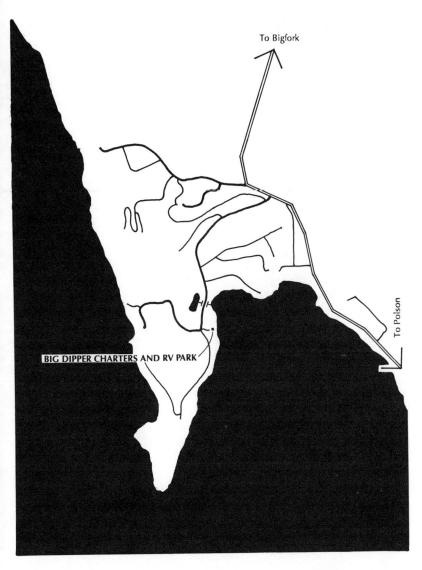

To Bigfork

To Polson

BIG DIPPER CHARTERS AND RV PARK

Woods Bay

North

BIGFORK

RESTAURANT / INN

BIGFORK INN
604 Main St., Box 697   837-6680
> Located in Bigfork, on the northeast shores of Flathead Lake, this fine country inn offers an eclectic menu, serving the finest food in the valley. Open seven days a week, year round. Our European style inn has a rustic lounge and dancing area, featuring jazz music for your enjoyment. Rooms available by prior arrangement.

MOTELS

BIGFORK TIMBERS MOTEL
Bigfork Highway 35 South, Box 757   837-6200
> Three diamond rating from AAA. Heated pool, jacuzzi, sauna, color cable TV, free coffee. Picture perfect, practically priced units, catering to fishermen. Open all year.

KALISPELL

GUIDES / OUTFITTERS

BIG DIPPER CHARTERS AND RV PARK
Woods Bay Marina (mailing address, 812 10th St., Kalispell 59901,)   257-3234
> Fishing charters, full or half days. Trophy mackinaw and Dolly Varden trout. All tackle furnished. Licensed skippers, with 15 years experience on Flathead Lake. For reservations and information, call: Days, (406) 837-4226, Woods Bay; Evenings, (406) 257-3234, Kalispell.

FLATHEAD RIVER

Map References 19, 20, 21

If ever a national contest were sponsored to judge a river system on the basis of its remote setting, diverse character, clear water, spectacular vistas, wild surroundings plus challenge to the floater, we think accolades and ribbons of merit would most definitely be awarded to the Flathead River. If the river could be granted one wish as its reward for this high rating, it might wish to add a better trout population, a wish that would certainly be endorsed by the fishermen who are frequently tempted to try its beautiful water.

The fishing quality here depends directly upon spawning migrations from Flathead Lake, namely by the Westslope cutthroat trout and the Dolly Varden or bull trout. Were it not for these two fish, with their instinctive command to leave the lake, enter the river, seek out tributary streams and finally perform their procreative compulsions, the fishing in this drainage would be considerably less than adequate. It would be a rare angler, indeed, who could look at the four large rivers in this system and not know in his heart that they are teeming with trout. The North, Middle, South and main Forks of the Flathead give the visual impression of being very productive fisheries, but in spite of their seductive appearance, their trout populations really are not impressive. Our overall observation tells us that the fishing here does offer a good challenge to the fisherman looking to catch that trophy, twenty pound bull trout and that acts as a natural complementary activity to a recreational float trip.

Some resident trout do live in the upper reaches of both the South Fork and Middle Fork, but these areas are quite remote and take some logistical planning and preparation to enjoy. As a general rule, you can expect the cutthroat to be small in size and the bull trout to be few in number. Kokanee salmon were once an important fish here, with fall spawning runs from Flathead Lake attracting hundreds of enthusiastic fishermen and literally hundreds of bald eagles that fed upon their carcasses. Only a few short years ago, between 100,000 and 150,000 salmon would crowd into the Flathead to seek the tributary streams such as McDonald Creek where they would complete their spawning activities. In 1987 an estimated three hundred salmon made this journey! The Flathead has a severe salmon problem and fisheries biologists have a difficult issue to address.

The three forks and the main river all have rapids and white-water areas that deserve the attention of float fishermen. There are some areas of water that are totally impassable, and some that have taken the lives of floaters who didn't realize the dangers confronting them. Several ranger stations located throughout the region can provide maps and valuable floating information to anyone planning to launch a boat here.

THE NORTH FORK—Originating in Canada this branch of the river continues south forming the border between Glacier National Park to the east and the Flathead National Forest to the west. Of its total fifty-eight miles in the U. S., the reach from the border down to the Camas Creek Bridge is classified as a "scenic river," as defined by the National Wild and Scenic River Law. It is designated "recreational" from Camas Creek Bridge to its confluence with the Middle Fork.

This is a medium size river most of the year, but during the run-off it's a formidable piece of water as it collects melting snow from the Canadian Rockies as well as the mountain ranges it bisects in Montana. The entire river can be floated, but it shouldn't be attempted by beginner boatmen. Only after run-off should it be navigated by intermediate rafters. As with all the forks of the Flathead, it should be either scouted beforehand, or run at least once with someone who has had experience on the reach to be floated. Access to the river is good from County Road #210 that parallels the river for its entire length in Montana. In addition to clear water and beautiful surroundings, a trip down this fork provides a good opportunity to sight game in the river bottom.

The run-off here lasts from May into July, but cutthroat will be found starting in April as they enter the lower river seeking suitable spawning gravel. From then through August the cutts and resident bull trout will be in the river as objects of angler's attention. The bull trout are here from July to October with their actual spawning taking place in September and October. Of the three forks, the north fork has the least fertile water and the fewest fish.

THE MIDDLE FORK—The water from the easternmost area of this river drainage is collected by the Middle Fork, which heads in the Bob Marshall Wilderness, flows northwest for about thirty miles through the center of the Great Bear Wilderness, then forms the southwest boundary of Glacier National Park and finally converges with the North Fork to create the main stem of the Flathead River. This fork has the steepest gradient of the three and has been nicknamed "Montana's Wildest River," a designation used to describe the river's physical character. The country through which it flows is remote and also has a wild nature.

For those wishing to reach the upper river on foot or horseback, the approach is often made from the Spotted Bear Ranger Station. This is the most interesting route, but also the most time consuming. For those wishing to make a faster trip, an airfield is located at Shafer Meadows about twenty-five miles from Highway 2, from which a float trip is made to Essex, near Bear Creek.

99

From Bear Creek to West Glacier, Highway 2 parallels the river and offers easy access for this next thirty-five mile segment of water. From its headwaters to Bear Creek the river carries a "wild" classification and is then rated as "recreational" down to its confluence with the South Fork.

There is foot access to the upper river on the "Big River Trail," a foot and horse pack trail that parallels the river. Whatever camping is done here is done under primitive conditions, so it is very important to be aware of the presence of grizzly bears and take normal precautions when hiking, cleaning fish and storing food. Information can be obtained from the Forest Service as to safeguards one should take to avoid problems.

The upper river requires very technical floating skills, particularly when the water is high. Optimum floating takes place from June to mid-July. After the first week in August the water may have dropped so dramatically that the river has become too low to float. The water of the upper reaches is rough and requires expert boating skills in many stretches. Commercial operators float here on white-water trips which provide plenty of thrills and challenges. Large boulders and downed timber combine with pounding rapids to give you a thrilling ride. It's a good idea to carry extra oars and to keep your life jacket snugly buckled.

The trip from Shafer Meadows to Essex can be made on a weekend should your time be limited. You could fly to Shafer early on Saturday morning, camp that night and float out on Sunday. This would involve steady floating and not much fishing, but it can be done. The fish here are, as on the North Fork, primarily spawners from Flathead Lake. Both cutthroat and bull trout are present and the most productive period would be after run-off from July through August.

The fishing below Bear Creek, along Highway 2, is considered marginal, not only because of the nature of the fishery, but also because there is substantial fishing pressure caused by the easy access.

THE SOUTH FORK—Unlike the Middle Fork, there are no airstrips on the upper reaches of this river, so the only way in is by horse or hike, approximately thirty miles in either case. There are two primary trail heads that access the headwaters of the South Fork. One is located at Holland Lake south of Condon off Highway 83, and one a few miles to the south out of Seeley Lake, over Pyramid Pass and down Young's Creek. In both cases you reach the river deep in the heart of the Bob Marshall Wilderness where the river originates. This fork has been classified "wild" from its headwaters to the confluence of Spotted Bear Creek and "recreational" from there to Hungry Horse Reservoir.

This fork is also floated, mostly by professional outfitters, and also contains some rough water. As a matter of fact, it is rough enough to have taken some lives, so anyone planning to float will need to make proper preparations ahead of time, use only good equipment, and plan to portage around some impassable hazards. The water is high through June and usually clears by mid-July when fishing begins for cutthroat to fifteen inches, bull trout averaging four to eight pounds and some resident whitefish. The fish here are not spawners from Flathead Lake because the dam at Hungry Horse Reservoir prevents their passage upstream. These fish are from Hungry Horse Reservoir and they move up into the river to seek tributary streams in which to spawn. After spawning most of them return downstream to the still water of the reservoir.

The water below Hungry Horse Dam down to the main river fluctuates drastically and is considered poor habitat for trout. The river upstream from Hungry Horse, on the other hand, is considered to offer the best fishing of the three forks. There seem to be no "secret" fly patterns used here, as these fish aren't overly selective, so standard caddis dressings and attractor flies work well, as do the popular spinning lures. Large spoons fished deep work most satisfactorily for the bull trout.

THE MAIN RIVER—The water below the confluence of the South and Middle Forks, essentially from Columbia Falls down to Kalispell, seems to be the favorite reach of the local anglers. The water below this stretch can often be off-color due to the sediment loads carried by the lower Stillwater and Whitefish Rivers. This main stem of the Flathead is a large river and provides good fishing for the fly fisherman as well as the spinning devotee. There seem to be more resident fish occupying this reach and both cutthroat and bull trout are taken; the best time to fish here is during June and the first part of July. There are many runs up to twenty-five feet in depth and also some very shallow riffles that spill into deeper water, creating a variety of holding water for the angler. The floating angler should keep an eye out for these areas as they present water character somewhat different from most of the water in the channel. Hatches of caddis and small stoneflies come off throughout the summer and standard dry patterns are used successfully. Sometimes the fly fishermen will hook large bull trout by fishing deep with Woolly Worms and streamers. This water can be waded on a limited basis in a few areas, but to really cover it well it should be floated.

THE LOWER RIVER—The river below Flathead Lake is very large, subject to sudden changes in volume, holds a few trout and a few northern pike, is slow and flat in some stretches and not an extremely appealing section of river to many anglers. It can flow for a time at four thousand c.f.s.. and within a few hours be up to ten thousand c.f.s. because of power demands placed on the Kerr Dam. On the average, the summer flows will average six thousand to seven thousand c.f.s.. and winter flows are somewhat smaller. This part of the river flows through the Flathead Indian Reservation, so be sure to purchase the required fishing permit in addition to your Montana license if you plan to fish here.

The Flathead River system drains some of Montana's most beautiful country. Just "being here" has as much value as fishing here, if not more so. The residents of this region are proud of the land in which they live and want to maintain it in as natural an environment as is consistent with the activities of man. As visitors we can certainly appreciate their pride and concern and should do our part in treating the natural resources with the respect they deserve.

KALISPELL

As you leave the immediate area of Flathead Lake and proceed northwest toward Kalispell on Highway 82 and then Highway 93, the valley opens into a vast, flat area of small farms which grow hay and grain, but you're always within sight of hills and mountains across the distant vista. To the north lies the Whitefish Range, to the east the Swan Range and the Salish Mountains dominate the western horizon.

Before the arrival of the railroad in 1891, the area was referred to by the Pend d'Orielle Indians as the "prairie above the lake," which in their language was "Kalispell." No longer a prairie, the city now is the seat of Flathead County and has a population of nearly 11,000 residents. Arrival at Kalispell by train has been replaced by air travel into either Glacier International Airport seven miles northeast of town, or into Kalispell City Airport at the southern edge of town. The latter provides charter air service and a surfaced, lighted runway of 3,600 feet for small aircraft. Most visitors, however, arrive via one of the two highways that span the state to intersect in this city; Highway 2 bisects Montana from Idaho to Nebraska and Highway 93 connects Idaho to Canada.

The economy of Kalispell is based on logging, lumber production, ranching and a local aluminum manufacturing plant. Tourism here, as in many areas of the state, is becoming an increasingly important factor in the economy. Accommodations and dining possibilities are, of course, numerous in this, the largest city in northwest Montana (north and west of Missoula), but visitors wishing to camp will also find many sites available on the loop from Flathead Lake through Kalispell and bending east to Hungry Horse Reservoir. If you're pulling a boat and wish to put it on the Flathead River, launch sites are convenient near town.

Activities for the family include a visit to historic Conrad Mansion, a restored residence built in 1895 by Charles Conrad, the "founder" of Kalispell. This beautiful twenty-three-room residence with many original furnishings is recognized as an historic site and has a place on the National Register of Historic Places. You can spend a lazy afternoon or a more physical period with a visit to Woodland Park. This is the city's largest park and it includes gardens, a lagoon replete with an impressive population of ducks, a small bird zoo, tennis courts and a public swimming pool. Several other parks in the city can be enjoyed for purposes of picnicking or merely contemplating world problems and solutions!

One of Montana's largest golf facilities stretches out with twenty-seven holes at the Buffalo Hill Golf Course. In addition to playing both nine-hole and eighteen-hole layouts you can practice on the driving range, rent equipment at the pro shop and enjoy a meal at the restaurant. When the golf scorecard has been laid aside—or framed for posterity—you can visit the Hockaday Center for the Arts which features works by artists and craftsmen from around the world, or, if your timing is right, enjoy a symphonic performance, a repertory theater presentation, a circus, a horse show or the Northwest Montana Fair and Rodeo held each year in mid-August.

As you see, Kalispell is a center of activity located conveniently between Flathead Lake and Glacier National Park.

Kalispell Area Chamber of Commerce: 15 Depot Loop, Kalispell, M o n - tana 59901 - Phone: 755-6166

Flathead National Forest: P.O. Box 147, Kalispell, Montana 59901 - Phone: 755-5401

WHITEFISH

If you enjoy participating in activities other than fishing or wish to combine fishing with other forms of water sports, you'll want to consider Whitefish as a location to do so. Although timber and railroading were once the main economic resources in this town of 4,000 residents, tourism has now taken over the leading role in a big way and now it's considered to be northwest Montana's quintessential recreation community. You'll find dining, accommodations and outdoor activities to be plentiful aspects of Whitefish life during the summer as well as the winter months. Within seven miles of town the development of Big Mountain, with at least twenty-five miles of groomed trails, has created Montana's largest alpine ski area. This area receives plenty of snow in winter which promotes a healthy interest in cross-country skiing as well.

The southern tip of seven-mile-long Whitefish Lake extends within the city limits giving access to fishermen who delight in hooking what are considered to be some of Montana's largest lake trout and northern pike. The town itself derived its name from the lake, which had gained its name from the abundant population of mountain whitefish swimming in its cool waters. Fishing for this species also provides good sport for many fishermen. The lake is the site of other water sports including motor boat races, swimming, wind-surfing, pleasure sailing and weekly sailboat races—breezes permitting! Once each summer a nationally recognized canoe race takes place starting at Whitefish and terminating at the town of Bigfork on Flathead Lake. The family can build sand castles or swim at the two beaches on the lake; one is at the Whitefish State Recreation Area, the other is in town at the City Beach.

In addition to all of this activity, weekly bike races are held here and golfers can shoot for eagles on any of the twenty-seven holes at the Whitefish Lake Golf Club which is open to the public and has a pro shop, restaurant, club house and driving range. At Baker Street Park, on the Flathead River, picnic facilities and tennis courts are available to the public. To enjoy great views of the surrounding countryside you can ascend the heights of nearby Big Mountain either on foot along the many hiking trails or by a less strenuous route via the chair lift. The chair lift starts up the mountain side at an elevation of 4,750 feet and terminates at the Summit House which rests at 7,000 feet.

At one time in its history, prior to the arrival of the Great Northern Railroad, Whitefish was called "Stump Town" because of the tree bottoms left by loggers. The railroad, now named the Burlington Northern, left a more practical remnant of its sojourn here in the form of the prodigious, two-story depot placed along tracks now used by the AMTRAK system to bring visitors into this area. No matter what form of transportation you use to arrive here, once your bags are unpacked, you'll find plenty of activities to keep you busy!

Whitefish Area Chamber of Commerce: 525 3rd Street, Whitefish, Montana 59937 - Phone: 862-3501

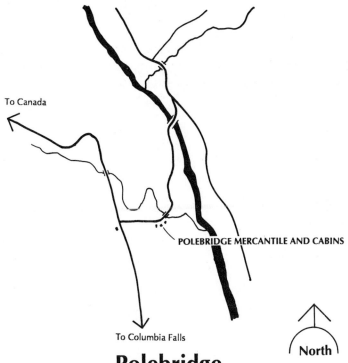

To Canada

POLEBRIDGE MERCANTILE AND CABINS

To Columbia Falls

Polebridge

North

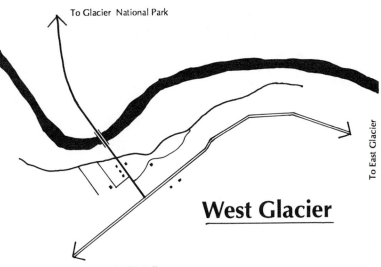

To Glacier National Park

To East Glacier

West Glacier

© Stream Stalker, Inc. 1988

To Columbia Falls

POLEBRIDGE

GENERAL STORE / CABINS

POLEBRIDGE MERCANTILE AND CABINS
1-1/2 miles south of Polebridge entrance to Glacier Nat. Park, Gen. Del. 888-9926
> Supplying this remote area along the North Fork of the Flathead River since 1914. Now on the National Register of Historic Places. Groceries, fishing tackle, gas and rustic cabins available. Open year round.

GALLATIN RIVER

Map References 22, 23

Most of us recognize the river flowing north from Yellowstone Park along Highway 191 as being the Gallatin River, and indeed it is. But it is also known by the name West Gallatin River, which adds a small note of confusion, particularly because there is also a West Fork of the Gallatin and an East Gallatin River that joins the Gallatin River near Manhattan creating what is sometimes referred to as the "main" Gallatin. To dispel some of this confusion, we will refer to the entire length of the river from the Park to the Missouri as the Gallatin, and we'll call the East Gallatin the East Gallatin.

The Shoshone Indian name for the river is interpreted to mean "swift water," and swift it is, particularly in the canyon area. This section is but one of several different faces worn by the river in the one-hundred mile journey to its end in the Missouri Headwaters State Park. Four different reaches distinguish themselves as one drives downstream, so we'll characterize each section starting at the Yellowstone Park boundary.

The first area is the upper river and it will take us from the Park down to Big Sky. This reach starts where the valley is relatively wide, flows through a narrow canyon and then opens out again before reaching Big Sky. The road stays in close proximity to the river for the entire distance and there are plenty of opportunities to select the type of fishing water you prefer. Access points to the river are numerous along here and fishing pressure is quite high. The river throughout this section is approximately thirty feet wide, flowing over fairly small cobbles and maintaining a relatively shallow profile without deep holes or undercut banks. The lack of complicated currents and obstructed channels makes this easy water to fish.

At the confluence of the Taylor Fork, the valley begins to narrow and the river picks up a bit more speed. The Taylor Fork is notorious as a sediment carrier. The run-off period usually starts about the third week of May and peaks by the last week of June. The river begins to clear by the third week of July. Throughout this period, and after every summer rain, the Taylor Fork can be counted on to muddy the Gallatin below.

You're traveling through some very scenic country here and what starts out as a corridor of sage and evergreen changes to a more rugged character of vertical rock faces and pinnacles. The white, and various shades of red, rocks in the river add to what is already a marvelous view. It was certainly a high tribute to President Thomas Jefferson's Secretary of the Treasury, Albert Gallatin, when William Clark named the river in his honor.

As you continue your journey toward Big Sky and the confluence of the West Fork, you see the valley again widen and the river flow through willow bottoms behind occasional fenced property. The water in this section of the river is cold throughout the year but particularly so in the spring. This is the time of the nymph for fly anglers and prior to run-off, popular patterns include stonefly imitations, Hare's Ears, Prince and Sandy Mites. The fish in this reach are primarily rainbow, with occasional brooks, cutthroat, cutt-bow hybrids and plenty of whitefish. The river bottom contains cobbles in the six to twelve inch category with very little small gravel, making a careful approach to wading a necessity.

The Gallatin is known to have a very good salmonfly hatch, but the river is often unfishable in the lower reaches because of very high, roilly water. When conditions are favorable, however, the hatch will come off as the water clears and anglers will get good action on artificials. Spin fishermen fishing this section of river will want to use small lures such as Panther Martin, Mepps, Thomas Cyclone, and Rooster Tail.

The next easily definable section of river spans the distance between Big Sky and the mouth of the Gallatin River Canyon, a distance of approximately twenty miles. Immediately below Big Sky a fence bars access to the river, but soon the river enters the canyon where access to the long pools, splashing riffles and powerful runs is no problem. Large river boulders start to appear here in great quantity, and it becomes obvious why kayaking enthusiasts enjoy practicing their skills in this section of the river, which is now forty to sixty feet wide. The angler can start to stretch out a bit more also as the channel has widened with the infusion of new of water contributed by the tributary streams. Added to the step-downs from riffle to pool, the boulders create enough pocket water, slicks and seams to offer the angler a wonderful assortment of water types from which to choose.

The river here is more closely wrapped in lodgepole pine and Douglas fir that grow right down to the water on both banks, providing a true forest setting for the angler. You'll notice that some of the lodgepole have been killed by the Mountain Pine Beetle. Although these trees have lost their former beauty, such beetle infestations are a normal event in nature's scheme of things and their demise allows room for the growth of future generations of trees. To the west of the canyon lies the Spanish Peaks Wilderness area, with its fifty thousand acres of meadows, streams, lakes, waterfalls and mountain peaks rising to over eleven thousand feet. Hikers can take trails from the highway to enter this area, and detailed information about the wilderness is available at the Squaw Creek Ranger Station.

One non-angling activity enjoyed by some people is rock climbing. You'll

Gallatin River

notice tiers of rock outcroppings the length of the canyon, but unfortunately much of the rock is unstable and unsafe. Climbers have been injured on several occasions in this area, so devotees of this sport should acquire information from the Forest Service before attempting a climb.

As with the water above, rainbow are the predominate fish here. They prefer the deep channels and slow, dark water behind the boulders. Nymph fishermen enjoy this type of water because they can use a short line to permit the life-like natural drift of a weighted fly in these vagarious currents. There are many nooks and crannies under the dancing surface of the river in which the trout find refuge, and the adept nymph fisherman can do well here any time of the year.

As winter's chill wanes under the spring sunshine, nymphs will provide almost one hundred percent of the angler's action. Through April and May the caddis and mayfly larvae imitations will be the best choice. Hare's Ears, Prince, Peeking Caddis and Muskrat are always popular in size #12 to #16. Toward the end of May when the large salmonfly nymphs begin to appear, switch over to big, dark brown and black stonefly nymphs in size #2 to #6. The hatch itself will be on in June amid the normal rush of high water when mid-stream fishing is futile. The best bet under these conditions is to fish close to the bank with both nymphs and dries using any of the standard, high-floating adult patterns. Because Taylor Fork is predictably emptying a dense concoction of silt into the river during run-off, you might wish to move above the

107

confluence and work nymphs in the clearer water. As the canyon waters drop and clear in early July there's an opportunity to fish the golden stonefly hatch that follows closely on the tail end of the salmonfly activity. Artificials here will be somewhat smaller, sizes #4 through #8, and the lighter colored dressings are appropriate for the golden insect.

After run-off in July, when the boisterous charge of the river has settled into a more normal condition, the fly angler will do well on nymphs and attractors during the day, phasing into Elk Hair Caddis and Goddard Caddis as the evening hatches begin. In addition to caddis activity, there's a spruce moth on the water in August above the West Fork mouth, and a #12 Elk Hair Caddis will work well as its imitation.

The Gallatin in these two upper reaches is not a large river by Montana standards, so the fly fisherman can feel comfortable using rods from four- to six-weight. We recommend they be at least nine feet long, however, to maximize line control over the river's capricious currents. They need enough backbone to throw the early summer stoneflies as well as the air resistant grasshopper imitations from mid-August to mid-September. Casting these patterns into the grassy banks works quite well as summer begins to fade into autumn. Typically the surface fishing slows down as September wears on, and nymphs and steamers become the most common offerings.

Spin fishermen throughout the summer will have been using the old favorite Panther Martin, Mepps, Kamlooper and Krocodile. Small profile lures that sink quickly are preferred in this area of deep pools and strong currents.

Before we leave the upper half of the Gallatin, let's briefly look at the two main tributaries we've mentioned. The Taylor Fork has been maligned because it is a carrier of high sediment loads during run-off and rain storms. This condition is a fact of life because the stream pushes through areas of silt and clay with unstable, eroding banks. When flows are stable and the water is clear, this comfortably-sized stream is heavily fished in its mid-section for rainbow in the eight- to fourteen-inch class and a few smaller cutthroats. Access is from a Forest Service road that follows the stream from the highway for seven and one-half miles, after which a trail extends two and one-half miles more to Taylor Falls.

The West Fork of the Gallatin is a small stream, about twenty feet wide, entering the main river at Big Sky. Its source is the North and Middle Forks, and it has access from a Forest Service road following its course through flat meadow land. The stream flows for the most part through Big Sky Resort property and is fished heavily for eight to twelve inch rainbows.

As the canyon environment along the Gallatin starts to give way to a broader valley setting at the Williams Bridge, the environment becomes less alpine and more agricultural. Hay meadows replace rock walls, and the river pulls to the west through the farm country of the Gallatin Valley. We've just left what many consider to be one of the more scenic drives in the state and we now enter a countryside that more typically shows off the "big sky" of Montana.

The third section of river we'll describe is from the canyon to the mouth of the East Gallatin River. The Gallatin Valley was settled in the 1860's as farmers came to this area and realized they could raise wheat in the rich soil of these bottom lands. Abundant water encouraged irrigation efforts from both the Gallatin and East Gallatin Rivers; first with modest ditches and eventually with more elaborate canals, diversions and pumping stations to pull water from the rivers. The river slows here and glides past hay meadows, braids into smaller ten to forty foot wide channels around cottonwood islands and presses tight against willow banks. The gradient has eased and the river has relaxed. This is the home of the more tolerant brown trout. No one guaranteed this fish would have an easy life here, and at times he doesn't! During July and August the irrigation draw-downs can reduce the flow of water by up to ninety percent, particularly below the Cameron Bridge. This event makes it awfully tough for the fish to keep their fins wet, and they all head for the deepest pools they can. Obviously as the water temperature rises, the fish become less than ravenous, and trying to fool one into taking a fly requires long leaders, fine tippets and a careful, stalking approach. They can be extremely selective in this situation so the angler has to use all the finesse he can muster.

In the areas that aren't affected by water depletion, this section of river fishes well with caddis, attractor dries and nymphs. This section of river fishes better in the evening than during mid-day and Elk Hair and Goddard Caddis from #14 to #18 work well at that time. During the day the Royal Wulff, Royal Trude, Bitch Creek and Yuk Bug attractors work well. When the wind blows in August and September try a hopper or beetle pattern next to the bank on the surface. Try this above the Cameron Bridge where the effects of irrigation are less severe.

In the fall, of course, the switch is made to big nymphs, particularly rubberlegs, plus the sculpin patterns and Woolly Buggers. Black bodies, olive bodies and a touch of flash adds to their appeal.

The lower river is that section between the mouth of the East Gallatin River and the Missouri River, where the Gallatin terminates its long and varied journey. This area is predictably the widest section of the river, more on a par with the Madison and Jefferson. Some very deep pools exist here along with attractive riffles of about two feet in depth. This is a relatively undisturbed bottom land, winding through an agricultural setting, with hay meadows south of the river and grazing land to the north. Of all sections of the river this is the best for spotting wildlife including deer, moose, otters, beaver, geese and blue heron.

Floating here is relatively easy year-round as long as the oarsman keeps an eye peeled for the occasional log jam. When you put in at Manhattan and float to Logan you can enjoy a leisurely half-day trip with plenty of time to fish or take a similar trip provided on the float from Logan to Three Forks. If you wish to cover this entire distance, pack a lunch and plan to spend the entire day for there are plenty of opportunities to beach the boat and work the especially appealing runs and pools.

This part of the river is home to migrating rainbows and browns on spawning runs from the Missouri, so the population here is a mixture of the two, with some of the browns reaching trophy size. Summer flows can be off-color due to irrigation returns, but when the water is relatively clear, anglers prefer to fish in the evening and morning when water temperatures are somewhat cooler.

Fall is the preferred time on this stretch when fly fishermen prefer a six-weight rod to throw large streamers and big nymphs into the undercut banks, deep pools and runs; Woolly Buggers and rubberlegs are favorite patterns. Spin fishermen will use 6-pound line with 3/8 ounce to 5/8 ounce spoons and spinners.

For access to this section of river you have four choices: the Four Corners Fishing Access Site near Manhattan on Secondary Road 346, the Nixon Bridge, the Logan Bridge west of Logan, and the take-out on the Missouri River just below the Gallatin mouth. This latter site is within the Headwaters State Park and provides the convenience of a boat ramp. To the west of the Logan Bridge the railroad right-of-way follows the river and offers access to the wade fisherman.

There you have it! We've taken you down the Gallatin River and pointed out its pleasures and pitfalls. This is a free flowing river without the controls imposed by a dam and impoundment, so the effects of nature in spring and early summer vary from year to year based upon snow pack in the surrounding mountains. Planning a trip to fish the river in June can be risky, so obtain information from tackle shops in Bozeman or West Yellowstone before taking a chance at this time of year.

EAST GALLATIN RIVER

This river is formed just north of the town of Bozeman from waters draining the Gallatin and Bridger Mountain Ranges. It is a short river—only about twenty miles long measured by highway distance—but when the meanders are measured you could possibly walk its bank for closer to thirty-five miles.

This is a meadow stream flowing through farm land in a channel hugged by willows that are sometimes very dense. Its bending and turning current glides over a relatively low gradient, but its steady push has cut out six- to ten-foot deep holes under banks. Because there are no designated access sites here, you'll need to ask permission of the ranchers. Their business, of course, is raising crops and they do so most productively by irrigating. Because of the irrigation return, water during July and August can be cloudy. The lower river seems to be affected most; less plant life covers the banks here so their resultant instability adds even further to the sediment load in the river.

This problem notwithstanding, the East does contain respectable trout, mostly rainbows between eight and eighteen inches in the upper river and mostly browns of the same size in the lower river. The run-off in May and June shuts down attempts to fish the river, but as it clears in late June anglers will take fish on large nymphs, particularly the rubberleg patterns in size #4 to #8. These big, dark flies seem to work best over this river's silted bottom when they are given some motion. Spin fishermen should use spinners having black bodies.

During the summer small dries and nymphs are effective, particularly Tricos in the morning and caddis in the evening. Hoppers are good in August and small Blue Winged Olives imitate the Baetis hatch in September. Nymph patterns include Gold Ribbed Hare's Ear and Prince Nymph in #12 to #16 and Pheasant Tails in #14 to #18. As with most Montana rivers, fall fishing is best using streamers and large attractor nymphs.

Because of the narrow channel and tight corners of the upper river, floating is a less-than-ideal way to fish this section of river but the stretch from Belgrade down to the mouth can be floated with little difficulty.

BIG SKY

The resort of Big Sky, located on the Gallatin River half way between West Yellowstone and Bozeman, exists largely because of the vision and enthusiasm of one man, well-known NBC commentator and native Montanan, Chet Huntley. Although Mr. Huntley has since passed on, his imagination and promotional efforts have transformed a working cattle ranch into what is now a successful, year-round destination resort. Completed in 1974 the resort is now under the ownership of Bogue U. S. A. Resorts.

The resort consists of two separate villages, Meadow Village in the lower valley and Mountain Village at the base of the ski area six miles to the west. The ski-oriented activities take place in the Mountain Village and the summer activities in the lower Meadow Village. Both areas, however, have similar amenities including restaurants, shops and services.

From either location guests take advantage of many seasonal activities including hiking, horseback riding on the fifty miles of trails in the Spanish Peak Mountains, riding the gondola to the top of 11,166 foot Lone Mountain, fishing in nearby streams and lakes, rafting or kayaking on local rivers, playing golf on the eighteen-hole course in Meadow Village and playing tennis at facilities in both villages.

Most visitors arrange air transportation through Bozeman's Gallatin Field Airport or the municipal airport at West Yellowstone and recent negotiations with the airlines have made these necessary activities much easier and more comfortable.

BOZEMAN

Prior to the 1860's, the ground of the Gallatin Valley felt the quiet footsteps of many Indian tribes such as the Blackfeet, Cheyenne, Crow, Flathead, Piegan and Shoshone who used this area as a corridor between mountain ranges as well as a neutral hunting ground on which to gather game for their families. The valley also served as a trail to the more westerly mining camps of Virginia City and Bannack. The most notable wagon master to utilize this trail was John Bozeman, who, in the early 1860's, decided it would be more profitable to sell supplies and provisions to the miners than act as their trail guide. In 1864 he and some friends laid out the town of Bozeman and shortly thereafter, in 1867, the town was significant enough to be declared the Gallatin County seat.

While most miners passed through the area in search of riches from placer gold and valuable ore, a few stopped near Bozeman and settled in this fertile valley to farm and raise crops. Today the raising of grain, cattle, swine, sheep, horses and dairy cattle make agriculture the number one source of income in 2,500-square-mile Gallatin County. In addition a few small lumber mills operate here.

The second-ranked, income producer in Gallatin County, once called the "Valley of Flowers," by the Indians, is tourism, and certainly Bozeman is a center of tourist attention and activity. This is an upbeat community, interested not only in tourism and farm-support functions, but the arts and academe as well. Of the city's total population, approximately ten thousand are students at Montana State University. This represents almost one-third of the entire population of 36,000. The school was founded in 1893 and continues to add a scholastic and cultural overtone to the heartbeat of the city. As a part of the university the Museum of the Rockies, located on campus at the south edge of town, was founded in 1957. The museum now enjoys regional significance with its diverse displays of dinosaur bones, the Plains Indians, early explorers, miners, trappers and settlers. There is a fully-furnished, full-scale replica home and sections on geological and archeological history. In addition, there are separate galleries of western paintings, sculpture and photography.

The Gallatin County Historical Society founded the Gallatin County Pioneer Museum in 1982 and it specializes in the local heritage of the valley with displays of photographs, fashions, farm tools and a library. Interestingly, this museum is located in the former county jail which in itself adds an unusual dimension to the other displays.

Other cultural and recreational activities that can be enjoyed by visitors to Bozeman include summer theater, both indoors as well as in local parks, and performances by the Bozeman Symphony. The city has six developed parks and two nine-hole golf courses, one public and one semi-private. Other local attractions include two nearby ski resorts, the Bozeman Hot Springs pool at the former site of a large Blackfeet Indian Camp and the Fish Cultural Development Center on Bridger Canyon Road at Bridger Creek. In operation since 1896, this is the oldest operating federal hatchery in the northwest and one of only five such centers in the country. Hikers can enjoy many areas nearby, including the mountains of the Hyalite Range and the Spanish Peaks Primitive Area south of town as well as trails in the Bridger Range north of town.

Within easy driving distance to the west is the Missouri Headwaters State Park and the Madison Buffalo Jump State Monument; to the south is the Gallatin Petrified Forest, adjacent to and within Yellowstone Park. This forty-square-mile area off Highway 191 offers the fascinating sights of petrified standing trees as well as many petrified stumps. Collection of pieces of the stone-like wood is allowed only with a permit issued by the U. S. Forest Service.

Of no mean importance to fishermen visiting here is the fact that three major rivers—the Madison, the Gallatin and the Yellowstone—enhance the countryside nearby. So in addition to many other attributes, Bozeman is also a center of angling activity.

Bozeman Area Chamber of Commerce: 1205 E. Main St., Bozeman, Montana 59715 - Phone: 586-5421

Gallatin National Forest: P.O. Box 130, Federal Building, Bozeman, Montana 59715 - Phone: 587-6701

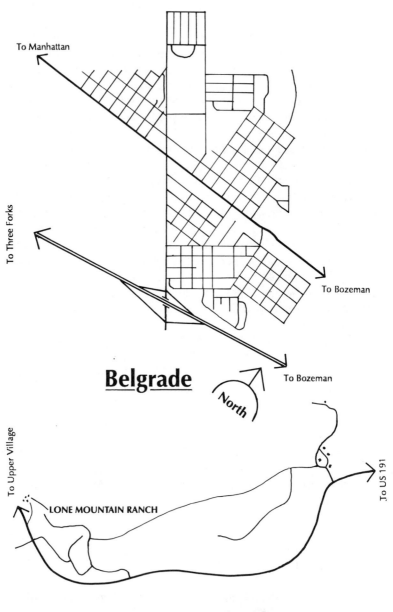

To Manhattan

To Three Forks

To Bozeman

To Bozeman

Belgrade

North

To Upper Village

LONE MOUNTAIN RANCH

To US 191

Big Sky

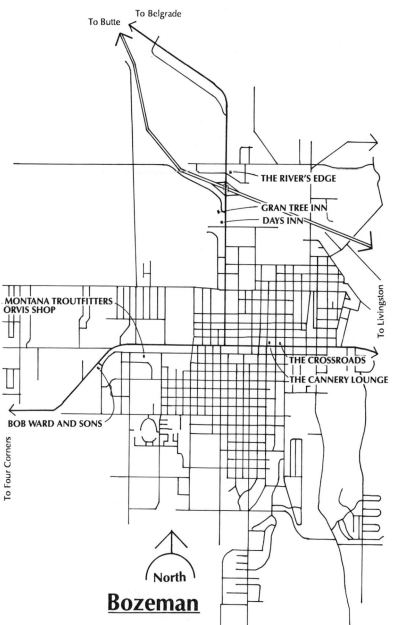

To Belgrade

To Butte

THE RIVER'S EDGE

GRAN TREE INN

DAYS INN

To Livingston

MONTANA TROUTFITTERS
ORVIS SHOP

THE CROSSROADS

THE CANNERY LOUNGE

BOB WARD AND SONS

To Four Corners

North

Bozeman

© Stream Stalker, Inc. 1988

BIG SKY

GUIDES / OUTFITTERS

GALLATIN RIVER GUIDES
Hwy. 191, 1/4 mile south of Big Sky entrance, Box 212   995-4369
> Located on the banks of the Gallatin River. We offer expertly guided float and wade fishing and the area's finest selection of flies, tackle and outdoor equipment.

JAKE'S HORSES
3 miles south of Big Sky Resort, (mailing address, 5645 Ramshorn, Gallatin Gateway, MT 59730) 995-4630
> Sparkling mountain lakes, surefooted horses, spectacular scenery, professional guides; the perfect combination for a supreme fishing trip and excellent vacation experience. Day trips and overnight pack trips. Brochures available. Jake and Katie Grimm, your hosts.

LONE MOUNTAIN RANCH
4-1/2 Miles west of Hwy. 191 toward Mountain Village at Big Sky, Box 69 995-4644
> FISHING- Top quality, Orvis endorsed, guided float trips. Walk-in, wade and horse pack fishing trips to the Madison, Gallatin and other famous Yellowstone area destinations. Orvis Fly shop. Western ranch vacations for the whole family. Plenty of recreation, even for the non-anglers!
>
> GUEST RANCH- Top quality western ranch vacations for the entire family! Beautiful surroundings, great food, clean, comfortable lodging. Horseback trips, guided fishing trips, naturalist hikes and much more! A great vacation destination for anglers with non-fishing family members.

GUEST RANCHES

LONE MOUNTAIN RANCH
4-1/2 Miles west of Hwy. 191 toward Mountain Village at Big Sky, Box 69 995-4644
> FISHING- Top quality, Orvis endorsed, guided float trips. Walk-in, wade and horse pack fishing trips to the Madison, Gallatin and other famous Yellowstone area destinations. Orvis Fly shop. Western ranch vacations for the whole family. Plenty of recreation, even for the non-anglers!
>
> GUEST RANCH- Top quality western ranch vacations for the entire family! Beautiful surroundings, great food, clean, comfortable lodging. Horseback trips, guided fishing trips, naturalist hikes and much more! A great vacation destination for anglers with non-fishing family members.

MOTELS

BEST WESTERN BUCK'S T-4 LODGE
On Highway 191 at Big Sky, Between West Yellowstone and Bozeman, Box 279 995-4111 or 1-800-822-4484
> On the Gallatin River at the Big Sky resort, Buck's is centrally located to fish the Gallatin, Madison and Yellowstone Rivers, and the streams and lakes of Yellowstone National Park "The right place at the right pace." Surprisingly affordable for a destination resort!

CONDOMINIUM MANAGEMENT

GOLDEN EAGLE MANAGEMENT
Box 8, Meadow Village   995-4800 or 1-800-548-4488
> Fish the Madison, Yellowstone or Gallatin Rivers, which are all located near the scenic resort of Big Sky. Golden Eagle offers luxury condominiums or an economy lodge where your family can enjoy swimming pools, golfing, tennis, horseback riding and much more, while you enjoy fishing.

GALLATIN GATEWAY

ANTIQUE SHOPS

BROKEN HART ANTIQUES
73800 Gallatin Road, at the end of Gallatin Canyon   763-4279
>Come browse for the most interesting and complete collection of antiques available in Montana. Located south of Bozeman in the Gallatin Valley, we specialize in Montana collectibles.

LODGING

CASTLE ROCK INN
65840 Gallatin Road   763-4243
>We have complete facilities for the angling family. Clean, reasonably priced cabins, a full service cafe, trailer and RV parking with full hookups. Hunting and fishing licenses and all manner of fishing tackle available. Come stay with us and fish the famous Gallatin River.

RAINBOW RANCH LODGE
Highway 191, 45 miles north of West Yellowstone   995-4132
>Located on the Gallatin River in the Gallatin National Forest. Excellent trout fishing begins right from the front lawn. Day trips to the Madison, Firehole and Gibbon Rivers. A deluxe lodge.

RESTAURANTS / BARS

THE CORRAL
42895 Canyon Route   995-4249
>One of the last "Old West" Montana bars, cafes and motels, nestled in the Gallatin Canyon, 5 miles north of Big Sky. If you're hankerin' for a hearty meal, cocktail and a good night's sleep, we have them at the most affordable prices. Open daily year round.

BOZEMAN

FISHING SHOPS

MONTANA TROUTFITTERS ORVIS SHOP
1716 W. Main St.   587-4707
>Bozeman's complete Orvis fly fishing specialty shop, offering Orvis endorsed float trips and fishing guide service on the Madison, Gallatin and Yellowstone Rivers. Established 1978.

THE RIVERS EDGE
2012 N. 7th Ave., Box 4019   586-5373
>Bozeman's most complete fishing shop and guide service. We have absolutely everything you need to enjoy the great fishing in the Bozeman area, on the Gallatin, Madison and Yellowstone Rivers. We have top of the line clothing, equipment, flies, fly tying materials and accessories to outfit you and enhance your visit to Montana. Our guides are licensed, insured and experienced to make sure you have an enjoyable, safe angling excursion.

SPORTING GOODS

BOB WARD AND SONS
2320 W. Main St.   586-4381
>Located at the gateway to fabulous Yellowstone National Park. We are surrounded by the finest trout streams in America. Open seven days a week to serve all your angling needs.

MOTELS

DAYS INN
1321 N. 7th Ave.   587-5251

> After fishing some of Montana's finest rivers and streams, enjoy our spa, sauna and clean, comfortable rooms. Non-smoking rooms available. A free continental breakfast is served in our lobby.

GRAN TREE INN
1325 N. 7Th Ave, I-90 at exit 306   587-5261 or 1-800-624-5865

> Located within minutes of the country's finest Blue Ribbon trout streams. Full service hotel, complimentary airport shuttle. Ample boat parking. Fish freezing available. Big Sky hospitality.

RESTAURANTS / BARS

THE CANNERY LOUNGE
43 W. Main St., Corner Willson and Main   586-0270

> Bozeman's best kept secret for lunches. Fishermen and their ladies will feel right at home. We have an 1890's back bar with an all-beverage lounge. A "must" stop while you're in Bozeman.

KITCHEN WARE / GIFTS

THE CROSSROADS
27 E. Main St., Just east of Tracy St., mid-block   587-2702

> In addition to a complete line of kitchen ware, we have Bozeman's only gourmet kitchen gallery. We have many fine gifts and a complete selection of imported wines and gourmet foods.

BELGRADE

GUIDES / OUTFITTERS

BRIDGER OUTFITTERS
1500 Rocky Mountain Road   388-4463

> Get off the beaten path! Go where the fishing is really good! We offer summer pack trips by horseback into the Yellowstone back country. Experience solitude, scenery and great fishing.

GEORGETOWN LAKE

Map Reference 24

If you're a still-water fisherman and you want to find an area in Montana where you can combine good lake fishing with attractive scenic rewards, abundant historical remnants and outstanding camping facilities, Georgetown Lake would be your choice of a destination. This lake is rich in aquatic life and the surrounding hills echo a rich history of mining activity that took place during the last half of the nineteenth century. Gold was first discovered at Georgetown in 1865. Nearby to the east, at the ghost town of Cable, a gold nugget presumed to be the largest ever mined was taken from the Old Atlantic Cable Mine.

Farther to the east, eighteen miles from the lake, you can visit historic, copper-rich Anaconda. This mile-high city was originally named Copperopolis in 1883, but that name, thought to be a bit too cute, was changed to Anaconda in 1894. Fourteen miles to the north of the lake you can visit historic Phillipsburg, site of Montana's first silver mill. Nearby Granite, referred to in 1890 as the "Silver Queen," is one of the state's best preserved ghost towns. The Granite Mountain Mine here was reputed to be the richest silver mine in the world, producing $40,000,000 worth of silver during a ten year period in the late 1880's and early 1890's.

Georgetown Lake is actually a reservoir which flooded a meadow after the dam was constructed. The water covers an area of approximately 3,000 acres at an elevation of 6,350 feet. It is a shallow, nutrient-rich body of water with a maximum depth of thirty feet and a bottom densely covered with vegetation during the warm months of summer. Fishing pressure here is as heavy as on any still water in the state, but in spite of the crowds, fishing quality remains high. Along with the great fishing, you'll have an opportunity to sight waterfowl. Moose and bear make occasional approaches to the water's edge from the forests that surround the lake.

This is primarily a rainbow fishery with a variety of strains including the Arlee, Kamloops and Eagle Lake. These fish average twelve to sixteen inches with fair numbers to three pounds and a few trophy size specimens to ten pounds. When they reach these larger proportions, they feed primarily on the extensive and popular kokanee salmon population. Of lesser importance to the fisherman are small populations of brook and bull trout. The brook trout, although few in number, average a respectable twelve to fifteen inches in

Georgetown Lake

length, with the occasional fish to three pounds.

The lake has been referred to as a "fish factory" and the fish themselves have been called "prodigious," so you can imagine why the lake undergoes such severe angling pressure. Along with high quality fishing, there are other factors that play a role in attracting sportsmen and recreationists to fish here. The lake is conveniently located adjacent to Highway 10A between Phillipsburg and Anaconda. Boat ramps are available in several locations along the road. It is quite easy to fish from shore, but the majority of the fishing is done from boats either by trolling, still fishing or casting with lures or flies. Fly fishing from float tubes continues to become more popular, not only because of the extensive areas of shallow water extending considerable distances out from shore but because sudden mountain storms that chase the boats to shore do not affect these craft so severely. Although plenty of fish are caught by those fishing from the water's edge, the larger fish seem to be taken out at least one hundred feet from the shoreline. Weed growths that proliferate during July, August and September can create an impenetrable problem for all anglers, especially for those who prefer to troll. The weeds, however, are also home to a copious population of damselflies and other aquatic insects. The damselfly imitation, in particular, can be a most rewarding pattern when fished just above the weed beds. In many areas there are channels between the patches of weeds and accurate casts will allow you to place flies and lures in these open spaces and avoid entanglement.

The damselfly hatch takes place in June when the nymphs wiggle and crawl to the shoreline to shed their nymphal skin and subsequently hover above the water as slender adults. Not only is this an exciting time to fish the nymphal patterns, but the adult representations also work well and provide explosive actions on the surface. Another fly pattern that produces well here is the Woolly Bugger, either in all black or olive body and black. Favorite lures include Thomas Cyclone, Mepps and Panther Martin.

Fish can often be seen from the road when their rise forms give an obvious indication as to their whereabouts. When fish aren't showing, however, you'll usually find them holding in bays and off points; a few favorites include Phillipsburg Bay, Rainbow Bay, Stewart Mill Bay and Denton's Point where trollers enjoy fishing for small kokanee salmon. Another favorite target for boaters is along shelves where shallow water suddenly becomes deep. If the wind picks up, there's usually a cove close by where you can seek protection. On the lake's eastern shore natural springs seep into the lake and these areas often attract both fish and fishermen. The heaviest concentration of consistently larger fish is in the deeper water near the dam.

Lake Notes

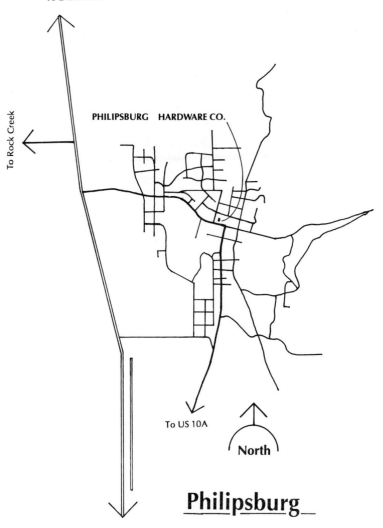

To Drummond

To Rock Creek

PHILIPSBURG   HARDWARE CO.

To US 10A

North

Philipsburg

To Georgetown Lake

HARDWARE

PHILIPSBURG HARDWARE CO.

109 E. Broadway, Box 39   859-3561

For all your hardware and fishing equipment needs, stop in and see Rick. We're located i
the beautiful Flint Creek Valley at the base of the "Pintlars."

GLACIER NATIONAL PARK

Map Reference 17

There is probably no region in the lower forty-eight states that better portrays the rugged splendor of high mountain wilderness than Glacier National Park in northwest Montana. If you'd like to paint a mental image of mountains literally being sculptured by the invincible force of billions of tons of glacial ice slowly cutting a path through solid rock, this is the choice location to do so. Take a look up any of the long, straight valleys here and envision it filled almost to the top with an ocean of ice so thick that only the tops of the highest peaks poke through toward the sun. Imagine ice thousands of feet thick moving imperceptibly downhill pulling rock upwards with its base surface and tearing huge sections from the mountains with its high flanks. This is the way these craggy peaks were formed—chiseled and bulldozed by solid ice.

Even today glaciers are evident in the park, though they are small and insignificant in size when compared to glaciers of the ice age. Currently up to fifty of these ice fields exist in the park but they do not shape new mountains for our ancestors to view from the roadside; quite to the contrary, they are in the process of slowly melting. Some of the rock showing on the park's mountain peaks is up to one billion years old and it's not likely they will again be violated by glaciers until the next ice age.

As the huge ice floes of the past formed these northern mountains, they also carved the large, bowl-like cirques at the upper ends of the valleys and deposited crushed rock and stones to form moraines at the lower ends of valleys. These moraines and deep deposits of glacial out wash now impound water that forms many of the parks approximate total of two hundred lakes. One might think that such a number of lakes would translate to an area of outstanding fishing but, unfortunately, that isn't the case. To be sure, the park's lakes and streams do hold fish, but the main attraction here is to experience entire ecosystems, as complete as nature can produce them, with a minimal influence from man. Fishing is not promoted to a significant degree and the waters are not stocked with fish, and haven't been for many years.

The park is set between the Blackfeet Indian Reservation to the east, the Flathead National Forest to the west and Canada (both British Columbia and Alberta) to the north. The North Fork of the Flathead River forms the western edge of the park and the Middle Fork of the Flathead forms the southwest boundary. The park is bisected by only one road, but it is almost totally circumscribed by roads near its boundaries. Driving across the park is usually confined to the period from mid-June to mid-September, depending on weather conditions and snow pack.

The million-plus acres in the park are of most interest to sightseers, campers, hikers and boaters. It is a region that contains all of this country's large, wild mammal species and one of the few areas containing the grizzly bear. Over two hundred bird species live here as do nearly one thousand species of flowering plants. Spruce trees, fir, pine and cedar are all represented in the park. The tallest peaks aren't high by Rocky Mountain standards, none over an elevation of eleven thousand feet, but they are rugged, and spectacular. The park has been referred to as the "Switzerland of America," "Crown of the Continent" and "Queen of our Parks;" special areas have individual names such as "Many Glaciers," "Moose Country," and "Goat Lick." The fifty mile-long blacktop road that bisects the park is called "Going To The Sun Road." With names like these you get the feeling that this is a pretty wild area— and that it is. It's an area that these authors heartily recommend experiencing, even if it's only from the roadside so by all means take the time to drive between St. Mary and West Glacier and enjoy the magnificent scenery.

Although fishing quality is marginal and fishing is not a major activity, the park waters contain rainbow, brook, cutthroat, bull trout, lake trout, kokanee salmon, whitefish and arctic grayling for those who wish to pursue them. Most of the fishing takes place on the lakes; a few of them can be reached by car, many require a hike of up to twelve miles. Large, trophy-sized lake trout are caught in some of the lakes. Stream fishing for the most part is away from the road and because the glacial water here is lacking in adequate nutrients, fish populations are small in size and normally few in number, especially when compared to other streams in Montana. Stream fishing is usually done as a secondary activity to hiking and backpacking. Serious backpacker/fishermen might wish to carry a small inflatable boat or float tube to facilitate fishing the deeper parts of lakes.

Fly fishermen will do well with most standard patterns, as these fish aren't known to be super-selective. The growing season here is short, however, so insects tend to be on the small side, particularly in the lakes, and small artificials seem to produce more consistently than larger patterns. Lures are used extensively in the lakes and favorites include Mepps, Panther Martin, Vibrax, Rapala, Daredevle, Super-Duper and Thomas Cyclone. Special regulations apply in the park, so be sure to check in at park administrative offices to obtain current fishing rules, maps, hiking information, grizzly bear information, etc.

Montana Campground Association: P.O. Box 215, West Glacier, Montana 59936

HUNGRY HORSE RESERVOIR

Map Reference 21

It hardly seems believable that a heavily timbered valley in a wild area of northwest Montana would have a dam built across its lower reaches with dimensions so large that when built, it was rated the fourth largest dam in the world. But in 1953 that is exactly what occurred and today the Hungry Horse Dam restrains the water of the South Fork of the Flathead River and controls its discharge through energy producing turbines. This mighty barricade stands 564 feet high and measures more than 1/3 mile across. A self-guided tour and visit to the dam's visitor center will provide you with details on how the power generated here is utilized throughout the northwest. Also at the visitor center you may obtain maps and literature describing the surrounding area.

Hungry Horse Reservoir is a long, slender body of water with 22,000 surface acres. It measures thirty-four miles in length and from one to four miles in width, averaging about a mile and a half. Its eccentric shoreline is a progression of bays, inlets, coves and protrusions. Access to the water is facilitated by a gravel road which encircles the reservoir. This road follows the South Fork upstream for a distance of fifteen miles to the Spotted Bear Ranger Station and Spotted Bear River. The road here also provides access to the trail heads that lead into the Great Bear Wilderness to the east and the Jewel Basin Hiking area to the west. This latter region has been set aside for use by hikers only and no horses are allowed. The thirty-plus miles of trails connect a series of over twenty lakes spotted throughout this remote region. The vicinity around the reservoir is wild and forested except where areas of verdant forest have been marred by clear-cut logging operations. An abundance of wildlife lives here and hikers and fishermen occasionally sight elk, deer, moose, black bear and grizzly bear.

Human habitation around the reservoir is of a temporary nature and is accommodated with campgrounds on both shores. Boat landings are also provided on both shores and allow put-ins and take-outs throughout the summer but during fall the water level drops severely enough to leave the landings above water level. The shoreline is relatively steep, making boats the preferred way to approach the most promising fishing areas. If needed, telephones are available for use on both shores, at about midway from both ends, at Anna Creek on the west side and at Betty Creek on the east side.

Hungry Horse is considered one of Montana's leading "lakes" for the natural reproduction of both cutthroat and bull trout. The many tributary streams to the reservoir act as nursery water during summer and fall for these two species and the mountain whitefish. The cutthroat, which average in size from ten to sixteen inches, congregate at the stream mouth during May and June and are caught in both reservoir and streams throughout the summer. Trolling is the method most practiced on the reservoir, but many anglers also enjoy casting. Favorite lures for the troller include Roostertail, Mepps, Triple Teaser and Rapala. Spin casters prefer Mepps, Daredevle, Roostertail and Thomas Cyclone. Fly fishermen can also enjoy hooking cutthroat using a variety of wets and dries in both imitator and attractor patterns.

The bull trout here are also caught in the summer and fall, but summer sees them rather widely dispersed whereas in the fall they head for the tributaries with strong spawning instincts as their stimulus. These fish average from two to ten pounds in size and respond best to wood plugs and big spoons. Trolling off stream mouths with lures running at thirty- to fifty-foot depths is a favorite fishing method. The south end of the lake is a favorite area of fishermen as a good number of these large fish move up into the South Fork and Spotted Bear River to spawn.

Whitefish are in the South Fork and Spotted Bear year-round, but during October and November their numbers increase substantially as spawning fish move from the reservoir into tributary streams. These nine to twelve inch fish are here in good numbers and are often caught on bait as well as with flies.

River Notes

JEFFERSON RIVER

Map Reference 27

If you're looking for a more relaxed setting with fewer fishermen on the river and a somewhat more pastoral environment nearby, the Jefferson fits the bill. When the Lewis and Clark party passed through this region in 1805 they referred to the river as the "North Fork," while the Madison was the "Middle Fork" and the Gallatin the "South Fork" relative to their respective juxtaposition when coming together to create the Missouri River. Because this fork carried the greatest volume of water, it was named after the country's president at that time, Thomas Jefferson.

The Jefferson begins where the Beaverhead and Big Hole Rivers meet just north of Twin Bridges. It continues its journey to the north and east by passing first through the agricultural, cattle country of the upper Jefferson Valley, then bites through the limestone walls and diverse rock formations of the Jefferson Canyon to finally find refuge in the cottonwood bottoms of the lower reaches above Headwaters State Park. The traveler along this course, whether in a highway vehicle or a water craft, will enjoy the rugged, glaciated peaks of the Tobacco Root Mountains filling the vista to the east, and the somewhat softer, less dramatic Highland Mountains to the west.

Some say the river is under-fished, whatever that means, while others claim it's a "sleeper" and holds more angling potential than people realize. True, the Big Hole, Madison, Gallatin and Beaverhead do have better reputations as fisheries, and maybe with good reason, but the "Jeff" is a pleasant river to fish, it isn't crowded with anglers, and it contains fish of an average size of twelve to sixteen inches, which is equal to most of the other southwest Montana rivers.

Of the Jefferson's approximate sixty-mile length, the upper river above the canyon is the most popular area from the angler's point of view. It reportedly has the best population of trout and it's water is the coolest during the warm months of summer. It is very floatable, very wadable and generally has sloping, cobble banks which don't obstruct movement up and downstream. The river is 150 to 200 feet wide and has an obvious unhurried pace, with a riffle/pool character and enough deep holes and bank cover to provide appealing holding water to the predominant brown trout. In the not-too-distant past estimates had put the brown to rainbow ratio at about ten to one. Now, under an active program to increase rainbow populations, the ratio is

121

Jefferson River near Twin Bridges

estimated to be nearer seven to one in the upper river. Anglers should be sure to check current regulations affecting the "Jeff" as they are definitely protective to Salmo gairdneri. The river also has a large population of whitefish throughout its length.

The Jefferson Canyon extends approximately twelve miles from La Hood down to the Sappington Bridge and the river in the upper half is fairly accessible over the railroad tracks from Highway 10. Shallow riffles empty into long pools throughout this reach, and evening shadows begin to cover the water sooner here than outside the canyon, so the evening dry fly fishing starts earlier. When floating this stretch, you pass the entrance area to the Lewis and Clark Caverns at the State Park on Cave Mountain. A visit to the Park is certainly worth the time as this is the only developed cave in Montana and it offers the visitor a look at truly impressive stalactite and stalagmite formations.

The lower river winds fairly slowly through cottonwood bottoms. In this area you'll have the greatest opportunity to sight wildlife. Whitetail deer are plentiful and waterfowl abundant. Timid otters will sometimes show themselves and the magnificent moose is an occasional visitor to this area of the river.

This stretch of water is the slowest, warmest and largest of the three rivers in Headwaters Park. It braids considerably, but also has some riffle/pool water as well as wide, gentle turns within the one-hundred-yard wide riverbed.

Although many of the former flood-type irrigation systems have been converted to the use of sprinklers, mosquitoes are still known to gather in impressive numbers, so we recommend you carry your repellent!

Fishing begins here in February, particularly in the lower reaches and gets into full swing by the end of June. Run-off starts in May, peaks around June 1, then the river starts to drop and clear. Irrigation commences in mid-July and continues until mid-September. This activity, of course, has a significant effect on the river as it influences the water temperature, water level, water clarity and, to a degree, the schedule of insect hatches. Irrigation return and rain storms in the valley also contribute to the already murky water of the lower Beaverhead. Fishing can be productive during the summer months, but don't expect to cast over sparkling clear water as found on many of Montana's other rivers. The Jefferson is not controlled by a dam, so sediment loads in the water do settle out in the slow stretches of the river.

The ecosystem of the Jefferson seems to have developed into one somewhat atypical of its sister rivers. The insect population is suppressed, but the sculpin and bait fish seem to reside here in good numbers. For this reason lures and streamer flies are fished throughout the year. The lower river is home to the crayfish which adds another interesting food type not found in many rivers. The Jeff doesn't produce a salmonfly hatch, but golden stones do live here and often emerge coincidentally with run-off, and are therefore difficult

Lower Jefferson River

123

to fish in normal years.

Mayflies are a factor on the river, but not as extensively as on other waters. The dominant insects here are the Callibaetis, Pale Morning Duns and caddis and they hatch from April to October. The Elk Hair Caddis is a favorite dry pattern in sizes #14 and #16 and is particularly effective in the evenings and on overcast days. Small caddis emergers work well when action with the adults tapers off. When fish are rising, whether to caddis or mayflies, you should concentrate your casts above the head-and-tail rise forms of the trout in order to avoid hooking the whitefish which reside here in great numbers.

The fish of the Jefferson are usually found where you would expect to find them. Not many mysteries exist here. During the dog days of summer you'll find the fish in the deeper holes, particularly against the banks, under snags, and along the angular rock rip-rap; in autumn they move out into the shallower runs and riffles. In the low, cloudy water of August throw big Yuk Bugs, Bitch Creeks, Girdle Bugs, Muddler Minnows, Spruce Flies or Woolly Buggers into the deep holes with a sink-tip line. Put them as close to the bank as possible and give them some movement as they swing out. Lure fishermen prefer Mepps, Panther Martins, Thomas Cyclones and hammered lures in medium sizes. They should sink quickly, and show well to the fish; light colors in clear water and darker colors in cloudy water.

Although grasshopper patterns don't seem to be particularly effective in the upper reaches, attractor dries are worth trying even when no fish are seen rising. Royal Wulffs, Royal Trudes, Humpies and Dry Renegades can all have their moments, so be sure you have a supply in your fly boxes. The artificial hoppers are, however, effective on the lower river, so don't leave them in the car. Imitator dries include not only the caddis, but Adams, Pale Sulphurs, Pale Morning Duns and Callibaetis in sizes #14 to #18.

The fall months provide those crisp days when we want to throw big streamers and rubberleg nymphs into the riffles. The water is now cooling and clearing and the fishing remains good right into November. The bottom rocks have collected a growth of weeds and algae during the summer, but they have little effect on fishing or wading. It's a good idea now to work the fly over the gravel rather than casting futilely over a silt covered bottom.

Access to the Jefferson is generally good. There are several bridges over the river, a state fishing access site at Parrot Castle and a BLM boat launch site as well. Some of these sites are suitable for launching heavy drift boats, some are better suited to lighter weight prams, canoes and rafts, while others have access for foot traffic only. Be sure you've taken a good look at chosen sites to assure that you can take out before dark and be certain the logistical demands are within the scope of your capability.

The first boat put-in is on the Beaverhead River at the bridge in downtown Twin Bridges, and the last take-out is on the Missouri River immediately below the Gallatin River mouth in Headwaters State Park. Don't try this entire float in one day; the average float speed on the Jeff, allowing for a stop or two to fish extra-prime-looking water, is one-half to one mile an hour.

For an experienced oarsman, the river should present few problems. It is large and slow enough to allow you to look ahead and pick a course. Care should be taken to avoid log jams, water diversions, which can require a short portage, and channelization. For the most part the floats are relatively relaxed, and sometimes the main problem you face is floating upstream. On days when strong winds are charging up river, they can literally stop you dead in the water, particularly at low water levels and especially if a raft is the craft being used. Many floaters prefer trimmer boats such as canoes and prams because they're less affected by the wind and they can be paddled or rowed through the long tail-out areas more quickly than a raft. This is particularly important in the lower river. The lighter boats are also easier to put in and take out at some of the access sites. Vehicle shuttle service is usually available at a reasonable fee by making local inquiries.

TWIN BRIDGES

About midway between the junction of the Beaverhead River and the Ruby River to the south and the Beaverhead River and the Bighole River to the north, rests the town of Twin Bridges. From the perspective of a trout fisherman, this has to be a rather salutary site at which to rest. The town is small and offers few of the larger-city amenities, but for the angler fishing in this area, meals, accommodations and professional advice about water conditions, insect hatches and trout responses is close at hand.

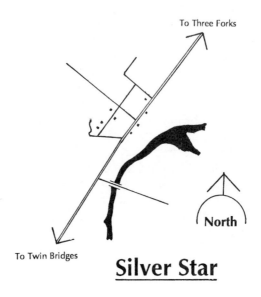

To Three Forks

North

To Twin Bridges

Silver Star

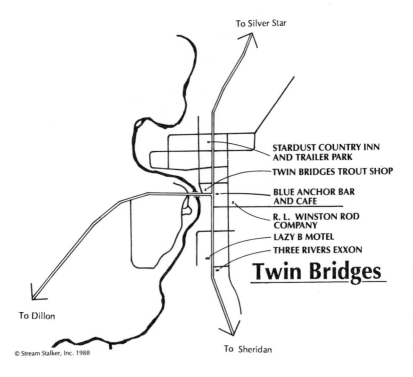

To Silver Star

STARDUST COUNTRY INN
AND TRAILER PARK

TWIN BRIDGES TROUT SHOP

BLUE ANCHOR BAR
AND CAFE

R. L. WINSTON ROD
COMPANY

LAZY B MOTEL

THREE RIVERS EXXON

Twin Bridges

To Dillon

To Sheridan

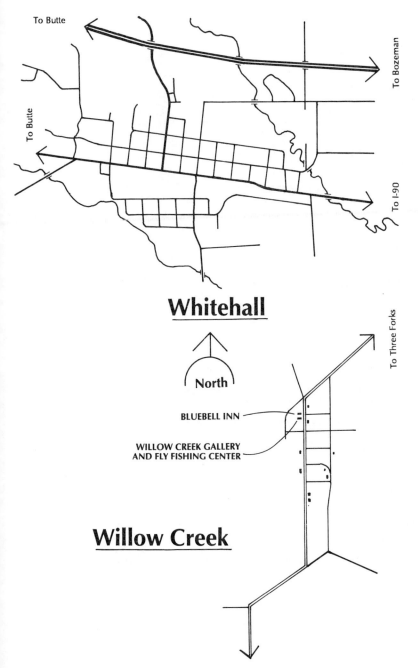

To Butte

To Bozeman

To Butte

To I-90

Whitehall

North

To Three Forks

BLUEBELL INN

WILLOW CREEK GALLERY
AND FLY FISHING CENTER

Willow Creek

TWIN BRIDGES

FISHING SHOPS

TWIN BRIDGES TROUT SHOP
Intersection Highway 41 and 287, Box 303   684-5773
> Located on the banks of the Beaverhead River, the Twin Bridges Trout Shop offers a complete line of tackle and guided trips on the Beaverhead, Ruby, Big Hole and Jefferson Rivers and other local private waters.

ROD MAKER

R. L. WINSTON ROD COMPANY
E. 3rd Ave., Drawer T   684-5533
> Winston has been building fine fly rods since 1929. Our designs have evolved from our wide range of fishing experiences. Stop by our shop to see and cast our rods.

RESTAURANTS / BARS

BLUE ANCHOR BAR AND CAFE
102 N. Main St.   684-5655
> Home cooked food. Banquet facilities. Open 7 days a week.

MOTELS

LAZY B MOTEL
307 So. Main St., Box 306   684-5639
> Twelve homey kitchenette and large family units, with cable TV. Float trip raft rental agent. Reasonable rates for weekly or monthly rentals.

STARDUST COUNTRY INN AND TRAILER PARK
409 North Main St., Drawer Y   684-5561
> Small, distinctive motel. Private cabins with kitchens, cable TV and queen beds. Free morning paper and coffee served to your room daily. Resident angling expert available for advice. Reasonable rates!

SERVICES

THREE RIVERS EXXON
325 So. Main St., Box 261   684-5733
> Convenience store and gas station. UPS mailing service, dry cleaning pick up and drop off, laundromat and propane. Open 7 days a week. Hours: Summer 7:00 AM to 10:00 PM, Winter 7:00 AM to 9:00 PM.

TWIN BRIDGES AREA CHAMBER OF COMMERCE
Box 444   684-5733 or 684-5519
> What does Twin Bridges have that West Yellowstone doesn't? Trout with virgin lips and 10,000 fewer fishermen! C'm on, tickle our lips! For information call or write, Chamber of Commerce, Twin Bridge, Montana 59754. Representing the Ruby, Beaverhead, Big Hole and Jefferson Rivers!

WILLOW CREEK

FISHING SHOPS

WILLOW CREEK GALLERY AND FLY FISHING CENTER
1st and Main St., Box 188   285-3885

> One of Montana's most unique fishing shops, featuring not only a fly shop, but an expansive fine arts gallery, specializing in sports art. We do float trips and personalized guide trips on all of the local rivers.

RESTAURANTS

BLUEBELL INN
1st and Main, Box 156   285-3162

> People travel from all over Montana to dine at this excellent restaurant. Our varied cuisine appeals to everyone. Every tired, hungry angler fishing this area should stop by and visit us.

KOOTENAI RIVER

Map Reference 28

Even when the Kootenai River is flowing at its minimum volume, it falls into the category of a large river. When that minimum volume is sextupled by water releases from the Libby Dam, you can witness a truly formidable rush of water! Envision your favorite trout stream, the one you really like to wade while casting flies to both banks from the middle of the channel. What flow does it have—two hundred, four hundred, maybe even six hundred c.f.s.? In contrast, low water on the Kootenai is 4,000 c.f.s. and it swells to 24,000 c.f.s. when at its maximum volume. This water flow classifies it as Montana's second largest river; only the Clark Fork has greater volume. The Kootenai originates in British Columbia, makes a tour through the northwestern corner of Montana and northeast Idaho and returns to British Columbia. It ultimately empties into the Columbia River. The river was named in honor of the Kootenai Indians who lived in northwest Montana. The word "kootenai" means "deer robes."

Approximately one hundred miles of the river flow through Montana and of this one hundred miles about fifty are impounded behind the steel and concrete structure of the Libby Dam. The dam controls the flow of the river based on electrical energy needs of users throughout the northwest, so the water level can, and does, fluctuate considerably. The river can rise or drop up to a foot an hour, and fishermen have been known to get caught in midstream during a rising river and have been forced to climb a mid-river boulder to seek safety. The river can fluctuate up to a total of four feet!

Moose, bear, deer and big horn sheep are found in abundance throughout the Purcell and Cabinet Mountain Ranges that surround the Libby area. These mountains have provided the fur, metal ore and timber resources that have been the basis of the economy in this region for over a hundred years.

From the fisherman's point of view we'll divide the river into three sections for ease of reference. The upper river will include the seventeen miles of water from the Libby Dam down to the town of Libby; the middle river will encompass the twelve miles from town down through the gorge below Kootenai Falls; and the lower river will take us twenty miles from the gorge to the Idaho border where the river departs Montana at the state's lowest elevation of 1,820 feet. When we asked a local sport shop owner about access to the river, he replied, "Hey, you're in Libby, Montana—access is no

126

problem." He was right. The entire length of the river in Montana is paralleled by roads and is easily accessible. Because of its size and capricious nature, the best way to fish it is from a boat. A variety of types are used here, including prams, canoes, drift boats and rafts.

Most of the river offers little technical challenge to a competent oarsman, but some areas require attention and some are to be avoided entirely. In the upper river, 7-1/2 miles above town, there is an area where the river has been pinched into a relatively fast chute in the middle of which are several vertical concrete standards. If you plan to float this section, you should scout it beforehand to determine the proper line.

Three areas of the middle reaches require the attention of the floater. Just below Libby is a stretch known as "the rocks," so named because of the many boulders situated mid-stream. Some of these rocks are of a size you'd use to landscape your driveway; others are the size of a car you'd back out of that driveway! Some of these obstructions protrude above the water's surface while others lie just below and the problems confronting the boatman change with fluctuating water levels. Farther downstream are three areas to be avoided entirely: the white-water portion known as China Rapids, the spectacular Kootenai Falls and the two-mile-long gorge immediately below the falls. To attempt floating here would mean certain destruction. The Kootenai Falls consist of two separate terraces with a total vertical fall of two hundred feet and there is a series of five rapids downstream from the base of the falls. There is a small park with picnic tables and an ungroomed trail leading to the river and the falls. There is also a foot bridge over the river about one thousand feet downstream from the falls from which you can enjoy a great view of the whole area.

The lower river is relatively easy to float with the exception of one problem area at the mouth of the Yaak River. Standing waves occur here and they can cause problems for less stable boats and rafts.

For the most part the river moves at a rate of four to six feet per second. There are few bank obstructions and no tight turns. This is a wide river, up to two hundred yards, so there's plenty of room to maneuver. Anglers try to avoid the flat bedrock and sand-bottom reaches in favor of deeper holes, cobble-stone bottoms, and the large mid-stream rocks that offer good protective lies for the fish. Obviously, holding lies change as water levels fluctuate and familiarity with the river's changing nature goes a long way toward achieving consistent fishing success. It's difficult to predict when water levels will change because discharges from the dam are unregulated and can occur at any time without prior notice. Information about anticipated releases can be obtained by calling the Libby Dam Site at 406-293-3421. A recorded message will give you details of anticipated flows and give short and long range projections. Sometimes during the summer months, presumably in deference

Kootenai River

to the desires of fishermen, the flows will be reduced on weekends, then increased again during the week. The lower volume does facilitate fishing the river, but it usually takes a day or so for the fish to adjust to the change in flow and resume normal feeding patterns.

Not only do the insects and fish have to constantly adjust to changing water volumes, they must adjust to varying water temperatures as well, particularly during the summer months. Water from the dam is released on a selective withdrawal basis, which means that water can be drawn into the dam structure from a pre-determined level of the reservoir. This level is not always the same and is changed as required to avoid sucking large numbers of fish into the turbines should fish be gathered at a particular level of water. Changes in water level mean changes of water temperature. An example of the effect on the creatures of the river would be to have the water temperature at sixty-two degrees due to natural thermal warming of the river, then suddenly have a release from the dam drop the river temperature to forty-eight degrees. This imparts a substantial thermal shock to the aquatic life and it takes time to make the adjustment back to normal behavior patterns. Some insect species that were native to the river prior to the construction of the dam have since disappeared because they couldn't adjust to the sudden temperature changes. Fortunately, many others have survived the problems and are able to cope with the variations. The river water remains cold through June because of the effects of tributary run-off, but starts to temper in July. During run-off, when

128

the water is off-color, the fish will move to the river's edge and fishermen can expect more success if they place their casts to likely looking water next to the bank.

During the 1950's and 1960's the Kootenai was almost entirely a cutthroat fishery. Today the river harbors very few cutts, and instead is home to a strong population of rainbow, a large number of whitefish and a smaller, scattered population of bull trout. Suckers also inhabit the river and provide forage for the larger trout. There are a fair number of large fish in the section between China Rapids and Kootenai Falls, but this is a difficult area to fish and most angling efforts are directed to those sections above the rapids, on up to the dam, where greater numbers of both fish and insects reside. The rainbows average from ten to fourteen inches in length but many go to five pounds. Each year both rainbows and bull trout over ten pounds are taken.

The Kootenai is a year-round fishery for both lure and fly fishermen. The Libby area doesn't normally experience severe winter weather conditions and many days from January through March are suitable for fishing. Fly fishermen can do well with nymphs as well as small dry flies at this time. Little Iron Duns and Blue Winged Olives can be very effective during January and February. The month of May, however, is the time when dry fly fishing really comes into its own with hatches that start then and continue on through the summer. Although the big Pteronarcys californica salmonfly isn't found here, hatches of smaller stoneflies do occur. A yellow stone in a size #12, a Red Quill and several caddis species appear in May. Fly fishermen should carry two small caddis patterns, both in size #16, one that is brownish-black in color, fished in May and June, and the other, a yellowish-tan color, which can be fished throughout the summer. Also expect to see a pale green caddis in size #14 and #16 from May through October. In June, Pale Morning Duns in #14 will appear along with a pale yellow crane fly in a #12 and an olive stone, also a #12. This is the time of run-off, so turbid water should be expected and nymphal patterns are a logical choice of flies to try. Attractor nymphs such as Bitch Creek, Yuk Bug and other rubberleg patterns thrown against the banks can be very productive. The dry mayfly imitations are generally small, with a #16 being fairly standard, although some exceptions do occur, such as a #8 Black Ant which is effective during the summer months. Don't expect to do well on hoppers on the Kootenai. Unlike many other rivers of Montana, this just isn't hopper water.

The dry fly fishing here is particularly challenging for a couple of reasons. The fish here are "narrow minded," to use a description expressed by Glen Overton of Libby. These fish just don't move more than a couple of inches to either side of their feeding lane. This trait necessitates extremely accurate casting with the fly rod. To compound this problem, the surface currents of the river are totally capricious; each square yard flows at its own desired pace, independent of its neighboring square yard. Downstream and slack-line casts are often necessary, so don't expect long, made-in-heaven drifts of your offerings. If you should be working a rising fish and do manage to get perfect floats and still the fish ignores you, give the fly an occasional short twitch to get his attention. This technique will sometimes trigger a strike. At times attractor patterns, both wet and dry, will take fish on the Kootenai, but most often, you'll get better results by using imitations of the naturals being taken by the fish. These trout seem to be both size and color conscious as well as reluctant to move laterally, so hatch-matching efforts will most often produce results.

With the exception of the early small stoneflies, the river is one primarily of caddis and small mayflies. The green drake is not present here, but the large October caddis, or Giant Orange Sedge, is a fly that does make an appearance. The imitation is large, tied on a #8 hook, with an overall orange/brown coloration. Other big flies include streamers, Muddler Minnows and Woolly Buggers. Sculpin do exist in the river and Muddlers tied in a range of colors from cream to brown to black in sizes up to four inches in length will work well when drifted through deep holes using a fast-sinking line and an eight- or nine-weight rod. Some of the holes on the Kootenai are fifteen to twenty feet deep and when you're fishing for big fish with large flies, a big rod is required to handle them. Woolly Buggers are always effective and can be tied considerably smaller, with an overall length of two inches, in combinations of black or brown hackle with black, brown or olive bodies. A bit of flash material tied into the tail adds a little attraction value. The area near the mouth of Libby Creek is popular and a good spot to try leech patterns. Another good fly is a #10 Black Woolly Worm fished from six to eighteen inches beneath the surface with a bit of action imparted to it. Some local anglers like to fish this fly as a dropper with a streamer used as the point fly.

Dry fly fishing here is usually done with a six-weight rod for a couple of reasons. In the first place, accuracy is of paramount importance, therefore long casts are not! Secondly, this is not a windy region as is true in the more arid, southwestern part of the state, so it is not necessary to buck a weight forward line into the teeth of a gale. Nine- to ten-foot rods are preferred, as are long leaders, up to fourteen feet. Spin fishermen will probably want to use a medium action rod of about eight feet, with line between six- and ten-pound test. Favorite lures include Krocodiles, Kastmasters, Thomas Cyclones and Panther Martins. A favorite method of fishing lures is to bring them back with a bouncing action rather than a purely steady, straight retrieve.

If we were to compile a list of "bests" for the Kootenai, the list would probably read something like this: the best time to be here is June through August, the best water level is between four thousand and six thousand c.f.s., the best time of day to fish is in the evening and the best water condition is when it has stabilized for a couple of days after a release. This summary, however, in no way implies that the fishing conditions must always be perfect. Not often do our fishing trips put us at the right place at the right time. The first time these authors approached the Kootenai it was from the south bank, the water volume was running at 22,000 c.f.s. and the water was reaching far back into the grass and willows. We caught fish nonetheless!

Even though this region of the state contains a large population of wildlife, it is not plagued with mosquitoes or rattlesnakes. This isn't to imply that these creatures don't exist here, they are just not considered a problem to fishermen. Another common affliction not experienced here is the detrimental effect of irrigation draw-downs and returns which so drastically affect many rivers.

For the angler who wants a diversion from fishing the main river, there are many small streams and lakes in the region that offer fishing for small brook trout and cutthroat. The lakes provide the float tube enthusiast a wonderful opportunity to fish off the beaten path on water that sees relatively few fishermen; many of these waters are within a few hundred feet of parking areas. The folks here are very friendly and helpful, so local inquiry should put you onto some water you'll enjoy fishing!

LIBBY

As you enter the community of Libby you immediately perceive you're in a town supported to a large degree by the logging industry, as rigs loaded with timber of various diameters roll through town in all directions going to and from mills both local and across the state line into Idaho. The town itself presents the visage of being attuned to the importance of trees as the homes and businesses rest between the conifers, rather than having replaced them entirely, offering a feeling of balance between man's progress and nature's durability. Logging, lumber, mining and tourism are what Libby, the Lincoln County seat, thrives upon. The town's nickname is "Logger City" and its 2,800 residents take pride in the fact that they handle all of the above business responsibilities as well as anyone.

The first recorded activity of the white man in this region was that of David Thompson, a fur trader and geographer, who came to Libby from Canada via the McGillvray River (later to be called the Kootenai River) and built the area's first building from which he conducted fur trading with the Indians. That business continued until the 1850's when furs became scarce and the business was no longer profitable. During the 1860's prospectors arrived in the region and the community was named "Libby Creek," after the daughter of one of the prospectors, but the "Creek" was subsequently dropped. The town remained centered around the activities of mining until the arrival of the Great Northern Railroad in 1892. The railroad became a serious influence on commercial logging as the need for railroad ties, mine timbers and homes became more critical. Loggers emigrated from other states, settled here and began the logging tradition and industry that continues to thrive today.

There are a number of interesting summer activities in Libby, not the least of which is "Logger Days" held in July. This four-day event includes a number of lumberjack competitions including axe throwing, log rolling and sawing events. Non-loggers get involved in races on the river using small craft such as canoes, row boats and log rafts. Each spring an art festival takes place; in August the town sponsors the annual fishing derby; and the ebullient Nordicfest comes along in September with its craft show, athletic events, horse show, good food, music, parade, dancing and melodrama. Before winter sets in a craft festival is conducted in November.

In addition to those special events, the mountains of the Purcell Range, the Cabinet Mountains Wilderness Area and the 2-1/4 million acres of the Kootenai National Forest offer almost inexhaustible possibilities for camping and hiking. Closer to town several tennis courts and a city swimming pool are open to the public as is the Cabinet View Country Club which offers a nine-hole golf course on a ledge above town that provides spectacular view of the Cabinet Mountains. Also available here is a driving range, rental equipment, a pro shop and snack bar.

The Heritage Museum is located south of town in a twelve-sided log building which measures 130 feet in diameter. This recently built structure houses displays of history relating to Indian life, mining, the timber industry, early explorers and regional wildlife. Another attraction for visitors is the Montana City Old Town, a re-creation of an 1890's town complete with boardwalk, stores, and an opera house in which live performances are staged during the summer months.

Motor tours can be taken to the Libby Dam and Visitor's Center, Kootenai Falls, Yaak River Falls and the Murry Springs Fish Hatchery near Canada between Rexford and Eureka. Another local vehicle trip of interest is that to the Ross Creek Cedar Grove Scenic Area southwest of Libby off Highway 56. This area provides a mile-long, self-guided tour through one hundred acres of trees, ferns and flowers in a verdant forest setting with the main interest centering around the Western Red Cedar trees. Some of these specimens are over 500 years old, are 8 feet in diameter and reach 175 feet toward the sky. This is an interesting place to enjoy a picnic lunch while appreciating the timelessness of nature.

A commercial tour of interest locally is one through the Champion International Corporation's lumber and plywood manufacturing facilities at

Libby. The tour through these plants takes less than two hours and provides a comprehensive understanding of how a tree is transformed into building products. Two other enterprises of significance which don't provide tours, but nonetheless are of interest, include the ASARCO underground silver and copper mine to the west of Libby near Troy and the W. R. Grace Company open-pit, vermiculite mine that has been in production since 1923. This is the country's largest such mine and the vermiculite is used in hundreds of applications including soil conditioners, lightweight concrete and fireproof insulation.

Libby is reached by car, daily bus service, daily AMTRAK passenger service, or by small plane into the Libby Airport with its paved, lighted, five-thousand-foot runway which accommodates private planes and small jets. Rental cars can be arranged. For a small town in the mountains and woods of northwest Montana, you can see that Libby is a spot where things are happening!

Libby Area Chamber of Commerce: 905 W. 9th St., P.O. Box 705, Libby, Montana 59923 - Phone: 293-3832

Kootenai National Forest: Rt. 3, Box 700, Libby, Montana 59923 - Phone: 293-6211

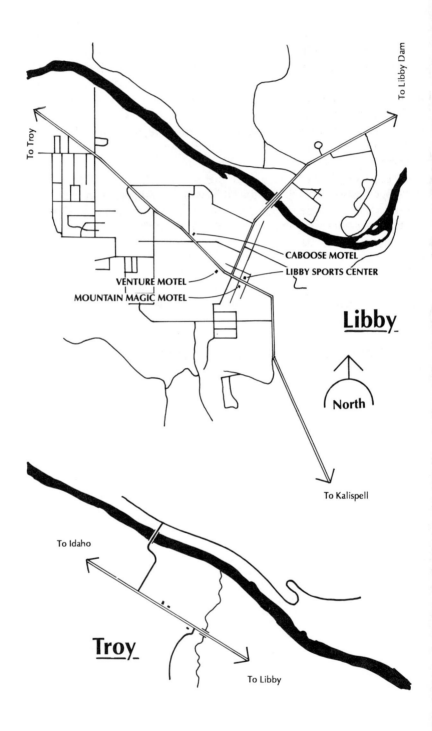

To Libby Dam

To Troy

CABOOSE MOTEL

LIBBY SPORTS CENTER

VENTURE MOTEL

MOUNTAIN MAGIC MOTEL

Libby

North

To Kalispell

To Idaho

Troy

To Libby

LIBBY

SPORTING GOODS

LIBBY SPORTS CENTER
116 9th St.   293-4641

Libby's only full line sporting goods store. Conveniently located in town on Highway 2. Tackle for spin and fly fishermen to use on the famous Kootenai River rainbows.

MOTELS

CABOOSE MOTEL
Highway 2 west, Box 792   293-6201 or 1-800-835-7427 ext. 258

Twenty-eight units, AAA rated, color cable TV, HBO, air conditioned with queen beds. Winter plug-ins for cars and trucks. Free continental breakfast. Direct Dial phones in each room. Restaurant and lounge right next door, open for meals til 1 AM.

MOUNTAIN MAGIC MOTEL
917 Mineral Ave.   293-7795

Eighteen reasonably priced, comfortable units, seven with kitchenettes. Heated pool, hot tub, water beds, color cable TV, HBO. Direct dial phones, air conditioning, electric heat, free ice.

VENTURE MOTEL
443 Highway 2 west   293-7711

Libby's finest lodging and dining facility. Seventy-one rooms, with indoor pool, hot tub, sauna and exercise room. Lounge and restaurant on the premises. Banquet and meeting rooms available. AAA rated, 3 diamonds. Amex, Visa, Master Card, Diners Club and Discover cards accepted.

LAKE KOOCANUSA

Map Reference 29

If ever you had a desire to run your sprint power boat flat-out for a full ninety miles, Lake Koocanusa is a water on which you could fulfill that ambition; in addition you'd become an international traveler during the experience. This impoundment straddles the boundary between Montana and British Columbia and forms a reservoir that has a shape more closely resembling a river than a lake; a free-flowing Kootenai River occupied the valley floor prior to 1972 when Koocanusa commenced filling against the north face of Libby Dam. Montana claims forty-eight miles of the reservoir's total length.

Construction of the dam began in 1966 and it was dedicated in 1975. It's definitely an impressive structure. If you take a stroll across the dam's crest you'll cover .6 of a mile. The base of the dam is slightly wider than the length of a football field. If you'd care to don a diving suit, jump from the crest and sink down to bedrock, your air lines would need to be 420 feet long. The five 105,000 kilowatt turbine generators located in the base of the facility can produce 3.7 billion kilowatt hours of electrical energy annually, which can be transmitted to 8 western states.

When visiting in the area, you can drive to the dam, spend some time at the visitor center and make arrangements to take a guided tour of the facility. The reservoir is reduced in volume during the winter and early spring months and fills again during the late spring and early summer run-off period. When full it covers an area of 46,000 acres and has a maximum depth of 370 feet. There's plenty of room here for the fish to practice swimming!

The fishing on Koocanusa gets started after ice-out in the spring, with particular angler interest directed to the mouths of tributary streams from mid-April through May and possibly into June. This is the time of year when the rainbows and cutthroat gather at the stream mouths before proceeding upstream to spawn. In addition to this activity, the lake's bull trout are also spawning in the streams, so fishermen can usually expect a successful day on the water from one or more of these species. Whitefish, ling and kokanee salmon are also present in the reservoir to add to the choice of targets. Several hundred thousand cutthroat trout are planted each year by the Montana Department of Fish, Wildlife and Parks and, in addition, the Canadians make plants of kokanee salmon which seem to thrive here and make up a large

Lake Koocanusa

percentage of the total numbers of game fish caught. These fish average a healthy sixteen to eighteen inches in length, making them some of the largest kokanee caught in Montana.

Although fewer in number, the bull trout are favored by fishermen because of their size; many are over three pounds, with some to ten pounds. More bulls are caught by bait fishermen in deep water near the mouths of the tributaries than by trollers using lures. On the other hand, the trolling fisherman will catch more kokanee than will those using more stationary methods and faster-than-usual trolling seems to be the secret in hooking larger-than-usual numbers of salmon here. Most fish taken by trollers in the early season will be hooked in the first ten feet of water depth; later in the summer, as the fish seek colder water, fishermen go deeper, sometimes using leaded line with long, eight pound test leaders.

The tributaries most preferred on the reservoir's east shore include Five Mile Creek, McGuire Creek, Pinkham Creek and Tobacco River. West side favorites are Bristow Creek, Parsnip Creek and Big Creek. These mouth areas are popular not only during the spring spawning runs, but throughout the summer and fall as well.

The tributary mouths are fished by anglers using a variety of methods. Boat fishermen will troll with light spinning gear; fly anglers will throw nymphs, streamers and shrimp patterns; bank fishermen will use lures or bait. All seem to catch their share of fish. With such a large area of water to fish and with such a variety of species to pursue, it's only natural to use a wide assortment of lures. Favorites include Thomas Cyclone, Krocodile, Hotrod, Jensen Needle Fish, Rapala, Mepps, Panther Martin, Kamloops, Triple Teazer and Daredevle. Maybe you have a favorite of your own not on this list. By all means give it a try!

Most of the campgrounds and boat launching facilities are in the first ten miles above the dam, but paved roads on both sides of the reservoir provide good access almost as far as the Canadian border.

Lake Notes

MADISON RIVER

Map References 30, 31

From an overhead view the Madison River would appear as a shallow, one-tire skid mark a hundred yards wide at the bottom of the Madison Valley. Starting below Quake Lake it slips and slides a bit on its course to the town of Ennis and there veers ever so slightly toward the east where it comes to its end at the Missouri Headwaters State Park. Throughout this journey the skid mark maintains a very consistent width and depth as it slides down the very consistent incline of the valley. The one exception to this description takes place near Ennis where the channel divides and braids around mid-stream islands both above and below town. The water can be deeper in some places here, averaging to four feet with the deepest hole up to six feet.

The eighty mile journey the river has taken between the lake and the Missouri is rarely detained by traditional impediments such as sharp bends, deep pools, formidable boulders, rock walls and downed timber. The river bottom is essentially flat from bank to bank. The riparian character is primarily range grass and sage, with occasional areas of willow adding a different challenge to consider when casting to the banks.

When floating, the current moves the boat at a remarkably consistent pace, averaging about five miles per hour; when wading, one is surprised at the pressure against the legs. The river contains no rapids as such except through the seven miles of the Bear Trap Canyon Primitive Area below Ennis Lake where rapids are substantial and not recommended for floaters, but the steady push of water on your waders tells you the river has a destination and intends to reach it without delay. The cobble under your feet will be from one to four inches in diameter in most areas which is comfortable to the foot but they also can be very slippery, so attentive wading is advised. Felt soles are a must and if you feel more secure in stream cleats, by all means wear them.

To both sides of the river the banks rise to flat benches covered with range grass and small rocks which seem to preclude agriculture in most areas. Both flanks consist of private ranch land extending up to the base of the mountains in the Beaverhead National Forest. To the east of the river is the Madison Range with peaks near eleven thousand feet. Generally the base areas show just range grass or hay meadows with occasional herds of grazing cattle, while the upper elevations are spotted with a variety of individual evergreen trees and random splashes of dense timber. Rising to the west are the lower, more

Madison River at the Channels

rounded hills of the Gravelly Range and to the north, the jagged Tobacco Root Mountains.

Because the Madison is born at the confluence of two rivers that are trout streams in their own right, the Gibbon River and the Firehole River, it is a productively fishable river for its entire length. As the river leaves Yellowstone National Park it has actually been within the border of Montana for about three miles and at this point flows but a short distance before entering the Madison Arm of sizeable Hebgen Lake. After leaving Hebgen Dam it again flows a short distance in a definite river channel before entering the much smaller Quake Lake. Upon leaving Quake Lake it tumbles a short distance over rubble caused by the earthquake disaster, then settles into its age-old channel for the fifty mile run to Ennis Lake and finally makes a free-flowing sprint to its mouth at the Missouri River. The river has been flowing down this same general path for an estimated two million years.

Overall the river flows for approximately 120 miles. The stretch from Quake Lake to Ennis is by no stretch of the imagination a classic piece of trout water. It's commonly referred to as "one big riffle," the "fifty mile riffle" or "the world's longest riffle" due to its totally unrestrained character. The bouncy surface is a significant reason why the Madison is a wonderful river for beginners to fish. The trout are usually not shy and when a fly passes through their window of vision, they must "take it or leave it" as the river's speed will quickly take the morsel out of range. Its character also makes it more forgiving o a bad cast than slower, more flat water might be.

Access to the river is quite good for most of its total length. Because the roads are not immediately adjacent to the river bank you can't just stop the car and step into the water as is possible along some rivers situated in narrow, less agricultural valleys. There are, however, fourteen formal access points between Quake and Ennis Lakes; some are little more than boat ramps, others provide tables, water and toilet facilities.

For a discussion of fishing the Madison, we'll break the river into two sections. The upper river is the water above Ennis Lake, the lower river includes the reaches below the lake. In both areas the fishing is generally considered best in spring and fall. During the summer after the run-off the lower river warms to dangerous levels due to extreme temperature rises in Ennis Lake. The lake was created in 1900 and has been a depository for run-off sediments since that time. The average depth now is considered to be less than ten feet, causing water temperatures to rise to over eighty degrees under the intense summer sun. Above the lake, summer water temperatures reach levels to sixty-five degrees, not high enough to discourage feeding by resident trout populations. The most active feeding occurs in the morning and evening hours and it is during these times that anglers find the most rewarding fishing. Also, those who are in the river at these times will gratefully encounter less boat traffic.

As with any wadable river, the angler will normally feel some degree of frustration if he is limited only to wading because of the relatively short distance he can cover in a day's time. The floater, conversely, will often feel he moves too briskly down a river, not giving all the fish in a likely area the privilege of viewing the delectable fraud he so diligently presents. The compromise is to float-fish the good water then park the boat and wade-fish when exceptionally appealing targets come into view. Most craft on the Madison are of the drift boat variety, although a raft is a perfectly acceptable form of transportation.

Throughout the year the fly fisherman would do well to use a nine-foot, six-weight rod for most of his fishing, particularly from a boat, as the total gamut of conditions and situations can be encountered in the course of a day. A four- or five-weight can certainly be used on special occasions, such as when dry fly fishing on a calm evening. An eight-weight is none too heavy when the wind roars up the valley or when you want to throw large streamers or big, weighted nymphs.

The spin fisherman will feel comfortable using his 5-1/2 to 7 foot rod capable of throwing lures up to 1/4 oz. with 6 to 8 pound test line. With the catch-and-release areas of the river being popular, many spin fishermen use a float and a fly instead of traditional lures. Favorite spinners here are the Panther Martin and Mepps. Gold blades are preferred and black bodies with yellow or orange spots work well throughout the year.

Resident fish in the Madison include browns, rainbows, cutthroats, cuttbow hybrids and whitefish. In the upper river, particularly above Varney Bridge, the rainbow is the most prevalent species—maybe eighty percent—with the balance primarily browns and very few cutts and hybrids. In the Varney Bridge area the population starts to turn toward a more even balance between the browns and rainbows. Below Ennis Lake, the brown comprises about eighty percent of the population. Whitefish are found throughout the entire river.

The Madison has been in the forefront of regulation experimentation in Montana for several years and progressive changes in the rules continue to improve a previously abused fishery. Back in the 1930's and 1940's the limit was twenty-five fish per day and anglers then would expect to hook five pound fish at each outing. The Madison was renowned for large fish, and plenty of them. Such fame, as would be expected, attracted more and more fishermen, which meant more and more killing of these sizeable fish and through the years the limit went to twenty and fifteen and ten and five and now, wisely, the regulations state that a portion of the river is set aside for sport fishing only, mandating catch-and-release techniques. We applaud such a policy, for we recognize it to be the most meaningful manner in which to preserve and eventually improve a heavily used resource. Because the regulations in Montana are progressive and are frequently changed to benefit the fish, the angler should read them before fishing any given stretch of any river. Maybe in the not-too-distant future we'll again enjoy the thrill of anticipation knowing we have a reasonable chance of hooking a five pounder. At the present, the average Madison fish will measure ten to fifteen inches. A twenty incher in the upper reaches is considered a very respectable trout. A slightly larger average can be expected from the channels above Ennis to the mouth at the Missouri River.

For the vacationing public in Montana, the fishing season generally starts in June, but for local residents, and maybe a traveling salesman or two, the fishing licenses had better be purchased early because dry fly fishing with midges can be very good starting sometime in February and continuing into May. Some people feel this is the best time of the entire year for dries, particularly in the upper river. Throughout this late winter/early spring period you can experience a spell of arctic-like weather, but on those calm, sunny days when the temperature permits, fish with imitations of those midges you'll see in quantity out of the main current on the soft water such as the slicks below boulders. Sometimes large fish will feed on the clumps of insects that form and drift downstream. The fly fisherman will do well to fish a #16 or #18 Griffith Gnat or an Adams on the surface, or try a small Brassie or Pheasant Tail in the surface film. Even very cold days can be productive because the water eleased from Hebgen Lake exits the dam at approximately forty-four degrees.

April starts the nymph fishing on the Madison, with favorite patterns including the Gold Ribbed Hare's Ear, Peeking Caddis, Prince and Sparrow, in sizes #8 to #12 and fished near the bottom with a dead drift. Larger patterns include dark brown and black stonefly larvae imitations such as the Montana Nymph, the Bitch Creek and Yuk Bug. The river has been low and stable throughout the winter making this a good time to fish streamers.

The spring run-off usually lasts from two to six weeks, starting in late May and peaking about mid-June. A long run-off could last to mid-July, but the extent of the high water is directly related to snow pack in the surrounding mountains. In low-snow years the run-off could have virtually no effect whatever on the river. Even in years when the river does rise, it can remain quite clear because the sedimentation from the park settles into Hebgen Lake and the silted water from Cabin Creek settles into Quake Lake.

Experienced anglers prefer the river flow to be from 1,000 to 1,200 c.f.s. When the water flow is less than 850 c.f.s., too many gravel bars are exposed and when it is more than 1,200 c.f.s., wading becomes appreciably more difficult. Even in very low-water years, such as was the case in 1987, good cooperation between the Montana Power Company (operator of Hebgen Dam), Montana Fish, Wildlife and Parks department and the state Tourist Bureau helped maintain adequate river flows even though inflow to Hebgen (300 c.f.s.) remained less than outflow (850 c.f.s.). Should you happen to be fishing the river during a period when a substantial rise or drop does take place, you'll need to allow about seventy-two hours for the river to stabilize.

In addition to the midge fishing on the upper river in May, caddis will start to emerge, as will a few mayflies. The Elk Hair Caddis and Goddard Caddis in sizes #10 to #18, plus a Blue Winged Olive in #14 and #16 will do the job.

The caddis hatches continue through June to about the end of July and provide the angler with good, dry fly activity throughout this period, particularly against the shady banks in the evening. Of most notable importance during this same time period is the annual emergence of the giant stonefly, Pteranarcys californica, referred to as the salmonfly because of the orange coloration of the adult's body. Normally, you could expect to see a token showing of these less-than-delicate insects over the water in the lower river starting in early June. By late June the insects are coming off the water near Ennis and the hatch progresses upstream each day until phasing out near the confluence of the river and the West Fork. These three-inch long insects not only attract the fish, but attract anglers from across the country and, as a result, this two- to three-week period is the busiest time of the year on the river.

Finding the specific stretch of river where the fish are responding most actively to these large flies is possibly the biggest challenge of all because the fish don't necessarily feed the heaviest where the insects are most numerous on the surface! Sometimes the catching is best when using nymphal or emerger imitations immediately upstream of the emergence. Local guides and outfitters are usually zeroed in as closely as anyone to the location of the most productive water. The intensity of this hatch varies from year to year, adding a further dimension of mystery and challenge to "hitting it just right."

Simultaneous with the salmonfly hatch, you can also expect the emergence of smaller, golden stones. They'll usually come off for seven to fourteen days and fish will sometimes take them as readily as they will the salmonfly. Try adults and nymphs in sizes #8 or #10 for the goldens, and the traditional #2 to #6 Sofa Pillow, Bird's Stonefly, the low floating "Stick" stonefly, Fluttering Stone and Jughead Stone for the salmonfly imitations.

July and August is a time of dry fly activity using attractor patterns such as Royal Wulffs, Royal Trudes, Grizzly Wulffs and Humpies. Hoppers also start to appear in July and will continue through August, for which we can be thankful because caddis and mayfly activity is at a minimum. Hopper imitations are most effective on hot days when afternoon breezes blow these terrestrials from the dry grass onto the water. Many fish will move to the banks under these circumstances, but don't neglect the shallower water in midstream with #8 and #10 imitations. If the "dog days" of August don't produce hopper fishing during the day, your best bet will be casting attractor patterns in the mornings and evenings in addition to using Blue Duns and Blue Winged Olives in #14 and #16.

As the leading edge of fall approaches in September the dry fly fisherman sets aside his hoppers and attractors in favor of large nymphs and streamers. In recent years the rubberleg patterns such as Bitch Creeks, Yuk Bugs and Girdle Bugs have become increasingly more popular when weighted and fished in large sizes. Popular streamers include old standbys such as the light and dark Spruce Flies, Muddlers, Spuddlers, Marabous and, the newer standby, Woolly Buggers, particularly those laced with a bit of flashy material and rubber legs.

The lower Madison is different from the upper river not so much in character as in water temperature. Although the number of fish in the lower river is high, the thermal heating of Ennis Lake in June and July so adversely affects the water temperature that the trout's lethargy renders the river unproductive to the best of angler's efforts. An irritating growth of weeds on the river bottom catches wet flies and lures on altogether too many casts. From late July through early September we'd suggest concentrating on the cooler water above the lake. In the spring before run-off and again in the fall, however, the lower river offers some very worthwhile fishing with streamers and large, attractor nymphs. In addition to those sizeable patterns you'll experience some dry fly activity in May using small midges, Blue Winged Olive in #14 through #18, particularly on overcast days, and if you should

Madison River at Gray Cliffs

happen to be on the lower river at just the right time, you can take advantage of the little known "Mother's Day Hatch." The start date of this caddisfly emergence dependably occurs between May 8th and 10th and fly fishermen can enjoy good dry fly fishing with Elk Hair Caddis and Goddard Caddis patterns in size #14 and 16 as well as soft hackle and sparkle pupae patterns just under the surface.

Of all the seasons on the lower Madison, fall is considered to be best. The water is cool and at stable levels, the predominant brown trout is preparing to spawn while putting on weight for the upcoming winter and there are few anglers on this somewhat remote and scenic section of the river. Although most fly fishing will be done using the large nymphs and streamer patterns, there still remains an unusual hatch of white mayflies, thought to be of the genus Ephoron. You might catch this emergence in October, late in the day, when fish will respond to White Wulffs dry and white Hare's Ear type nymphs in sizes #12 and #14.

There are fewer accesses to the lower river than to the upper river, particularly when fishing without the use of a boat. Heading west from Bozeman over the rolling, agricultural countryside one should continue southwest on Highway 289, which rises to the top of some beautiful hills before dropping into the valley and meeting the river. The river at this point is about a hundred yards wide, with a steady speed and a gently riffled surface.

The highway continues upstream offering hike-in access to the Bear Trap Canyon Primitive Area, while the Madison road parallels the river downstream for a couple miles before pulling away to the east, leaving access behind.

Between this point and the community of Three Forks, two public access sites are available. The first site is the Gray Cliff Access, a dead-end loop offering toilets, tables, camping and a boat ramp. You'll notice the road splits to the south and if followed for about a mile, leads to another campsite. Throughout this area the river braids around willow-covered islands and offers excellent fishing potential. In late fall the water must reach at least forty-five degrees before there is good response from the fish. Use a floating line, put the fly close to the bank and give it a couple of twitches. You can expect some eighteen- to twenty-inch fish here and you can lose flies easily, so we'd suggest OX tippets.

Downstream from Gray Cliff is another access named "Cobblestone." A short walk from the parking area to the river, through Darlington Spring Creek and over a levee, is required to reach the river. The creek holds trout and can be fished under special regulations for a change of pace from the river. Wading in the Madison here is difficult because the banks are compressed, causing a deeper channel. If you wish to drag or carry the boat some distance to or from the river, this can be a put-in for a raft or a take-out for the float from Gray Cliff. The shortest distance is next to the fence at the north boundary of the access. Scout this area first as some work is involved here! As you float, watch the east bank for a sign stating "Cobblestone 2." This means it is two miles to the cobblestone take-out, so pull into shore occasionally, climb the bank and look for your vehicle! If you intend to float past Cobblestone, don't stop too often to fish all the beautiful water that beckons a few additional casts because a straight-through float to Three Forks can take up to seven hours. The lower take-out is at Highway 10 near Three Forks.

Some additional observations:

1. The river between Varney Bridge and Ennis is closed to activity between late February and late May to protect nesting ducks and geese. Check the regulations for specifics.

2. From Varney Bridge to Ennis you can expect to hook larger fish because of the presence of deep holes and cut banks offering good holding lies for the bigger trout.

3. From McAtee Bridge to Varney Bridge there is little access to the river except by boat.

4. For private floaters, there are four or five floats that can be made, mostly from four to six hours each, and shuttle service is available in Ennis.

5. To fish the "channels" immediately above Ennis Lake by wading from the Valley Garden Access, a walk of a mile or two downstream is required to really get into the best part of this water. The true channels start about a mile above the lake.

6. Best all-around dry flies on the Madison include the Royal Wulff, both standard and parachute Adams and, in the upper river, a #20 and #22 Trico. For wet patterns the Bitch Creek and other rubberleg nymphs work very well. The Woolly Bugger is a tough streamer pattern to beat.

7. The Beartrap Primitive Area contains rattlesnakes, so be on your guard as you fish this section of river.

8. On the Madison you should fish the "windows" of soft water. Fish the quieter water next to a current, next to the bank, over slight depressions or below boulders.

9. Don't drag an anchor to slow the speed of your drifting boat. This practice is far too common and is harmful to bottom organisms, not to mention that it is alarming to the fish.

10. Throughout the length of the river you can expect to sight wildlife including ravens (locally called dumpster chickens), ducks, deer (in big numbers in the channels section), herons, eagles, Canadian geese and osprey.

11. In the heat of summer, the fish seem more active farther upstream because the water is cooler.

12. The river was named by Lewis and Clark to honor Secretary of State James Madison.

SOUTH FORK OF THE MADISON RIVER

This feeder stream to Hebgen Lake receives most of its angling pressure in the fall as the brown trout instinctively enter its mouth to continue upstream in search of suitable spawning gravel. Streamers, of course, are the most common type of artificials used at this time.

Summer fishing really isn't very popular here for a couple of reasons. First of all, access is not good because of private property along the river's banks above the highway and secondly, the water carries a very large population of whitefish in proportion to the trout population

During the summer months, "gulper" fishing is fairly popular where this stream enters Hebgen Lake, as explained in the section on Hebgen Lake. A gravel road along the lower reaches of the stream provides river access to this area as well as to the South Fork Campground.

WEST FORK OF THE MADISON RIVER

This small tributary to the Madison enters the main river from the west, nine miles downstream from Quake Lake. The West Fork Bridge is reached from Highway 187, a campground is available and access to wade fishing is plentiful.

The West Fork isn't an important fishery, particularly in light of its size and proximity to a river of the Madison's quality. It does offer a totally different type of experience for the angler if one is looking for light-tackle, small-fish fishing. There is a wide section of the stream called Smith Lake that reportedly offers good brown trout fishing. In late July and August the fish will respond well to offerings of grasshopper imitations.

A gravel road extends about fourteen miles upstream along the West Fork and provides access to it and its several channels and beaver ponds. Unfortunately the stream can be off-color, particularly after a rain, but does offer fishing for eight to twelve inch rainbow and a fair number of whitefish.

HEBGEN LAKE

Although called a lake, this body of water is, in fact, held in place by a dam at its northwestern edge. The earth-filled structure was constructed by the Montana Power Company in 1915 as an impound facility for hydroelectric generation at sites downstream. Surprisingly, the dam is still intact after dropping nine feet in elevation during the earthquake of August 17, 1959. At the time of the quake the north shore of Hebgen dropped while the south shore rose, causing the water to shift and bury the highway that hugged the north shore. Some of the remains of that road are now used as boat ramps.

The lake is located about eight miles northwest of West Yellowstone, Montana near the west entrance to Yellowstone National Park. The unusual shape of the impoundment is due to the "arms" which bring water into the lake from the east and south. These include Grayling Arm, Madison Arm and South Fork Arm plus what could be termed the outlet arm which presses against the dam. The lake measures approximately sixteen miles long and three miles wide and has fifty-seven miles of shoreline. At the dam the water is ninety-five feet deep. Hebgen is an attractive lake, surrounded by low mountains and evergreen trees. Although commercial and residential structures do circle the lake, its appearance is that of a relatively wild environment. The dam is situated in a forested canyon where the water outflow forms a short stretch of the Madison River above Quake Lake.

Fishing on Hebgen takes place year-round. In mid-winter many hearty fishermen brave the well-known, arctic chill of this region and fish through the ice in an attempt to hook some of this lake's population of large fish. In mid-summer the lake is transformed into a playground for camping, picnicking, water skiing, boating, sailing and, of course, trout fishing. The trout population consists of thousands of regularly stocked Eagle Lake rainbow and McBride cutthroat, resident brown trout of trophy size, whitefish and the Utah chub. The stocking programs are continued in an effort to establish a self-sustaining population. The growth rate of the fish in the lake is rapid due to feeding on the abundant chubs.

A wide range of fishing techniques are used here from relaxed angling in canoes to deep trolling from cabin boats. Brown trout are more easily caught early in the season as the ice goes off in May and June while the rainbows and cutthroat seem more responsive to angler efforts later in the summer. Bank fishermen and trollers do well on Mepps spinners, Thomas Cyclones, Cobb spin-jig and Rapala lures. Bait fishermen will anchor over the deeper, colder water in the summer because the big browns (over ten pounds) prefer these cooler depths.

Fly fishermen are pleased to find that a good variety of flies is successful on Hebgen including imitations of scuds, damselflies, dragonflies, Mayflies, caddisflies, leeches and minnows. In the spring, just at ice out, they will put on their fins, step into their float tubes and cast Woolly Buggers along the open shoreline where trout feed on minnows. Streamer fishing comes into its own during late September, October and November when the trout are gathering at the inlet mouths prior to making their spawning runs. Don't be surprised if you catch rainbows as well as browns during the autumn because it seems the bows make a false spawning run along with their neighbors. Try using Spruce Flies, rubberleg Woolly Buggers and Muddlers. Give them plenty of action by giving a strong fin kick followed by a good line tug, making the fly dart and then slow down. When casting into water twenty to thirty feet deep, allow the fly and line to sink, but don't retrieve. Merely kick and tug so the fly stays deep enough to attract the larger fish.

To the best of our knowledge the term "gulper" originated on Hebgen Lake. It refers to the sound made by trout from mid-June through August as they inhale mayflies from the surface. The insects involved are an olive-bodied Trico that comes off about 7:00 a.m. to 8:00 a.m. and the Callibaetis that will be seen on the water close to noon. Both insects are predictably present every day of the summer.

The most popular area for gulper fishing is the Madison Arm, although this fishing can be good anywhere on the lake. For both the Trico and Callibaetis a #16 or #18 parachute Adams is the most commonly used fly. Whether fishing from shore or from the water's surface in a float tube or boat, the technique involves finding a feeding fish, getting in tune with the rhythm of its rises and placing your fly where you next expect him to gulp. In addition to fishing an Adams on the surface, it is sometimes a good idea to try a small Hare's Ear or Pheasant Tail nymph just in or under the surface film. Because of the nature of this technique, you'll want to use tippets down to 5X, but expect to lose a few fish in the weeds. You can also expect the wind to blow on Hebgen.

When serious fly fishermen think of fishing Yellowstone Park in the fall they instinctively think of Hebgen Lake because of the "brown run" that occurs then as spawning brown trout migrate from the lake into the soft currents of the Madison River within the Park's borders. Old timers in West Yellowstone claim they haven't seen "slick" fish (those that leave the lake to enter the river to spawn have a milky substance on their sides) in the river prior to the first week of October. Some think that the run really doesn't start until the first part of November, with the peak occurring around Thanksgiving. It is also believed that those large fish caught during September and October are actually resident to the river. Although the Park fishing is closed as of November 1, the river from its boundary into the Madison Arm of the lake is in season and offers good potential to those who fish it.

QUAKE LAKE

A major earthquake caused a large piece of mountain to fall across the Madison Canyon in August of 1959 and for some time the Madison River ceased to flow beyond that point. A lake immediately started to form behind this natural dam of mountain side rubble and as the subsequent hours passed it was obvious that this new lake could back up all the way to the existing dam on Hebgen Lake. The possibility of this occurring caused grave concern because such a condition could have weakened the dam, leading to its failure and resulting in an even more devastating situation downstream. Earth-moving equipment was brought in immediately to cut a spillway through the slide debris. This action proved successful and the water of the Madison River was again allowed to continue on the course it had taken for an estimated two million years. The tree tops protruding twenty to thirty feet from Quake Lake's surface today remain as mute evidence that the lake bed was a forest floor not many years ago.

Although this long, narrow lake now provides us with a viable still-water fishery, the river that it has replaced was considered the finest section of the Madison for large fish. This was the truly "big fish" area of the river for both rainbows and browns. The lake is approximately four miles long with an estimated surface area of six hundred acres and a maximum depth of approximately one hundred feet. It contains rainbow, brown, cutthroat and whitefish. The most effective way to work this body of water is from a small boat or float tube and the angler can expect to hook fish in the ten to fifteen inch range, with a few browns and rainbows up to five pounds. The lake receives relatively little angling pressure and the fly fisherman can enjoy good fishing with Elk Hair Caddis and mayfly imitations in the evening, after the wind has settled down. There are times when the use of small Yellow Sally stonefly imitations can also be productive. Another effective time to fish the lake is at ice-out when shoreline fishing with Woolly Buggers and streamers can fool a few fish.

There are no beaches or camping facilities along the lake shore, but there is one boat ramp at the east end which was formerly a section of the highway through the canyon. Toilet facilities are available at this site.

There is a Visitors Center at the west end of the lake and we suggest you take a few minutes out of your schedule to learn of the devastating quake that caused the sight you witness here.

CLIFF LAKE AND WADE LAKE

Cliff Lake, the larger of these two lakes, covers slightly over six hundred acres with emerald green water. It's a narrow lake, approximately four miles long by up to one-third mile wide and over one hundred feet deep. A narrow canyon is the setting here and the main tributary is Antelope Creek, entering the lake's upper end at what is known as Antelope Prong.

The fishing is directed at rainbows averaging twelve inches, whitefish and a small population of browns. Efforts seem to be most rewarding on both lakes where the shallows drop off into the deeper water.

Although Cliff seems to be the least popular fishing destination of the two, it does provide more camping facilities. The lakes are reached from a good gravel road that connects Highway 287 and Highway 87 (the Raynolds Pass Road) west of Quake Lake.

Wade Lake, Cliff Lake's smaller companion, is 1/4 mile wide and about 1-1/2 miles long. It, too, is located in a steep canyon and lies just a half mile north of Cliff Lake.

Wade has a reputation as a trophy-trout lake, with the result that good numbers of fishermen visit here in summer. They catch ten- to fourteen-inch rainbows most of the time and occasionally larger browns, some up to ten pounds. The most productive fishing takes place from either a boat or a float tube as the steep banks encountered at lakeshore make fishing from here difficult.

ENNIS LAKE

Ennis Lake is also referred to as Meadow Lake for good reason. When the dam was built in the early 1900's, the sweet water of the Madison River was backed up to flood a hay meadow. Since that time the riparian character of the lake has changed very little and, even now, few trees are evident along the shoreline except among the commercial and residential areas on the north shore. The original purpose of the dam was to generate electric power, but new facilities located elsewhere have taken over and little power is now produced at this site.

The lake is located off Highway 287 approximately five miles north of Ennis. Its 3,800 surface acres form a roughly circular body of water approximately three miles in diameter, and its depth ranges from nine to fifteen feet, considerably less than when the lake originally filled. Annual siltation has decreased the depth dramatically over the years to the point where summer water temperatures become very high and threaten the well being of fish populations in the lake as well as in the Madison River below. Weed growth has recently become another problem and it's thought that the lake's traditionally substantial grayling population was severely damaged during an attempt to eradicate the weeds.

An access road follows the shoreline, but the best fishing is considered to be in the cooler waters at the lake's south end where the channels of the Madison enter. A boat ramp here permits fishermen to launch their craft and make their way toward the river's mouth, about a quarter-mile away. This is an area also used by float tube fishermen.

Because water temperatures in the lake reach into the low eighties at times, the fate of the rainbow trout population is in jeopardy. The state Department of Fish, Wildlife and Parks continues to stock DeSmet and Eagle Lake Rainbows in the lake to determine which will best withstand the effects of the warm water and also to help reduce the population of chubs. Only time will tell the fate of this fishery. The lake also has a population of brown trout, which are better able to flourish in warm water and their survival is more predictable. Studies are constantly being conducted to determine viable remedies to the thermal problem, but to date no answers are forthcoming.

In spite of its many problems, anglers can expect to catch fish in the twelve- to fourteen-inch range, with an occasional twenty incher. You might even be surprised by hooking one of the chub-eating Eagle Lake Rainbows that can often weigh in at five or six pounds.

Both spin and fly fishermen find the weeds to be a considerable problem, so once the weeds are up near the surface your best chance for strikes will be in the channels between the weeds. Let's hope a solution to the lake's problems is soon found.

WEST YELLOWSTONE

We can remember just a few years back when the rain puddles on Canyon Street reflected the deep azure sky over Yellowstone Park and the one-story store fronts just across the cracked sidewalk. Progress has brought curbs and gutters, plus a greater sophistication to this small town which hosts millions of tourists each year. The eastern border of this community is literally the western border of Yellowstone National Park and from Yellowstone Avenue you drive directly into the park through its west entrance.

Although the town of West Yellowstone is relatively new (incorporated in 1966), the first settlement took place in the 1880's and until 1920, it was simply called Yellowstone. In the early days it was the influence of the Union Pacific Railroad that really made the town tick. "West," as it is now called, was the end of the line for rail passengers arriving from Salt Lake City to visit Yellowstone Park. The first such train arrived in 1908 and at the train station visitors boarded stages in which they then toured the famous features of Yellowstone. In 1908 records reflect 3,705 people entered the park via the west entrance while today the year-round total numbers over two million.

Visitations to the park were severely reduced during the depression years and the Second World War, but auto traffic thereafter increased substantially, and in 1959 the railroad discontinued service to both the town and the park. Union Pacific did, however, offer to give its beautiful depot building to the community on the condition that the residents would create a legal town, which they accomplished by incorporating in 1966.

The Union Pacific Depot Building, which is listed in the National Register of Historic Places, has now evolved into the Federation of Fly Fishers International Fly Fishing Center. The center is open June 1 through October 1 and offers to the public, free of charge, the Fly Fishing Museum which features antique tackle, flies, books and other memorabilia of the sport. In addition, the center houses the Pat Lilly Gallery of Angling Art, the Federation of Fly Fishers' Library and the administrative offices for this international organization of over sixty thousand members. The purpose of the FFF, a non-profit organization, is to preserve and enhance our invaluable warm- and cold-water fishery resources, and to promote fly fishing as the most sporting method of catching fish. The building and its contents can be of interest to everyone, whether fishermen or not.

Other features and attractions in town include many motels, restaurants and retail stores, plus a museum of area history, a theatre with live, family entertainment, several fishing guide services, Yellowstone Park tour services and the Yellowstone Airport which is open June through September.

Chamber of Commerce: P.O. Box 458, West Yellowstone, Montana 59758 Phone: 646-7701

Federation of Fly Fishers: 200 Yellowstone Avenue, P.O. Box 1088, West Yellowstone, Montana 59758

ENNIS

Think for a moment of being employed at a post office in a small Montana town and handling hundreds of thousands of letters and packages with your name them! That is exactly what happened to the Ennis family for a remarkable period of eighty-four years. Mr. William Ennis was appointed postmaster in 1881 when the Ennis Post Office was first established and held the position for seventeen years. His daughter held the job for forty-two years after which time her daughter carried the title until 1965. But William Ennis is known for more than his life in government service! In 1842, at age fourteen, he arrived in America from his home in Ireland. In 1863 he headed out of Omaha, Nebraska with a large wagon train of supplies to be sold to the miners of Bannack and Alder Gulch, Montana. By 1873 he was living in Ennis as a merchant and stock rancher. He continued to develop needed businesses as the town of Ennis grew, but his life was prematurely ended when he was killed in 1898 at age seventy by a former friend.

The ranchers who live in the countryside surrounding Ennis raise sheep, cattle and crops. The town, which sits on the banks of the Madison River, has a population of about seven hundred residents. That number grows to nearly one thousand during the summer as people owning second homes here arrive to enjoy the many activities available, not the least of which is fishing. Between June and September the community gains much of its revenue from the visitors who vacation here and enjoy the angling rewards offered by the Madison River. Lions Park provides a stocked pond right in town where kids only can enjoy catching trout next to a playground in a pleasant setting. Other outdoor pursuits include tennis, golf at the local nine-hole course which provides equipment rental and clubhouse facilities, as well as swimming and boating on Ennis Lake.

Southwest of town tourists can enjoy visiting the Ennis National Fish Hatchery where seven different strains of trout produce ten to fifteen million eggs per year which are sent to other hatcheries around the country. This facility also raises fish to a stockable size for planting in the waters of Montana. In addition to the eggs and fish to be stocked, visitors can view the brood fish which may reach sizes to fifteen pounds. Other attractions in the vicinity

153

include the Lewis and Clark Caverns, Virginia City, Nevada City, Yellowstone National Park and the Earthquake exhibit on the upper Madison River below Hebgen Lake.

Commercial air transportation is handy at Bozeman, West Yellowstone or Butte. In addition, private aircraft have access to two fields at Ennis. Although the town is very tourist oriented, you never feel you're in a "tourist trap!" The folks of Ennis want fishermen to enjoy their community and have accordingly provided for their needs.

Ennis Chamber of Commerce: Box 291, Ennis, Montana 59729-0291

River Notes

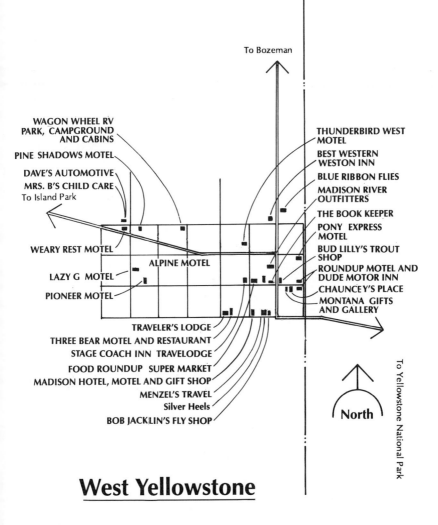

To Bozeman

WAGON WHEEL RV
PARK, CAMPGROUND
AND CABINS

THUNDERBIRD WEST
MOTEL

PINE SHADOWS MOTEL

BEST WESTERN
WESTON INN

DAVE'S AUTOMOTIVE

BLUE RIBBON FLIES

MRS. B'S CHILD CARE
To Island Park

MADISON RIVER
OUTFITTERS

THE BOOK KEEPER

PONY EXPRESS
MOTEL

WEARY REST MOTEL

BUD LILLY'S TROUT
SHOP

ALPINE MOTEL

ROUNDUP MOTEL AND
DUDE MOTOR INN

LAZY G MOTEL

CHAUNCEY'S PLACE

PIONEER MOTEL

MONTANA GIFTS
AND GALLERY

TRAVELER'S LODGE

THREE BEAR MOTEL AND RESTAURANT

STAGE COACH INN TRAVELODGE

FOOD ROUNDUP SUPER MARKET

MADISON HOTEL, MOTEL AND GIFT SHOP

MENZEL'S TRAVEL

Silver Heels

BOB JACKLIN'S FLY SHOP

North

To Yellowstone National Park

West Yellowstone

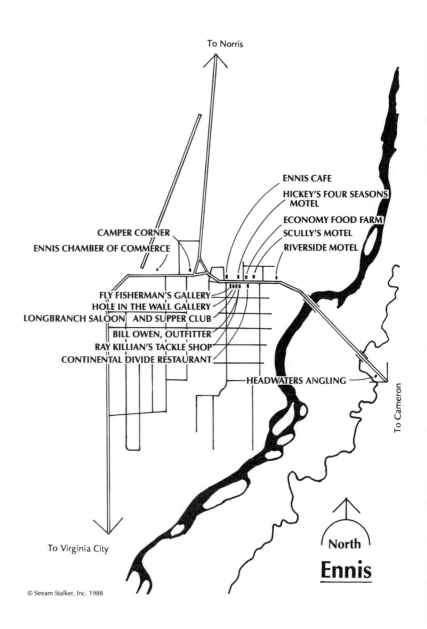

To Norris

ENNIS CAFE

HICKEY'S FOUR SEASONS
    MOTEL

ECONOMY FOOD FARM

SCULLY'S MOTEL

RIVERSIDE MOTEL

CAMPER CORNER

ENNIS CHAMBER OF COMMERCE

FLY FISHERMAN'S GALLERY

HOLE IN THE WALL GALLERY

LONGBRANCH SALOON   AND SUPPER CLUB

BILL OWEN, OUTFITTER

RAY KILLIAN'S TACKLE SHOP

CONTINENTAL DIVIDE RESTAURANT

HEADWATERS ANGLING

To Cameron

To Virginia City

North

Ennis

© Stream Stalker, Inc. 1988

WEST YELLOWSTONE

FISHING SHOPS

BLUE RIBBON FLIES
309 Canyon, Box 1037   646-9365

Complete fly pro shop, offering personalized guided trips to Yellowstone National Park and Montana waters. We offer a complete selection of flies tied by the west's best tyers, fly fishing and outdoor gifts, clothing and the largest available selection of tying materials for the fly tyer.

BOB JACKLIN'S FLY SHOP
105 Yellowstone Ave.,   646-7336

Quality fly and spin tackle, fly tying materials, custom U. S. tied flies. Dealers for Sage, S. A. Cortland, Hardy, Shakespear, Simms, Caddis and Eagle Claw products. Licensed professional outfitters with float and wade trips to Montana, Idaho and Yellowstone National Park. Fly fishing schools throughout the summer. Send for free information and maps.

BUD LILLY'S TROUT SHOP
39 Madison Ave., Box 698   646-7801

Guide service, complete tackle shop, quality merchandise, outdoor clothing, art gallery, books, fly tying equipment, maps. Best and largest selection of flies in the west. West Yellowstone's oldest and best fly shop.

MADISON RIVER OUTFITTERS
117 Canyon, Box 1106   646-9644

West Yellowstone's full service fly fishing shop, offering an outstanding selection of top quality equipment, fly tying materials and outdoor clothing. Experienced guides, float fishing trips on Montana and Idaho rivers, wading trips into Yellowstone National Park.

CAMPGROUNDS

MADISON ARM RESORT
Hebgen Lake, Box 40   646-9328

On the Lake, in the pines, 5-1/2 miles west of town on Forest Service road at Madison Arm. Ninety shaded campsites overlooking the marina and Hebgen Lake. Coin laundry, general store, fishing licenses, beach, swimming and boat rental. Clean cabins also available. Great fishing always!

WAGON WHEEL RV PARK, CAMPGROUND AND CABINS
408 Gibbon Ave, Box 608   646-7872

Complete camping facilities, located in a quiet shaded pine grove only three blocks from downtown. Overnighters are welcome. Laundromat, recreation room, tent village, hot showers and cabins are available. Tom and Dorit Herman are your hosts.

GUEST RANCHES

PARADE REST GUEST RANCH
8 miles north on Hwy 191 to Hwy 287, 1 mile west, 7979 Grayling Creek Road
646-7217

We offer you Montana's famed Madison and Gallatin Rivers, Yellowstone Park's Firehole and Gibbon Rivers, as well as our own private stream and many others, all near our true western dude ranch. Excellent food and authentic western accommodations, catering to fly fishermen and offering superb riding and fun for the rest of the family. We can arrange fly fishing float and guide trips.

MOTELS

ALPINE MOTEL
120 Madison Ave., Box 960   646-7544

twelve units, centrally located, AAA rated. Open early spring to late fall. Queen beds, Color cable TV and HBO. Electric heat. Visa and Master Card accepted. Close to restaurants and shopping. Early reservations are necessary.

BEST WESTERN WESTON INN
103 Gibbon Ave., Box 373   646-7373

Thirty-two large, comfortable units. Electric heat, tubs and showers, phones, color cable TV, heated outdoor pool, airport limousine service. Special family rooms available. Restaurants and shopping nearby. Open all year.

EINO'S TOO CABINS
Intersection Highways 287 and 191, 8 miles north of town, 8955 Gallatin Road
646-9280 or 646-9963

Open year round. Quiet location. Two bedroom cabins, fully furnished with kitchens. Great view of Hebgen Lake and Continental Divide.

LAZY G MOTEL
123 Hayden, Box 218   646-7586

Fifteen units in a secluded neighborhood. Patio, with barbecue. Excellent rooms, with color cable TV. We have fish cleaning and freezing facilities. Three efficiency units, $4.00 extra. Two, two bedroom efficiency suites, and one, two bedroom unit. No pets, please.

MADISON HOTEL, MOTEL AND GIFT SHOP
139 Yellowstone Ave. Box E   646-7745

If you're a history buff, make sure you don't miss this historic hotel, built in 1912, yet still renting to non-smokers. Modern motel units, both economy and deluxe rooms are also available A real find if you're looking for clean and inexpensive lodging. Color cable TV, HBO. Famous (huge) gift shop on the premises. All major credit cards and checks accepted. Open May 25 to October 10.

PINE SHADOWS MOTEL
530 Gibbon, Box 721   646-7541

Fourteen clean, comfortable units, including two log cabins. Kitchenettes also available in some units. Color cable TV, HBO in each unit. Outdoor hot tub and picnic area, with tables and grills. Guided fishing trips from the motel. Fly tying bench with materials. Smoker and freezer service. Ample parking for snowmobile trailers. Garage area for snowmobiles. Package deals available. Master Card, Visa, Amex accepted. Your hosts are Blaine and Vickie Heaps.

PIONEER MOTEL
515 Madison, Box 442   646-9705

Modern, clean units, cable color TV. Some large kitchen units. Quiet location with lots of room. Within walking distance to center of town. Running Bear Pancake House across the street. A great place to stay for the sportsman or tourist who will be in this beautiful area for awhile. Very reasonable weekly rates available.

PONY EXPRESS MOTEL
4 Firehole St., Box 908   646-7644
> Large one, two and three bedroom units, comfortably furnished. Located on a quiet street, two blocks north of the west entrance gate to Yellowstone Park and very close to shops and restaurants.

ROUNDUP MOTEL AND DUDE MOTOR INN
3 Madison Ave., Box 609   646-7301
> Forty-two AAA rated, units one block north of the Park entrance. Color cable TV, with HBO. Some kitchens. King and queen beds, electric heat, direct dial phones, heated swimming pool. Major credit cards accepted. Close to restaurants and lounges. Open all year.

STAGE COACH INN TRAVELODGE
209 Madison Ave., Box 160   646-7381 or 1-800-255-3050 for toll free reservations
> Full service hotel. Western atmosphere and friendly service. Color cable TV, hot tub and sauna area, restaurant, lounge with entertainment, poker. Banquet and meeting facilities. Airport transportation. AAA rate. Three blocks from Yellowstone Park.

THREE BEAR MOTEL AND RESTAURANT
217 W. Yellowstone Ave., Box 519   646-7353, motel; 646-7811, restaurant
> Three Bear Lodge. Across from the FFF Center and 2 blocks from the Park entrance. All the amenities you would expect plus executive suites, indoor jacuzzi and outdoor swimming pool. Meeting and banquet rooms available. Next to Three Bears Restaurant and Lounge.

THUNDERBIRD WEST MOTEL
216 Dunraven, Box 427   646-7677
> Nineteen units, offering clean, pleasing, modern accommodations. Color cable TV, HBO, some queen beds, tub/shower combinations. Two large family units available. Centrally located across from City Park, one block from shopping and dining. Mobil Guide Quality Rated. Reasonable rates. No smoking rooms available.

TRAVELER'S LODGE
225 Yellowstone Ave., Box C   646-7773
> There's more to this motel than meets the eye! Forty-three rooms with cable TV, HBO movies, hot tub, jacuzzi, sauna and heated outdoor pool. Large social room with video games and big screen TV. Common kitchen and laundry facilities for all our guests. Summer car rentals available at the motel office. We offer additional discounts for those renting a room and car in the summertime. Open all year.

WEARY REST MOTEL
601 Highway 20, corner Hwy. 20 and Hayden, Box 263   646-7633
> Ten unique fireplace and/or kitchen units, including two, four-bedroom chalets, suited to varied tastes. Varnished log exterior and sparkling clean knotty pine interiors reflect the western atmosphere visitors look for. Color cable TV, HBO. Open all year. We welcome personal checks.

RESTAURANTS / BARS

CHAUNCY'S PLACE
16 Madison Ave., Box Q   646-7788
> Chauncy's Place is a unique restaurant, offering an interesting variety of freshly prepared foods, excellent omelets, luncheon crepes, enchiladas, and a variety of salads and sandwiches you've never heard of. We appeal to both meat and vegetarian appetites. Located across from the Post Office. In season, 7 AM to 3 PM; off-season, 7 AM to 2 PM.

EINO'S TAVERN
North shore, Hebgen Lake, Hwy. 287, 16790 Hebgen Lake Rd.   646-9963
> Open year round. Casual restaurant and bar where we supply the steaks and burgers and you cook 'em the way you like. Off sale liquor.

TOTEM RESTAURANT AND LOUNGE
115 Canyon, Box 549   646-7630

Cafe and dining room offers fine family dining, serving breakfast, lunch and dinner. Adjoining liquor store and deli are open seven days weekly for spirits and take out items. Fishermen's lunches available.

ART GALLERIES

MONTANA GIFTS AND GALLERY
West Park Mall, Box 716 646-7885

Exclusive dealer for Gary Carter prints in West Yellowstone. We offer limited edition prints and original art by Paul Krapf, Morten Solberg, Paul Calle, Jessica Zemsky and many others. Open year round.

GROCERS

FOOD ROUNDUP SUPER MARKET
Corner Madison and Dunraven, Box 368   646-7501

The area's finest food shopping outlet. Fresh produce and meats, imported and domestic wines and beers, gourmet and fancy foods. Party and picnic supplies. Maintained off-street parking right in front.

HORSEBACK RIDING

DIAMOND P RANCH
2865 Targhee Pass Highway   646-7246

Enjoy beautiful mountain views, wooded trails and blue Montana skies, as you ride with friendly, capable guides. We outfit individuals or groups with good horses, selected to fit your personality and riding ability. Families are our specialty. Tiny tots, too! Join us and enjoy Montana.

RETAIL SHOPS

THE BOOK KEEPER
104 Canyon, Box 10   6469358

Full line book store with one of the west's largest selections of fishing books on the Yellowstone Park and Montana area. Catalog available.

Silver Heels
115 Yellowstone Ave., Box 54   646-7796

Gold, silver, precious and semi-precious stones. Custom jewelry by owner Greg Huth. Located in the Montana Outpost.

SERVICES

DAVE'S AUTOMOTIVE
300 Hayden, Box 462   646-9574

Complete automotive and RV repairs. Auto rental. Prompt, courteous service. Reasonable rates.

MENZEL'S TRAVEL
127 Yellowstone Ave., Box 27   646-7666

Bus tickets, domestic airline reservations and tickets, rental cars, tours and accommodations in Yellowstone National Park. Located in Menzel's Curio Store, two blocks from the Park entrance.

MRS. B'S CHILD CARE
300 Hayden, Box 462   646-9795
        Supervised child care.

CAMERON

CAMPGROUNDS / CABINS

MADISON VALLEY CABINS
Highway 287, Box 525   682-4890
        Located 37 miles south of Ennis on the Madison River. We have housekeeping cabins and full RV hookups. We cater to hunters, fishermen, cross-country skiers, snowmobilers and sightseers.

WEST FORK CABIN CAMP
On the banks of the Madison River, 35 miles west of West Yellowstone at the junction of the West Fork, Box 545   682-4802
        On the world-renowned Madison River, 7 miles downstream from Quake Lake. Fish Wade Lake, Cliff Lake, Hebgen Reservoir and Henry's Lake as well as the Madison River. We have full RV hookups, housekeeping cabins, tent spaces, overnighters, laundry facilities, showers and a store.

ENNIS

FISHING SHOPS

HEADWATERS ANGLING
Highway 287, 1/2 mile east of Ennis, Box 964   682-7451
        In our fly shop, we stock Orvis, Sage, Simms, Winston, Cortland and Patagonia products. The guide service, established in 1975, offers float trips on the Madison, Jefferson, Missouri and Big Hole Rivers, and extended overnight expeditions on the Smith River.

RAY KILLIAN'S TACKLE SHOP
127 Main St. , Box 625   682-4263
        We are here to make your fishing trip more enjoyable and successful and we are eager to help you with all of your needs, whether they be current fishing information, quality tackle, a guided fishing trip, or accommodations in the area.

GUIDES / OUTFITTERS

BILL OWEN, OUTFITTER
Box 1424, Belgrade MT 59714   388-1272 winter, 682-4263, summer
        Float and wade fish the famous waters of southwestern Montana with Bill Owen, an independent licensed and insured guide and outfitter, with nine years experience on the Madison, Jefferson, Missouri, Gallatin, Beaverhead and Bighorn Rivers.

RANDY BROWN GUIDE SERVICE
Box 444   682-7481
        Fly fishing for trout on the Madison, Bighorn and all Montana rivers, as well as light tackle spin and fly fishing for bonefish, tarpon and permit on the flats of the Florida Keys.

T LAZY B RANCH
532 Jack Creek Road,   682-7288
        We cater strictly to fly fishing and upland bird hunting. Superb log cabins and main lodge on the banks of privately controlled Jack Creek. We specialize in float fishing trips on the Madison River, and serving you a great meal after a great day. Maximum occupancy, eight persons.

CAMPGROUNDS

CAMPER CORNER
On Highway 287, in Ennis, Box 579   682-4514
> Delightful, shady campground, one block from downtown Ennis. Full hookups, showers, laundry and rest rooms. Ann and Jim Davis, your hosts.

LAKE SHORE LODGE
North Ennis Lake Road, Box 134, McAllister, MT 59740   682-4424
> LAKE SHORE LODGE- Beautiful, shaded, quiet resort on the north shore of Ennis Lake. Modern housekeeping cabins, lakeside RV hookups, fishing boats. marina. Licensed outfitter, guided river float trips., lake fishing.

MOTELS

THE EL WESTERN MOTEL AND RESORT
Highway 287 South, 1/2 mile east of Ennis, Box 287   682-4217
> Located conveniently, 1/2 mile east of Ennis, on U. S. 287. Eighteen acres of beautiful grounds. Its 28 log cabins range from comfortable sleeping units to luxurious cottages with fireplaces, kitchens and all the amenities you could ask for.

HICKEY'S FOUR SEASONS MOTEL
222 Main St., Box 687   682-4378
> Located in the middle of Ennis, Montana, with 23 units to fit all price ranges. Queen beds and free coffee in the rooms. Heated pool and jacuzzi in season. Color cable TV.

LAKE SHORE LODGE
North Ennis Lake Road, Box 134, McAllister MT 59740   682-4424
> LAKE SHORE LODGE- Beautiful, shaded, quite resort on the north shore of Ennis Lake. Modern housekeeping cabins, lakeside RV hookups, fishing boats, marina. Licensed outfitter, guided river float trips, lake fishing.

RIVERSIDE MOTEL
Downtown Ennis, Box 688   682-4240
> We have 11 clean, comfortable, reasonably priced units, some with kitchenettes, all with color cable TV and small refrigerators for ice, pop and sandwiches. Next to Lion's Community Park, which has a kid's fishing pond. One-half block from the Madison River.

SCULLY'S MOTEL
301 Main St., Box 248   682-4384
> Nine units, some with kitchenettes, all with refrigerators and coffee machines. Located in downtown Ennis, two blocks from the famous Madison River. Color cable TV in each unit. We also have one condominium unit for larger groups.

GROCERS

ECONOMY FOOD FARM
232 Main St., Box 38   682-4213
> Economy Food Farm, your one stop shopping store in Ennis. Fresh meats, produce, in-store bakery, ice, film, beer, wine and pop. A friendly place to shop, with competitive prices.

RESTAURANTS / BARS

CONTINENTAL DIVIDE RESTAURANT
Main Street, Box 622   682-7600

Jay Bentley's passion for trout fishing is exceeded only by his love of serving fine cuisine. He can converse as well about Pale Morning Duns as duck breast in raspberry sauce or blackened salmon. His 3-star Michelin rating attests to that. Jay and Karen would love to have you drop by and prove it to yourself. Specializing in Creole and French cuisine. Dinners only.

ENNIS CAFE
108 Main St., Box 87   682-4442

On Main Street in Ennis, on the edge of the famous Madison River. We open early for the fishing crowd and serve homemade pies and great home cooking. Breakfast, lunch and dinner. Open all year.

LONGBRANCH SALOON AND SUPPER CLUB
Main Street, Box 148   682-9908

Longbranch Saloon and Supper Club! Great food, nice atmosphere. Come see our hand carved bar. Your hosts are Sam and Chris Johnson.

ART GALLERIES

FLY FISHERMAN'S GALLERY
119 Main, Box 330   682-4599

The west's only exclusive angling art gallery!

HOLE IN THE WALL GALLERY
123 E. Main, Box 608   682-7235

Original oils, acrylics, watercolors, bronzes, wood sculpture, specialty art, limited edition prints, specializing in western art and wildlife. Three convenient locations in Ennis, Big Sky and West Yellowstone.

SERVICES

ENNIS CHAMBER OF COMMERCE
Madison Valley Complex, Box 291   682-4388

The best kept secret in the continental U.S., 60 miles north of West Yellowstone on Highway 287. Ennis is a year round, full service community, geared to all of your fishing and recreational needs. Call for information today.

MARIAS RIVER

No Map

While the Marias isn't a river to be totally ignored by floaters, it really isn't one to be considered as a destination river for trout fishermen. This is basically a prairie river flowing casually through the grassland east of Cutbank near which it has its origins.

The river was originally designated Maria's River by Captain William Clark in honor of his cousin, but time and usage finally caused the apostrophe to be omitted and today's designation has prevailed. The river's path takes it along a 130-mile course through farming country, into the Tiber Reservoir, finally to depart the dam and continue toward its confluence with the Missouri River near Loma.

The badland terrain below the reservoir is neither aesthetically nor ecologically associated with quality trout water. There is, however, a population of trout within a few miles below the dam where rainbow are stocked and caught. A campground here is the access point for fishermen. This section of river also contains walleye pike, northern pike, perch, some brown trout and a substantial population of large whitefish. From fifteen miles below the dam to its mouth, the river becomes warm, silt-laden and better suited to ling, sturgeon and catfish.

There are small populations of trout and whitefish above the reservoir, along with a number of carp and other rough fish, but this area isn't considered a respectable trout fishery.

MISSOURI RIVER

Map References 30, 31

Surveys have shown that the majority of fishermen on the Missouri River above Great Falls are fly fishermen. In a way this is a surprising revelation about a river nicknamed "Mighty Mo" and "Big Muddy," both terms seemingly contrary to standard conceptions of a pristine, mountain, trout stream. It's also a bit difficult to imagine a river of one-hundred yards' width as having the character of a spring creek, but indeed it does. This is a big river, formed at Three Forks from the confluence of three rivers—the Gallatin, the Jefferson and the Madison—all fine trout rivers in their own right.

Prior to the explorations of Lewis and Clark in 1805, the Missouri was a transportation thoroughfare for the Indians. Once the white explorers discovered the potential of the river, fur traders took advantage of the great abundance of game here. Then gold was discovered nearby and more and more settlers arrived and the river became host to steamships moving miners, ranchers and cattle. This conduit of commerce finally experienced its last days of commercial use when the railroad arrived. This entire region, now used for agricultural pursuits, was the subject portrayed in many of the frontier paintings of famous artist Charles Russell who established his log cabin studio and home in Great Falls.

The river's journey from Three Forks to Great Falls covers 150 miles and through this distance it is constantly being transformed in ways that couldn't have been imagined in the early 1800's. At the very point of its formation its temperature is drastically raised during the summer as it receives warm water from the Madison River. It also experiences a turbidity condition caused by irrigation returns into the Gallatin and Jefferson Rivers upstream. For the next few miles the river flows between the Belt Mountains to the east and the Elkhorn Mountains to the west until it is literally stopped and backed up for about five miles behind Toston Dam, a relatively small irrigation dam above the town of Toston. From here it flows freely for a few more miles before once again being halted by the shallow, still waters at the upper end of Canyon Ferry Lake behind Canyon Ferry Dam, a substantial body of water approximately twenty-five miles in length. Below Canyon Ferry the river flows into Hauser Lake, after which it continues again, only to flow into yet another impoundment, Holter Lake. From the base of Holter Dam the river will now flow unobstructed to Great Falls.

We have called these impoundments "lakes," because the maps designate them as such, but they are, of course, reservoirs of water stored for public use—in this case, irrigation water and power generation. In spite of the fact that these facilities have altered the wild nature of the original, historic river, they have created a type of fishery that wouldn't otherwise exist here. The water coming from the dams is cooler during the summer months and cleaner during run-off months than was true before the dams were built. That's good for fishermen. Additionally, the river sections now offer anglers the opportunity to hook not only the smaller, resident fish but also the considerably larger, migratory fish. These migratory fish play an important role in the overall fishing appeal of this river. Each year rainbows between six and ten pounds are caught as they move out of the reservoirs into the river. Browns run even larger with fish over ten pounds taken. Also the angler has an easier time locating fish in the spring and fall because the fish look for special, spawning grounds within the length of the river as well as stacking up somewhat immediately below the dam structures. Lastly, where fishing is allowed year-round, the water below the dams stays open, while the river farther downstream does freeze over in mid-winter.

This area of the river below Holter, in some places, really does display the characteristics of a river that might be gushing forth from a giant spring. The water is alkaline and its nutrients promote a carpet of weed growth in several areas. The weeds present little problem as far as wading is concerned—in fact this is an easy river to wade—but floating moss and weeds during the summer months do create a problem when fishing lures and wet flies. This is a common situation in many tail-water fisheries of the west and relief takes place only after frosty nights occur in the fall. By October the problem subsides and fishermen can again fish sinking lures with greater convenience.

Throughout the river fishermen will find few areas where wading is difficult, except, of course, where the water is too deep. The bottom isn't slippery and the rocks are generally quite small, so sliding off the side of a large cobblestone usually isn't a concern. You should, however, be cautious when standing on a gravel bar that contains loose gravel, as currents can undermine your footing.

Private boats are often used on the Missouri including inflatable rafts, motor boats, drift boats, prams and canoes. The river which has an average summer speed of four miles per hour is very easy to navigate due to its generally flat, broad nature. Aside from one tricky spot, the Half Breed Rapids below the Sheep Creek confluence near Cascade, the only problem the boatman encounters, particularly in late summer and fall, is frequent wind blowing upstream out of the north.

Although good fishing can be enjoyed by the wading fisherman, optimum opportunity to put your fly to feeding fish is offered to the floater. The fish here seem to congregate in pods, sometimes predominately trout, other times primarily whitefish. The fish often feed in foam lines where insects become concentrated into narrow, current lanes. These lanes change with changing water levels and the fish will seek them out to concentrate under the food supply. A boat provides the best mobility to search the river for this localized feeding activity. When fish are found the craft can be beached and if wading is possible the fish approached on foot. Whether wading or using a boat to find your fish, one point to bear in mind is this: if you are hooking fish but are disappointed because they're all whitefish, find a new location. This schooling trait of whitefish is highly developed here and when these fish are found it may be time to move on.

When trout are located and coming to the surface, it's usually best to cast directly to their feeding lane as they normally don't move far to take either an artificial or a natural fly. This fact is particularly true when insects are on the water in prodigious numbers. Accurate casting becomes important under these circumstances and the closer you can come to the fish, the better the drift you'll achieve. The currents on this river are not easy to fish; they tend to slip and slide around as if deliberately programmed to complicate your best efforts. Like on flat-surfaced rivers everywhere, make your cast as short as possible, cast downstream if necessary and throw plenty of slack line when appropriate to avoid the disastrous effects of these capricious surface currents.

Spin fishermen here are faced with their own problems, choices of lures to use and methods of retrieves to practice, but at least they don't have to face the subtle surface disharmonies the fly fisherman must overcome. Favorite hardware here includes hammered brass lures, Panther Martins, Mepps, Thomas Cyclones, Krocodiles, black leadhead jigs, Vibrax and sinking Rapalas.

Fly rod anglers will feel comfortable with rods from five weight to nine weight. In the fall when the browns are moving into the river from the reservoirs and you're throwing a size #2, weighted Muddler Minnow and the wind is blowing and you're trying to cover as much water as possible on the drift and swing, the nine-weight outfit is perfect. If you're casting tiny #20 Blue Winged Olives to very selective trout on a breathless, August afternoon, the five weight might be your first choice. The water here is so big, the fish behavior so changing in different seasons and the conditions so variable, that no single outfit will cover the range of needs. Even though few of us like to cast into it, the wind does serve a useful purpose on this river. For one thing it puts a ripple on the otherwise flat surface, somewhat disarming the fish into a slightly less wary attitude and as a result, it also allows you to approach slightly closer than might be possible on a calm day. Another obvious advantage in the summer is the greater susceptibility the terrestrial insects have to being blown onto the water. Those big streamers mentioned above star

158

becoming effective early in the year because of the strong population of sculpin in the river. Muddler Minnows and Marabou Muddlers are used whenever the river is fishable. During May the resident fish become more active at the approach of summer and other streamers will also work well particularly when fished deep on a sinking line. Flies like the Zonker, Woolly Bugger and Spuddler complement the use of the Muddler. May is also a good month to start using nymphs, as this is a time when golden stoneflies will start to appear. Good nymphs now, and throughout the year, include the Hare's Ear, Brown Hackle Peacock, wet Renegade, Prince and Pheasant Tail. Surface flies will also appear this time of year, in the form of #20 Midges and some Blue Winged Olives in size #14 to #18.

Run-off will show throughout the river in June but the dams really curtail the enormous rush of water seen on many other rivers. The water will discolor for a few days, but usually not for the extended periods common elsewhere. Hatches of caddis flies start this month, continue strong through July and August and phase out in September. Because the fish are starting to look skyward, but numbers of surface insects are still limited, this is an ideal time to start using attractor dries—Royal Wulff, Royal Trude and Humpy. These patterns remain effective throughout the summer.

The months of July, August and September see the peak of dry fly fishing on the river and those anglers who fish this water frequently will give it the highest marks for surface fly productivity. Caddis are on the water mornings and evenings, Pale Morning Duns appear as do Blue Winged Olives, and about mid-July the Tricos swarm over the water each morning. In addition to this potpourri of protein, the fish will also be taking ants, beetles and hoppers. These terrestrials continue to be seen through August and into September and can be very effective near the banks on windy days, particularly in the lower reaches.

During the ninth month of the year the streamer fishing gains momentum as insect numbers start to diminish. Floating lines are removed from reels and, when fishermen throw the big nymphs and streamers, sinking lines take their place. The spools are interchanged occasionally, however, as small mayflies and midges will continue into October.

The fish of the Missouri are healthy! They're well structured, nicely marked, strong opponents when hooked, but we've been told, are of poor eating quality. The predominant fish is the rainbow but there is a substantial population of browns. The bows average thirteen to sixteen inches, with fewer numbers from sixteen to nineteen inches; those over nineteen inches are the exception. Like many rivers of southwestern Montana the Missouri also supports a large population of whitefish. Spawning time for the rainbows is from March into the first two weeks of April. The browns generally start their annual peregrination about mid-October and go well into November.

Let's take an imaginary float down the river from its very beginning at Headwaters State Park to a take-out at Great Falls. To save time and energy, we'll truck the boat around the reservoirs and concentrate our observations on the river sections only.

The first section of river, down to Toston Reservoir, is the slowest moving we'll experience until Great Falls. Without the use of a motor here, the trip will take a full day. Floaters who make this relaxing trip will sometimes take out at Clarkston, about six hours from Three Forks, or camp there and finish the trip to Toston the following day. The Fairweather Fishing Access at Clarkston is the only vehicle access within this remote and barren stretch of the river. Due to high water temperatures during the summer fishing here is best during the spring and fall. This is good streamer and large, attractor nymph water.

The water from Toston Dam down to Canyon Ferry Lake is the next area we'll consider. This water covers approximately twelve miles and is known locally as the "Townsend Stretch." This is an agricultural area where the flat countryside supports crops of hay, wheat and barley and where cattle graze in the meadows. This is a full-day float through a single channel in the upper portion and then through braided arteries for a couple of miles above the reservoir. These channels provide good holding water for trout during the hot summer months when the shallow upper reservoir warms to fairly high

Missouri River at Toston

temperatures. They also hold browns in the fall when these fish seek suitable spawning gravel. The brown trout population in this area is thought to be considerably smaller than its potential would allow it to be and although the regulations are structured to protect the fish, apparently the kill rate is still too high.

This portion of river isn't particularly well known for its resident trout population, but it is noted for its migratory runs. During March and the first two weeks of April the rainbows journey from the lake into the river where fish to six pounds can be expected. The most consistent method of catching them is with the use of spawn sacks, but spin and fly fishermen can also enjoy good catches. Fluorescent orange spoons seem to top the list of favorite lures used by spin fishermen, while orange Girdle Bugs, egg patterns and streamers are preferred by fly fishermen. The water now is at its lowest volume of the year; it's cold and clear and perfectly complements the relatively warm air temperatures. Although the dams do temper the effects of spring run-off on the river, this area is affected from mid-April (after the rainbow run) until June. Water levels and turbidity will be higher than normal.

The summer months here are not as popular as they are on lower reaches. This isn't a particularly good dry fly stretch, although attractor patterns do take some fish. Normally anglers will concentrate their efforts just below the dam in the evenings using large Muddlers, Woolly Buggers and attractor nymphs fished deep. During late August and into September, evening dry fly fishing can be good using a large White Wulff or other white mayfly pattern in a size #10 to imitate what we believe to be the Ephoron hatch.

Fall is the season that stimulates the most angler interest here because of two fish migrations that occur. As expected, the browns move out of the lake to establish their spawning redds and these fish will average from two to five pounds. They can commence moving as early as mid-September but more predictably October into November would be a reliable time to plan a trip here. The companion rainbows will range between two and four pounds as they start their run up river in mid-October. Best lures are #4 and #6 Panther Martins and #2 Mepps and favorite flies include big, rubberleg nymphs and large streamers.

The reach between Canyon Ferry Dam and Hauser Lake is short, but contains good numbers of fish. This one-mile stretch is considered one of the most heavily fished areas in the state, and maybe rightfully so. Seems as if someone hooks a fish of twelve pounds here every year!

Another popular section of river is that from Hauser Dam down to Holter Lake. This is another area when large spawning fish move up from the lake. A favorite spot here is near the confluence of Beaver Creek, about two miles below the dam. The creek enters the river from the east and can be reached from the road out of the town of York, or by walking downstream from the dam.

It should be noted here that fishing from the several dams throughout this region or their adjacent structures is not allowed. Be sure to heed the signs and regulations posted for the safety of those afoot.

The water and countryside from Holter Dam to the town of Cascade is probably the most varied and interesting we'll see throughout this 150 mile trip down the Missouri. This is the stretch in which the spring-creek nature of the river really shows itself. The channel is approximately one hundred yards wide, there are several areas of islands and a good deal of rip-rap shows on the river bends.

Access to the dam is gained from either side of the river. From the Wolf Creek Bridge the Beartooth Road follows the river upstream on the east side to not only the dam, but beyond to the Holter Lake Recreation Area. On the west side a gravel road parallels the river from the Wolf Creek Bridge to the dam, with pullouts along the way giving easy access to the river. This is called the Holter Dam Road.

Below Wolf Creek as we head toward the town of Craig, we're impressed with the spectacular cliffs and rock uplifts rising above the banks. The islands we pass are good areas around which to fish, so don't neglect their potential. Downstream from Craig the river is moderately fast with gentle riffles as it proceeds through attractive, canyon terrain. This entire stretch is relatively easy to float at normal water levels, however, there is one piece of water just

Missouri River near Craig

below the confluence of Sheep Creek and Prewett Creek that deserves your attention. It's called Half Breed Rapids and, aside from being rapid, it is also punctuated with protruding rocks that will keep you on your toes—or at least on your oars! We recommend you scout this area before floating through it!

Below the rapids the terrain starts to flatten some, becoming more agricultural and showing more cottonwoods along the river banks. The river slows somewhat approaching Cascade, the rocky, canyon-style river banks change to mud banks and the river takes on a different character.

The fish population throughout this entire reach is quite abundant, with high counts of rainbows and fewer numbers of browns. The ratio is said to be about four to one. Whitefish also are present in impressive numbers. Overall the fish in this area are smaller than their counterparts upstream because they don't have a reservoir in which to relax and put on poundage. This isn't to say the fish here aren't of a respectable size, however, they just aren't typically as hefty as those above the lakes. Since there are more of them, it probably balances out. Also the fish are always here; they're not transient trout to the degree they are above. The fish do, of course, move within the confines of the river but they don't return to an impoundment for the balance of the year. The rainbows start their spawning activity in March and as farther above, fishermen do well on bright, Fluorescent orange offerings in both flies and lures.

Hatches here start to appear in April and continue until late in the fall. In addition to the Pale Morning Duns, Blue Winged Olives, Caddis, Tricos and midges found in other areas, this stretch of river is better suited to hopper fishing in August and September, particularly on a breezy afternoon.

As the season eases into autumn and colder weather approaches, the browns start their annual spawning moves, heading upstream toward the dam. Anglers prefer to cast into the riffles this time of year, fishing deep with large streamers and rubberlegs. Favorite areas include the base of the dam as well as off the mouths of Prickly Pear Creek and the Dearborn River.

The water below Cascade flows through plains country with a lower gradient, slower current, willow- and cottonwood-lined banks, less access and the water is usually more turbid. The lower Smith River often runs dirty where it empties into the Missouri at Ulm and, while the trout aren't greatly receptive to this condition, a population of walleye pike doesn't seem to mind. Trout certainly do reside in the waters below Cascade, but not in the numbers seen upstream.

So there you have it—the "Mighty Mo," a truly varied, interesting, challenging and productive river.

CANYON FERRY LAKE

This reservoir is an aquatic recreation site in the truest sense of the term. It offers swimming, water skiing, camping, picnicking, wind surfing, sailing, houseboating, canoeing and fishing. One can fish from shore, from boats, both moving and anchored, and when the ice forms thick on the surface, from holes through same. To assure that no one suffers from lack of angling success, the Montana Department of Fish, Wildlife and Parks stocks hundreds of thousands of fish each year. The fisherman has a choice of yellow perch, kokanee salmon, brown trout and two strains of rainbow trout. In addition to these there are good numbers of forage fish to keep the trout fat and sassy!

The lake doesn't attract fly fishermen, but bait fishing from the shore and trolling from boats are the two preferred methods of fishing from ice-out in spring to ice-up in early winter. Ice-out usually occurs about mid-March at which time shore fishing is very good and remains so into May. Shore fishing seems to be consistently productive along the southwest shore in the area of the Silos and across the lake on the east shore at the Confederate Recreation/ Duck Creek areas. Trolling starts in May and continues into fall; with June and July being the most productive months. Trollers use a variety of lures, but the Rapala seems to be the favorite. The usage of this reservoir is quite intense during the summer due to its proximity to four of Montana's larger population centers. From the fishing perspective, however, the months of July, August and September generally represent the least productive time. Shore fishermen and those trolling near the surface find fewer fish because the water temperature comes up and the fish go down to seek the relief of cooler sanctuaries at the lake's lowest levels. Deep trolling, however, can be rewarding during this time.

Areas have been set aside at the lake's south end to protect and encourage the nesting of waterfowl, but the lake extends for a distance of approximately twenty-five miles and is up to four miles wide, so there's plenty of water on which recreationists can enjoy their favorite pastime. Camping areas, picnic spots and boat ramps are numerous and fishing-shop personnel can answer your questions and give up-to-the-minute information regarding fishing conditions.

HAUSER LAKE AND HOLTER LAKE

These two impoundments lie downstream from Canyon Ferry Lake and although their combined size is considerably smaller than their upstream sister, they offer similar recreation opportunities on a reduced scale.

Hauser Lake is the first impoundment below Canyon Ferry and it offers fishing to a good population of rainbows, fair numbers of browns, plus perch, bass and walleye. At 3,700 surface acres, the lake offers swimming, boating and water-skiing in addition to camping.

Holter Lake is the farthest north of the series of impoundments on this upper stretch of the Missouri. It covers almost five thousand acres and measures approximately four miles by one mile in the main body of the lake north of the big oxbow bends. Trolling is done throughout the lake while shore fishing seems to be concentrated on the east side where the Beartooth Road follows the shoreline. This road offers good access to the lake and services three camping areas and boat ramps. As with the other lakes in the chain, Holter is used extensively for boating and appurtenant water sports. This is a more scenic area because of the rock formations which are evident especially at the "Gates of the Mountains" where high cliffs tower over the shoreline. This location is considered the most dramatic on the river for natural beauty and rugged terrain.

DEARBORN RIVER

This pretty little tributary of the Missouri River has its humble beginning at Scapegoat Mountain near the Continental Divide southwest of Great Falls. Its extremely clear water flows for about sixty miles to the east before entering the Missouri below the town of Craig. As were so many rivers in Montana, this one too was named in 1805 by the Lewis and Clark Expedition to honor then Secretary of War Dearborn.

Although this is a nice trout stream in many aspects, it also has its drawbacks from the angler's point of view. It's small, making it easy to fish; the water quality is high and it moves through some attractive countryside. However, access isn't particularly easy and under normal conditions the water level drops so low when the fishing gets good that it's difficult to float a boat on it—and floating is the means of access to its most attractive water. In July and August it's necessary to get out of the boat and pull it over the gravel bars and through the shallow riffles. The upper reaches of the Dearborn are reached only on foot and the fishing is limited to pursuing small brook trout and cutthroat.

Most floating and fishing is done downstream from where Highway 287 crosses the river, one of the few accesses available along its course. This access is about twelve miles from the river mouth as the crow flies. For practical purposes, the bends and twists taken by the river make this a two-day float trip. Part of this lower reach is bordered by subdivisions but the most interesting stretch runs through a vertically walled gorge where rapids, boulders and white water make it a place to scout before floating, and a place to be avoided by beginning boatmen.

This canyon section is a pristine area where the rainbows will average ten to fifteen inches with a few larger and where browns have been known to reach four or five pounds. Once again, be forewarned that as the fishing is picking up, the water is on its way down, so the chances of experiencing good summer fishing are less than optimal. Fortunately there's a little creek down below called the Missouri River that makes up for these shortcomings!

THREE FORKS

At the current location of the town the Missouri Fur Company established a facility in 1810 known as Fort Three Forks, but the fort was abandoned before it was totally completed because of repeated attacks by Blackfeet Indians. In 1864 this same area was laid out as a town by missionaries. The abundant water, fertile soil and relatively moderate weather conditions made this a logical townsite and, as others agreed and settled nearby, the town officially got its start in 1908.

This community of 1,300 residents nestles in the heart of the Gallatin Valley, surrounded on three sides by mountain ranges. Three Forks is essentially a farm-support town with limited light industry supplemented by a tourist influence during the summer. Local attractions include the Headwaters Heritage Museum on Main Street which displays replicas of 1890's living and working quarters and the Headwaters Public Golf Course which features a driving range and new clubhouse. A paved airstrip nearby accommodates small aircraft.

Three Forks is a focal point from which several interesting side-trips can be taken. Ghost towns are within short driving distance at both Elkhorn and Pony. Very nearby is the Madison Buffalo Jump State Monument, a site of 620 acres 7 miles south of Logan off Highway I-90. The area depicts how Native

Americans, for hundreds of years, killed buffalo by stampeding them over cliffs to fall to their deaths below. Picnic facilities are provided here. Five miles to the east of town the Missouri Headwaters State Park provides interesting plaque displays of the early history in this region of Indians and fur traders. From here you'll see the convergence of the Jefferson, Madison and Gallatin Rivers which forms the genesis of the Missouri River.

Of greatest interest to many visitors in the Three Forks area is the Lewis and Clark Caverns State Park, twenty-two miles southwest of town on Highway 10. Located in the northern foothills of the Tobacco Root Mountains, this is the largest limestone cavern in the northwest region of the country. As the Lewis and Clark Expedition proceeded along the Jefferson River it was unaware the caverns existed, but in 1908 President Theodore Roosevelt honored the explorers by using their names when dedicating the site as a national monument. It was in 1890, eighty-five years after the Lewis and Clark Expedition, that local ranchers happened across the caverns and shortly thereafter informal tours were initiated. In 1937 the area was deeded to Montana and then established as a state park. Today a staff of tour guides is on hand from May through September to conduct visitors through the caverns. The total time required is approximately two hours and anyone taking the tour should be prepared for a fifty degree temperature as well as areas where the cavern floor might be slippery. On the 2,800 acre site above the caverns visitors can enjoy the visitor center, utilize the picnic area, engage in a self-guided tour of the surrounding area and even find a place to camp overnight!

Three Forks Chamber of Commerce: Box 1103, Three Forks, Montana 59752

Lewis and Clark Caverns: Box 648, Whitehall, Montana 59759

TOWNSEND

The community of Townsend rests along the banks of the Missouri River a stone's throw from Canyon Ferry Lake in, appropriately enough, Broadwater County. It serves as a center for the fishing activity in the area as well as a support community for the region's agricultural industry. Founded in 1883, the town is now home to approximately 1,500 people.

In 1864 gold was discovered in the mountains to the east. History relates that at one location on the Missouri, a sand bar called the Montana Bar, seven hundred pounds of gold were recovered on one claim in one day; much more followed later the same year. The days of the bonanza are over and Townsend's stability now depends on farming and tourism. Visitors to town can take advantage of displays at the Broadwater County Museum, enjoy swimming at Swimming Pool Park or play a round of golf at the local nine-hole, sand-green course.

HELENA

The "Queen City of the Rockies" lies on land that slopes gently toward the north from Mount Helena. The peak of this mountain is at an elevation of 5,468 feet while the city of Helena is listed at 4,157 feet. Helena's elevation would depend on what particular spot the measurement was taken, however, as there is probably a hundred foot difference between the high side and the low side of town. A view from the city looking north toward the Helena Valley shows rolling, grassy hills, flecked with sage and small evergreens, backed by the distant Big Belt Mountains. Helena is surrounded on three sides by National Forest and in bygone years the hills and gulches of this area of Montana were teeming with prospectors and miners searching for the elusive placer gold and gold ore that made millionaires of a few of the more tenacious or more fortuitous.

Western Montana is replete with accounts of its colorful history, from the days of the Indians to fur trading, mining, the railroads, and agricultural settlement. Helena, although a relatively large, cosmopolitan community, fosters a strong historical curiosity and preservation. In the downtown area of the city you'll find a street named Last Chance Gulch with its pedestrian-only extension, the Last Chance Mall. It was here in 1864 that four prospectors called the "Georgians" discovered the gold that caused an immediate rush of other hopefuls to the spot that would eventually become the political and governmental center of the state. By 1865 the village had a newspaper and by 1866 more than 150 retail stores were open to the public and a sawmill had been put into operation by a leading citizen, Anton Holter. In 1881 the railroad arrived and the town was incorporated. Soon thereafter in 1894 Helena, although it had served as the territorial capital since 1875, was dedicated as the capital of the nation's fourth largest state.

Interestingly, the city wasn't named after any physical, personal or historical entity within the state, but rather after the Minnesota hometown of an early city leader. He may have been one of the city's estimated fifty millionaires that made Helena the county's richest per capita city. With a current population of nearly 26,000 people, the city now also serves as seat of the Lewis and Clark County government. With such a concentration of government offices located here, it follows that the highest percentage of employment is dedicated to government service.

In a city so devoted to historical preservation, the visitor has a wide selection of sights to see within the immediate community. As noted, Last Chance Gulch was the original mining district of town. Homes and business structures were made of wood and very susceptible to uncontrollable conflagrations, which tragically were a common occurrence then. After the fire of 1874 swept through the business district of town, the Helena Fire Tower was constructed and manned twenty-four hours a day to provide early detection of fires and sound the alarm when they occurred. The tower was named the "Guardian of the Gulch" and stands today as one of only four or five such structures in the country. Although now fenced for preservation reasons, the ground at its base offers a good view of the city. A visit to Reeder's Street is interesting in that this block-long area of buildings has been restored and the edifices now are used to house businesses, primarily arts- and crafts-oriented enterprises. Most of the red brick buildings were constructed by a mason named Louie Reeder in the 1880's.

The original Governor's Mansion was privately constructed in 1888, acquired by the state in 1913 and served as residence to nine governors until 1959 when a new residence was put into use. This original house is now one of the properties owned by the Montana Historical Society, has been restored essentially to its original condition, and is open to public tours. Another stop along the tourist trail would be the Montana Historical Society building which houses an extensive historical library, the state archives, a museum and three galleries. The museum features a wide selection of artifacts and relics from Montana's history. The Mackay Gallery of Charles M. Russell art offers a large and broad selection of his works. The Haynes Gallery features the work of frontier photographer F. J. Haynes, while the Poindexter Gallery displays periodically changing exhibits.

During the summer months guided, as well as self-guided, tours take place at the Capitol Building. The original building was dedicated in 1902 and the structure was enlarged in 1912. When approaching Helena from the north, one has the impression that this structure is the tallest building in town. There certainly are no skyscrapers here to detract from the traditional skyline. The sandstone and granite building, with its Greek Renaissance architectural style and dome of Montana copper, can be seen from a long distance. The interior of the building, with its statues and paintings of scenes from the days of mining, frontier cowboys and the relationships between Indian and white man, strongly reflects Montana's history. The most notable work in the capitol is considered to be the huge C. M. Russell mural entitled "Lewis and Clark

Meeting the Flathead Indians at Ross' Hole." Ross Hole is the area around Sula, Montana at the upper reaches of the East Fork of the Bitterroot River.

Another building of interest is the Cathedral of St. Helena, a Gothic-style structure patterned after the Votive Cathedral in Vienna, Austria, which was built in 1913. It features twin spires which reach to a height of 230 feet from ground level, plus beautiful stained glass windows and a marble interior. Other sights to see are the current Governor's Residence, the Pioneer Cabin, Carroll College, the Mansion District and the Historic Cemetery. Much of Helena's flavor can be tasted within easy walking, or short driving, distance and a tour train is available to take a one-hour tour of many of the more prominent points of interest.

Not far out of town, attractions including the ghost town of Marysville, a boat cruise through the limestone formations at the Gates of the Mountains on the Missouri River and Frontier Town may be enjoyed. Frontier Town, a log and rock reproduction of a typical frontier town, is located fifteen miles from Helena at MacDonald Pass on the Continental Divide and features the largest one-piece bar in the world, plus a spectacular seventy-five mile view to distant mountain ranges.

Another good view point is from Mt. Helena City Park, located on the mountain just southwest of town, which, with 620 acres, is one of the country's largest parks. Several trails wind through the park offering hiking possibilities and access to picnic areas. Parking is found at the trail head at the west end of Adams Street. Several other more traditional parks offering swimming, tennis and picnic areas are located throughout town. One next to the Lewis and Clark County Fairgrounds has a kid's fishing pond which is stocked by the Montana Department of Fish, Wildlife and Parks. For golfers, one municipal course is available with eighteen holes, pro shop, club house and driving range.

In addition to the many sights to be enjoyed in the city and surrounding area, special events occur often in Helena including an annual Jazz Festival, weekly band concerts, Community Theater, rodeos, fairs, marathons, triatha-lons and art shows. The knowledgeable chamber here can fill you in on all you wish to know.

Helena Area Chamber of Commerce: 201 E. Lyndale, Helena, Montana 59601 - Phone: 442-4120

Montana Department of Fish, Wildlife and Parks: 1420 E. Sixth Ave., Helena, Montana 59620

Helena National Forest: Drawer 10014, Federal Building, Helena, Montana 59626 - Phone: 449-5201

Travel Montana, Dept. of Commerce: 1424 9th Ave., Helena, Montana 59620 - Phone: 444-2654

Montana Chamber of Commerce: P.O. Box 1730, Helena, Montana 59624 Phone: 442-2405

Montana Historical Society: 225 N. Roberts, Helena, Montana 59620

CASCADE

Throughout the course of a year this little town, in addition to being a farm- and ranch-support community, acts as host to good numbers of anglers who travel to this area to enjoy fishing the Missouri River. When we use the word "little" it is certainly not done so in a demeaning manner. The town happens to be small—four blocks by nine blocks—but still provides the basic amenities such as dining, accommodations, groceries, etc. needed by the tourist.

For relaxation the Atkinson Memorial Park which has tennis courts, swimming pool, playground, picnic and camping facilities is available. The park is named in honor of Cascade cowboy J. Robert Atkinson who achieved national recognition as founder of the Braille Institute of America. Another nationally recognized individual who visited here, was married here in 1896 and held residency here for a short time is famous western artist Charles M. Russell.

To the east of town the visitor can take a scenic drive over the gently rolling hills of the Chestnut Valley to Castner Falls and the Smith River. Eighteen miles to the west of town you can visit the site of St. Peter's Mission, a Jesuit school that was operated by the Ursuline Sisters at the turn of the century.

Cascade rests snugly between Highway I-15 and the Missouri River and there's a fishing access just across the bridge at the lower end of one large island and very near the upper end of another. A very convenient situation!

GREAT FALLS

As members of the Lewis and Clark expedition made their way up the Missouri River in search of its headwaters, their progress was delayed by impassable water falls at what today is the site of Great Falls. Their equipment had to be portaged around the insurmountable cascade for a distance of eighteen miles, over a twenty-five-day period. Travelers in this time and place encountered the vast herds of buffalo so predominant on the plains east of the Rocky Mountains; in the Great Falls region the countryside was spotted with thousands of these impressive animals. Their only adversaries were the Blackfeet and Gros Ventre Indians who hunted here. So it was in the year 1805!

Local recorded history started in the mid-1800's with the establishment of a fur trading post at Fort Benton, forty miles north of Great Falls, followed by the building of Fort Shaw on the Sun River. These military establishments were placed in the region to protect the transportation routes used by miners and settlers who had begun to move into the area. During the 1870's farming and ranching began in earnest; the Great Northern Railroad came to Great Falls in 1887; and during the 1890's Cascade County was a leader in coal production, much of which was used in regional ore smelters.

The city of Great Falls came into being primarily because of the vision, foresight and talents of an engineer from Maine named Paris Gibson. He perceived the potential of the energy that could be derived from the Missouri River as well as the potential for growing crops in the fertile land nearby. He surveyed the townsite, laid out the street grid, inspired investors to initiate development, gave a name to the new community and became its first mayor when the city was incorporated in 1888. This was indeed an efficacious individual!

Great Falls has been nicknamed the "Electric City" because of the five hydroelectric dams constructed on the Missouri River. These dams and the several falls can be seen northeast of town. With a metropolitan population of approximately 81,000 residents, and as the seat of Cascade County, Great Falls prospers from the influence of farming and ranching and from the presence of the military. The city acts as the financial and transportation focal point for several surrounding counties in the "Golden Triangle" of grain producers. Agriculture is considered the backbone of the city's economy. Great Falls is the state's largest flour miller, has more farm implement dealers and grain elevators than any other Montana city and transports very substantial quantities of wheat and barley grown nearby. The military significantly affects the economy not only with the salaries paid to the 4,000-plus staff of Malmstrom Air Force Base but with the goods and services the base consumes. This defense complex is the control center of the country's first Strategic Air Command Minuteman Missile Wing.

In addition to the agricultural and military influences on the community, tourism also plays a role. The city is a resting point and attraction center for vacationers traveling to the recreation area of western Montana and is the major city en route to Glacier Park from the east. Fishermen also base here because of the convenient access to Missouri and Smith River fishing. Visitors have several interesting activities to choose from while in Great Falls, not the least of which is the opportunity to play golf on two separate courses, swim at four pools or play tennis on several courts throughout the metropolitan area. Several parks with gardens, ponds and picnic areas grace the city. A particularly interesting park is Giant Springs Heritage State Park where, in view of adjacent playgrounds and picnic area, cold water pushes from the earth at over 300,000 gallons per hour. The water is utilized by the State Fish Hatchery here where visitors can enjoy stopping at the visitor center. Southwest of town, you can visit the Ulm Pishkun State Monument. ("Pishkun" is an Indian word meaning "buffalo jump".)

From an historical/artistic perspective, three points of interest stand out. The C. M. Russell Museum Complex is the most well known. Included here in a contemporary, 15,000-square-foot museum is an extensive collection of this famous artist's work as well as that of several of his contemporaries. The log studio and the home in which Mr. Russell worked and lived throughout most of his incredibly productive career is included in the complex. His activities in this region began when, at age sixteen, he worked as a cowboy near the town of Cascade. In 1892 when he was twenty-eight he moved to Great Falls and started his life as the cowboy artist, producing thousands of oil paintings, watercolors, sketches and bronze sculptures. Another museum of particular interest is the Montana Cowboy Museum, opened in 1941. This attraction is housed in a log cabin building and features exhibits of guns, saddles, Indian artifacts, branding irons and a variety of other items out of the western past. The third museum of note, the Cascade County Historical Society Museum, is located in Paris Gibson Square where you'll also find the Center for Contemporary Arts.

Many special events occur throughout the year including performances by the Great Falls Symphony and Choir; the week-long State Fair in late July which showcases a variety of entertainment including a carnival and rodeos; a fall "Art in the Park" event; the Children's Pet and Doll Parade in July; theater group performances; and the nationally-known C. M. Russell Auction of Original Western Art, a twenty year tradition, and the largest such auction in the country. Information on these and other local happenings can be obtained from the Chamber office.

Great Falls Area Chamber of Commerce: 926 Central Ave., P.O. Box 2127, Great Falls, Montana 59403 - Phone: 761-4434

Montana Fish and Game Department: R. R. 4041, Great Falls, Montana 59405

Lewis & Clark National Forest: P.O. Box 871, Great Falls, Montana 59403 Phone: 727-0901

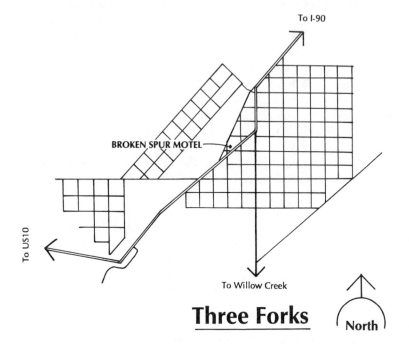

To I-90

BROKEN SPUR MOTEL

To US10

To Willow Creek

Three Forks

North

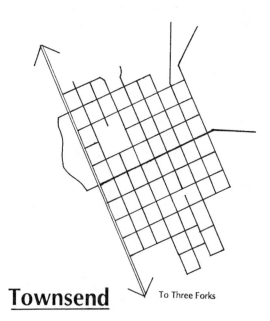

Townsend

To Three Forks

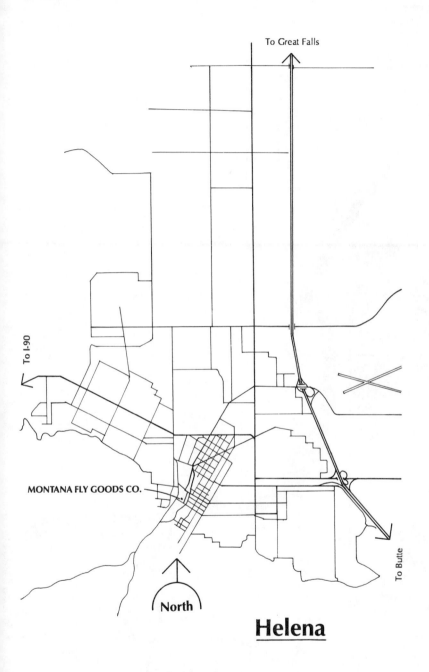

To Great Falls

To I-90

MONTANA FLY GOODS CO.

To Butte

North

Helena

To Lewistown

North

FLY FISHER'S RETREAT

Great Falls

© Stream Stalker, Inc. 1988

To Conrad

To Helena

THREE FORKS

CAMPGROUNDS

THREE FORKS KOA
Highway 287, off I-90 at exit 274, Box 15, KOA Road   285-3611

Countryside campground, with panoramic views of the Missouri River headwaters and surrounding mountains. World famed fishing on the fabulous Jefferson, Gallatin and Madison Rivers, within five minutes of the campground. Lewis and Clark Caves, Headwaters State Park and State Buffalo Jump just 20 minutes away.

GUIDES / OUTFITTERS

THE CANOEING HOUSE AND BLUE RIBBON GUIDE SERVICE
Highway 2, 6 miles southwest of Three Forks on the Jefferson River, R.R. I, Box 192 285-3488

FISHING AND FLOATING SERVICE. 1. Guide service for western rainbow and brown trout on the internationally famous rivers of Montana: The Jefferson, Madison, Big Hole, Yellowstone, Gallatin and Missouri. We float these rivers in McKenzie type river boats. 2. Canoe rental and shuttle service for day trips or canoe camping, 2 to 7 days. Groups welcome. (Canoe rental and shuttle, $20.00). 3. Shuttle service and private boat landing on the Jefferson River at The Canoeing House.

MOTELS

BROKEN SPUR MOTEL
Rt. 2 and Elm, Box 1009   285-3237

A new motel with old fashioned hospitality. AAA rated, gift shop, free continental breakfast, two queen sized beds in each room. A true home-away-from-home in a friendly western atmosphere.

TOWNSEND

CAMPGROUNDS

SILO'S CAMPGROUND
7 miles north of Townsend on Hwy. 287, 81 Silo's Rd.   266-3100

Drive in or fly in to Silo's. Complete RV camping facilities, store, tackle, RV dump. Access to Canyon Ferry Lake. 3200' landing strip for air access. Open all year. Homesites available for sale.

HELENA

FISHING SHOPS

MONTANA FLY GOODS CO.
330 N. Jackson   442-2630

Enjoy Montana's finest dry fly fishing on the Missouri River with one of our experienced guides. We specialize in personal service and custom flies, ties in our spacious, comprehensively stocked fly shop, located in historic downtown Helena.

GREAT FALLS

FISHING SHOPS

FLY FISHER'S RETREAT
825 8thAve.   453-9192

As the name implies, this shop is the "watering hole" for central Montana fly fishermen. It has everything you need in the way of equipment, fly tying materials and guide services. It also includes a comfortable corner where fishermen can drink coffee and swap stories.

MUSSELSHELL RIVER
Map Reference 35

The Musselshell heads at the very eastern edge of the Montana Rockies. Dropping from the Little Belt and Castle Mountains, the river flows east, parallel to and north of the Yellowstone River. After about 120 miles it takes an abrupt turn north and travels another 60 miles before entering the southernmost point of Fort Peck Reservoir. The twenty-five miles between the confluence of the north and south forks and the community of Harlowton have the most interest to the trout fisherman. A population of trout does exist below Harlowton, but the water temperature here starts to rise and severe dewatering for irrigation takes place, making this area less desirable than the upstream waters. From Martinsdale to Harlowton the trout population is predominantly browns with minor numbers of rainbows, brooks and, of course, the ubiquitous whitefish. From Harlowton downstream small mouth bass become prevalent; even farther downstream catfish and sauger are caught.

Your standard fly selection will work fine here, as will small Mepps and Panther Martins. This is good hopper water in August. One particular insect in abundance is the mosquito, so be sure to have repellent handy when fishing. Access to most of this water is available only through private property, so be sure to gain permission before entering private land.

RED ROCK LAKES

Map Reference 36

As you turn west from Highway 20 just south of Henry's Lake in Idaho, the gravel road winds considerably as it rises through patches of evergreen, aspen and willow to peak out at an elevation of 7,100 feet atop Red Rocks Pass. The road at this point enters Montana and continues west through the Centennial Valley which is one of the state's last undeveloped valleys. The valley derives its name from the fact that its first settlers brought in cattle and started ranching operations in 1876, just one hundred years after the Revolutionary War. From the pass the road drops into what the settlers would call a "hole," a barren expanse of grass, sage, hay meadows and thousands of cattle. The road follows Red Rock Creek for a short distance before entering the Red Rock Lakes National Wildlife Refuge, an area of forty thousand acres which was established in 1935 to protect the seriously diminishing numbers of trumpeter swans. During the early 1900's this beautiful bird had been reduced to nesting only in Alaska, Canada and the tiny tri-state area where Idaho, Montana and Wyoming meet. At that time fewer than one hundred swans were in this area. Today the population wintering here reaches up to 1,500 birds. The refuge is basically a wetland, with fourteen thousand acres of lakes and marsh connected by small waterways, creeks and channels winding through the marsh grass. To assist visitors to the area, the U. S. Fish and Wildlife Service maintains their headquarters office at Lakeview.

Activities for visitors to the refuge are controlled to assure the well being and survival of the swans and other waterfowl that nest and reside here. The season for fishing, canoeing, photography, etc. is relatively short—usually commencing in mid-June and continuing through September. Before entering the refuge, you should check with the office to familiarize yourself with the rules governing canoeing and fishing. Be sure to take your camera as you might have the opportunity to photograph not only the waterfowl, but eagles, sandhill cranes, moose, elk and antelope as well. Also be prepared to apply insect repellent, particularly during July and August, as mosquitoes come out in substantial numbers.

The lakes and ponds in this area were very well known in the 1930's and 1940's as producers of very large brook trout in tremendous numbers. To relieve the "pressure" of such a spectacular population, the limit on brook trout was set at one hundred fish per day. To further relieve this over-abundance of fish concentrated in one area, officials broke a dam to allow the fish to spread throughout the valley. That was the beginning of the end for that marvelous population of brookies that averaged five to six pounds. There are, however, remnants of that ancestral population that reside in some of the ponds and contemporary anglers can still enjoy to some extent the angling pleasures that once existed.

There are a significant number of creeks and ponds to choose from in this valley and we'll touch on each of them here in alphabetical order. To avoid some redundancy in the individual descriptions, the following general characteristics of the area are made. The ponds are very clear, mostly spring fed and hold good populations of trout. They are also quite weedy and require some care not only in the presentation of flies and lures, but also in the playing of fish. The ponds are well suited to float tubing and their waters contain good numbers of scuds and damselfly nymphs. This area provides a good opportunity to catch Arctic Grayling.

CULVER POND (Widow's Pool)—This shallow, spring-fed, thirty acre pond is 3/4 mile long and lies at the very eastern boundary of the refuge. It contains rainbow, cutthroat and grayling, but is best known for its large brook trout, some to five pounds.

ELK CREEK (Elk Springs Creek, Shitepoke Creek)—This stream heads at the outlet of Elk Lake, flows for about five miles and ends at Swan Lake. The upper mile, which lies along the road, offers some beaver pond fishing.

ELK LAKE—Located outside the refuge, but brushing its northeast corner, this 230 acre lake is home to grayling and cutthroat averaging thirteen to sixteen inches and lake trout to twenty-four inches. The water off the steep shoreline at the south end is preferred by trollers, while the more shallow north end appeals more to fly fishermen.

HELLROARING CREEK—This small tributary to Red Rock Creek is fished lightly for small brook trout and cutthroat.

HIDDEN LAKE—This lake is situated outside the refuge north of Elk Lake, south of Cliff Lake and is a good rainbow fishery.

LOWER RED ROCK LAKE—This lake, with a surface area of 1,100 acres, is not open to fishing. It is very marshy and very shallow and is strictly for the birds—the watching of which is excellent!

MACDONALD'S POOL (Buck Pond)—This spring-fed pond is only seven acres in size. Water is also supplied by Elk Creek and the average fish here is a respectable fourteen to eighteen inches and there is the occasional rainbow to five pounds.

O'DELL CREEK—This small stream contains small brooks, cutthroat and grayling and flows from the south into the refuge and eventually into Lower Red Rock Lake.

RED ROCK CREEK—Another small stream that flows through the upper end of Centennial Valley and into Upper Red Rock Lake, it is a nursery stream for spawning grayling. Fishermen can also hook small brook trout and a few small cutthroat .

SWAN LAKE—The smallest of the three "lakes" on the refuge, it is closed to fishing, but provides a wonderful source for bird-watching and photography!

TOM CREEK—This small stream enters Upper Red Rock Lake from the southeast and is not considered to be an outstanding fishery, but it does contain small brook trout.

UPPER RED ROCK LAKE—This is the largest body of water on the refuge at 2,200 acres and is closed to fishing.

WIDGEON POND—Located between Culver and MacDonald Ponds, it contains primarily cutthroats, grayling and a few brook trout.

Lake Notes

RED ROCK RIVER

Map Reference 37

If you traced the headwaters of Red Rock River to its source you'd find yourself near 7,100 foot Red Rock Pass on the Idaho/Montana border just west of Henry's Lake. The small stream here flows west paralleling the Centennial Range and the Continental Divide and passes through lakes and swamps in the Red Rock Lakes National Wildlife Refuge. Near the village of Monida the river enters the warm waters of Lima Reservoir before bending toward the northwest to feed into Clark Canyon Reservoir, nearly forty miles downstream. The river is warm and in short supply as it leaves Lima Reservoir and then passes beneath the red cliffs which prompted its name. Spring waters seep into the river eventually and the fifteen mile stretch of river above Clark Canyon is considered very respectable trout water. It rarely runs clear because of irrigation returns, but the resident browns, rainbows, whitefish and cutthroat seem to have adequately adjusted to it. Most of the fish here average between ten and fifteen inches, but in the fall fish over five pounds leave the reservoir to seek agreeable spawning gravel in Red Rock.

The river in these lower reaches is relatively small, but the channel is deep and the banks are dense with willows and grass. The combination of depth, width and speed have made float tubing an accepted method of fishing here. The stream's characteristics, dense banks, deep holes, uniform speed and a moss-covered bottom, are very similar to the Beaverhead below the reservoir, but on a smaller scale.

This lower, most productive, section of river pushes through large ranches where public access is essentially non-existent, so permission must be requested before entering private lands. When you do reach the river you'll find the surface insects consist primarily of caddis, with less numerous small mayflies such as light olive Pale Morning Duns, and occasional hatches of small yellow stoneflies. Wet patterns will prove the most consistently effective here with Woolly Buggers, Zonkers and Muddlers used extensively.

Spin fishermen might want to leave their gold and brass bladed spinners in the tackle box while trying Thomas, Mepps and Panther Martins in bright colors such as red and white, and green and black with yellow dots.

ROCK CREEK

Map Reference 38

Certainly no river can be all things to all people, but if a hundred trout fishermen were asked to describe the trout stream of their choice, including water quality, insect and fish populations, riparian environment, access and any other attributes they felt important, ninety-five returns would probably portray a river describing Rock Creek. The other five would have been completed by anglers who have never had occasion to fish in the Rockies! This tributary to the Clark Fork is ideal. Much of its watercourse pushes through national forest land, so access is generally good. Irrigation problems do not exist here, special regulations have been instituted to protect and improve the fishery and throughout the fifty miles of river from its headwaters to its mouth at the Clark Fork east of Missoula, it is a free-flowing stream.

The river heads at the base of the Sapphire Mountains west of Georgetown, at the confluence of the East and West Fork. The upper reaches flow through open countryside, mostly on private property, on a fairly calm course characterized by smooth runs, gentle riffles and some pocket water. The trout in the upper section are primarily cutthroat with an occasional brook trout. As would be expected most of the fish run small, averaging about ten inches. This section extends down to the area where Big Hogback Creek enters the river from the east. From this point downstream to below Harry's Flat Campground the river takes on a different character. It picks up speed and becomes much more riffle and much less pool. Holding water is less recognizable and, where found, it's more difficult to fish with proper line control. The fish population here is predominantly rainbow, about sixty percent of the total, and they average about fourteen inches in length. Protective regulations here have caused the comeback of the cutthroat, and they now comprise about twenty-five percent of the population.

The lower river, from Harry's Flat to the Clark Fork, contains a good deal more riffle/pool water, pocket water around rocks, downed timber and deep holes on bends. This is the type of water preferred by brown trout, and they dominate here with estimates to eighty percent of the total population. These fish will average between fourteen and eighteen inches, with larger fish from the Clark Fork making temporary residence during the fall spawning period. The minor numbers of rainbow in these lower reaches will range between twelve and fifteen inches. The river does contain bull trout averaging between

Rock Creek

one and three pounds, which are normally caught on spoons.

To the good fortune of the fishery, regulations permit fishing with flies and lures only, except that kids are allowed to use bait. This policy of quality fishing was instituted a few years back to revive a seriously depleted population of trout, and evidence of its success is demonstrated each summer as increasingly large numbers of anglers enjoy the river and the several camping facilities located along its banks. A variety of regulations are in effect here, including catch-and-release restrictions, so the rule book should be read before starting out to fish.

Rock Creek is one of the coldest rivers in the region and is also one of the slickest to wade. Felt soles are the minimum protection you want on the bottom of your waders, and cleats would give you an even greater feeling of security. Some fishermen also prefer to use a wading staff. There are several cable crossings located along the river for use by those wishing to cross in the heavy water.

Run-off occurs here normally between the first part of May and the latter part of June. In the middle of this high water period the salmonflies make their annual emergence on the lower river and are active for about three weeks. It's a time of year when fishermen can experience great angling by driving the gravel road that follows the river and stopping to fish when the insects are located in the air above the water. Fishing in advance of, or just behind the emergence of these creatures, can also be effective with both nymphs and dries using the standard Pteronarcys imitations. A local favorite is the Fluttering Salmonfly in a #4.

During late June both the Golden Stones and caddis begin coming off the water. Elk Hair Caddis in #14 and #16 is standard fare here and the Fluttering Golden Stone is favored in a #6. About mid-August the Spruce Moth emerges and gains the attention of both fish and fishermen. This is another annual event anticipated by local anglers and appreciated by visiting anglers. A #10 Elk Hair Caddis or Bucktail Caddis will do the job here and is most effective when fished between the hours of 9:00 a.m. and 2:00 p.m. Attractor patterns including Royal Wulffs and Goofus Bugs should be part of the angler's fly selection, particularly for those times when fish aren't obviously feeding. Small nymphs can be used to good advantage fished dead drift on a short line through obvious holding water. Stonefly nymphs, Hare's Ear nymphs, Sandy Mites and Prince nymphs work very well here. Caddis will continue to work on into September and hopper patterns thrown into the bank at that time can also result in fast action.

Spin fishermen use #2 Mepps, Colorado Spinners, Thomas Cyclones and Medium Rapalas here, but with the insect life available in this river, a bubble/ fly combination is also worth trying.

Aside from the necessity to match fly patterns to what the trout are taking at any given moment, there is another important factor that comes into play regarding success or failure on this river. It's very important to approach your target zone with some degree of stealth and care. This river receives a good deal of pressure during the summer months from visiting anglers as well as locals and the fish have become instinctively cautious. Long leaders, controlled drift and a covert attitude all help to pay big dividends.

RUBY RIVER

Map Reference 39

The Ruby has been described as a small Beaverhead River and its character justifies the comparison. It twists and bends its way down the Ruby Valley between the Ruby Range to the southeast and the Tobacco Root Mountains to the northeast. Its headwaters originate in the Snowcrest Range about forty miles south of Ruby Reservoir and it flows for sixty-five miles to its junction with the Beaverhead, three miles above the town of Twin Bridges.

This is the neighborhood where gold placer mining in the 1860's and dredge mining at the turn of the century was very big business. Names of nearby communities such as Nevada City and Virginia City are prominent in Montana history and this history is recalled vividly to thousands of people who visit these towns each year. Not far from the community of Laurin (pronounced low-ray) are the remains of a famous road house called the "Robber's Roost," a local hangout for the criminal element that preyed on both miners who had struck gold and the stage line that transported the gold through the valley.

The river has carried several names throughout its history beginning with the Shoshone Indians who called it "Passamari," which denoted the fact that it flowed through a cottonwood bottom. The river was renamed "Philanthropy" by Captain William Clark during his expedition of 1805-1806 in honor of what he considered to be a strong character trait of President Jefferson. During a later period, the river earned the name "Stinkingwater River" after the carcasses of rotting buffalo sullied the water one spring. In more recent times the river was assigned its present name because of the red garnets which are found in the river's bottom gravel.

Much like the Beaverhead, the banks of the Ruby are tightly pressed with thick willows and grass. Branches hang into the stream at every turn, making accurate casting both forward and back a necessity. In spite of the fact that this stream carries the name "river," it is really not much more than a creek, at least by Montana standards. For every mile the crow flies, the river probably meanders two or three miles within its twenty- to thirty-foot wide channel. Wading is normally not a problem at the tail-out of runs and that's good because the angler must cross frequently in order to be in position to cast to the deep side of the bends where the larger fish take refuge. This is not a boulder-strewn river; to the contrary, the bottom consists of stones from one

Ruby River

to four inches in diameter and the moss growth on them is not slippery.

When compared to other rivers in the surrounding vicinity, the Ruby receives relatively light fishing pressure in spite of the fact that it holds good populations of rainbow in the upper river and browns in the lower, mostly in the twelve to fifteen inch size range. The reason for light angling pressure probably is due to the small stream size and the brushy riparian character, as well as to the limited access on both upper and lower sections. Fee fishing is becoming more prevalent here with the result that "permission" is granted on less property. That, coupled with the fact that there is no official state access to the water, has caused access to be available only at bridges and from those ranchers who still grant permission. Four bridges offer access in the lower river.

The water of the Ruby will run cloudy a good deal of the time, but it clears somewhat in the fall. From the fishing point of view, the river is considered an early and late stream. In late May and early June there is a good a caddis hatch that lasts for two to three weeks. It occurs after the run-off has started but before the reservoir fills and the dirty water is released over the spillway. Once the reservoir fills and releases larger quantities of water, the river can be out of commission for several weeks. In August and September it fishes like a spring creek. The constant water flows, constant temperature and some weed growth makes the fishing that much more interesting. After September, the true fall-type fishing commences as resident and migratory browns from as far as the Missouri move into this nursery stream to spawn.

The portion of the river a few miles down from the dam isn't considered to have as good fishing as from Laurin down to the area below Sheridan. Spring water enters the river here, reducing the water temperature and promoting a more favorable ecology. As a matter of fact, there are some spring creeks available to anglers and details on their availability and location can be obtained by inquiring in Sheridan.

Unlike the Beaverhead, the Ruby does not contain a good crane fly population. The main insect here is the caddis which comes off in good quantities throughout the summer, plus a brown mayfly that is imitated well by a #14 March Brown or Ginger Quill. Some small stoneflies come off and are well represented with a Jack's Yellow Sally and in some years the late summer hopper fishing can be good. Favorite nymphs include the Pheasant Tail in a #14, Golden Stone Nymph in size #10, Hare's Ear and Prince in #12 to #16. Muddler Minnows work throughout the year while the larger streamers like Woolly Buggers, Matukas and Zonkers are preferred in the fall. Adams, Elk Hair Caddis and Goddard Caddis in #14 are all old standby dries during summer. To throw all of these flies, you'll need no more than an eight-foot, four-weight fly rod because casts are relatively short. If you normally use a nine footer in a five or six weight, that's fine also. Terminal tackle will consist of a nine foot leader tied to a 3X tippet for wets and 4X to 5X for dries. You will get hung up in the willows on occasion, so plan to lose some flies!

The river below Sheridan is wide enough to float, but it's not like cruising down a tree-lined boulevard; small craft are recommended and canoes are preferred over rafts because protruding sticks and branches are everywhere and can puncture the latter quite easily. Whether floating or wading it's always possible to sight moose and bear as well as blue herons and sandhill cranes. Both of these impressive birds are in the valley in large numbers.

A short distance above the village of Alder you'll see piles of raw talc that has been mined from the nearby Ruby Range to the southwest. The blacktop road zigzags its way out of the valley and up the hillsides to the earth-filled Ruby Dam. The reservoir behind it covers a long, narrow valley of sagebrush, grass and an occasional evergreen. This three-mile long and one-half mile wide impoundment has most likely always had a mud bottom, but through the fifty-plus years of its existence, it has filled in approximately thirty percent from siltation. Discharges for irrigation can draw the reservoir water down to very low levels each year making fishing from a boat impractical because the boat ramps might be thirty feet above the water's surface. When this is the case, the float tube becomes the sensible form of transportation.

The reservoir receives relatively little fishing pressure, with trolling during the spring months providing most of the angling. The predominant catch will be rainbows, but you'll also find small cutthroat, some large browns and a population of suckers that help make the browns grow even larger. If fishing is slow, you can always leave the water and concentrate on the ground where red garnets, some of gemstone quality, can be found in the stream bed as well as in silt deposits surrounding the reservoir.

The upper Ruby River is small and must be considered no more than a creek in anyone's terms. The valley here is bracketed by of the Snowcrest Range to the west and the Gravelly Range to the east, beyond which flows the Madison River twenty miles away. The fish of the upper Ruby consist primarily of rainbows in the ten to thirteen inch range, with the occasional brown and brook trout to add variety. These upper reaches below the forest boundary flow through privately-held lands and permission must be gained before fishing. Several ranchers here have started fee fishing programs that are available to the angling public.

There is one stretch of river below Warm Springs Creek that has recently been opened to the public, and local inquiry with the Forest Service or tackle shops can provide information about it. Due to private property limitations, areas of fee-fishing only, water level fluctuations and water clarity variations, we recommend fishermen make local inquiries here before visiting the river. Sound advice coming from the folks who live and fish here consistently can save a good deal of time and enhance your hours spent on the water.

SHERIDAN

The small town of Sheridan is located on a bench above the Ruby and Beaverhead valleys with views of nearby hills and distant mountains to the west. These same hills were viewed optimistically by gold miners in the 1860's when their hopes for riches didn't materialize in the gold-rich areas of Virginia City and Alder Gulch to the east. Some of these opportunity seekers stopped at Sheridan and established businesses which were to succeed and eventually encourage others to settle here.

Today Sheridan is home to about 1,200 residents who take pride in their community and make visitors feel right at home. It's a town where fishermen can talk fishing at local stores, pick up groceries, do some banking, or take a swim at the Ruby Valley Pool. There is access to the Ruby River from here and campgrounds are available on the road to Branham Lakes east of town.

To Sheridan

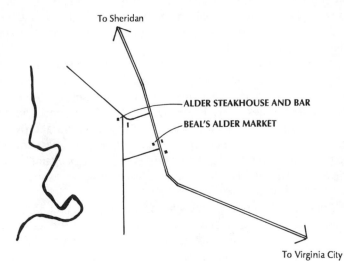

ALDER STEAKHOUSE AND BAR

BEAL'S ALDER MARKET

To Virginia City

Alder

North

To Sheridan

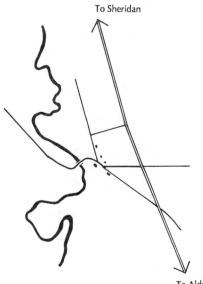

Laurin

To Alder

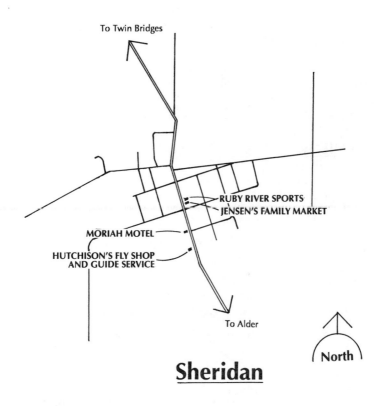

To Twin Bridges

RUBY RIVER SPORTS
JENSEN'S FAMILY MARKET

MORIAH MOTEL

HUTCHISON'S FLY SHOP
AND GUIDE SERVICE

To Alder

North

Sheridan

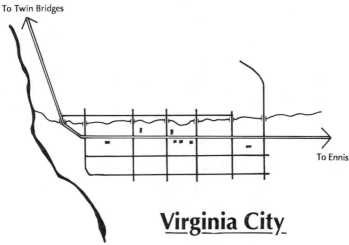

To Twin Bridges

To Ennis

Virginia City

ALDER

RESTAURANT / BAR

ALDER STEAKHOUSE AND BAR
Downtown Alder , Box 33   842-5159

> In the heart of Montana's hunting and fishing paradise, nine miles from historic Virginia City on the Old West Trail. Steaks, chicken, seafood and sandwiches. "Stale beer, cheep whiskey, lousy service - and the best damn steaks in the west." On the rong side of the tracks in Alder.

CONVENIENCE STORE

BEAL'S ALDER MARKET
Downtown Alder, Box 169   842-5679

> Your one and only stop in Alder for your gas, groceries, videos, ice cold beer and pop. Fishing and hunting licenses, supplies and friendly advice available.

SHERIDAN

FISHING SHOPS

HUTCHISON'S FLY SHOP AND GUIDE SERVICE
310 So. Main, P.O. Box 387   842-5868

> Complete fly fishing shop, carrying top of the line equipment. Float the Big Hole, Beaverhead, Jefferson and Madison Rivers. Float tube on mountain lakes, walk in on miles of private water.

RUBY RIVER SPORTS
107 So. Main, P.O. Box 527   842-5461

> For all your fishing and hunting needs, Ruby River Sports and the Pick and Pan Pharmacy, friendliest in the west. Stop in and say "howdy!"

GENERAL STORE

JENSEN'S FAMILY MARKET
115 Main St., P.O. Box 665   842-5821

> A full service general store, including groceries, sporting goods, fishing and hunting licenses; everything you need during your stay. Dennis is available to give good advice on local fishing and hunting spots.

MOTELS

MORIAH MOTEL
220 So. Main, Box 667   842-5491

> A new 7 unit motel in the heart of Sheridan. Each room has two queen-size Beauty Rest beds. Color cable TV and complimentary coffee. Within walking distance of restaurants and other shops in town.

SHIELDS RIVER

No Map

In addition to the Yellowstone River and the nearby spring creeks, the area close to Livingston offers one other stream fishing possibility in the Shields River. This stream isn't highly touted and for good reason, but it does provide another angling option, particularly in spring and fall.

The Shields heads in the Crazy Mountains north of Livingston and winds for about fifty miles to its mouth on the Yellowstone a few miles east of town. The upper reaches are typical of a mountain stream that produces small cutthroat trout; the lower three-quarters of the river plows through ranch land and that's where it begins to deteriorate as a trout stream. Erosion and siltation take their toll here with turbulent, bank-consuming flows during run-off, followed by significant irrigation draw-downs and thermal pollution during the summer. These extremes and their attendant impact on the stream bed, riparian environment and insect population create a rather harsh neighborhood in which the trout might set up housekeeping! The timber along the upper river was clear-cut in the 1950's causing changes in the hydrology of the river. Add to this the fact that this is fairly arid countryside and you can visualize the problem.

The river channel maintains a twenty- to forty-foot width throughout its lower reaches which makes it too small to float, but it's well suited to wading. The river holds a resident population of browns and the fall months see a migration of spawning fish from the Yellowstone. The river does channelize in places and the bank erosion has caused a fair number of trees to fall creating snags greatly appreciated by the browns and rainbows, but not particularly revered by fishermen; the numerous whitefish seem to display no preference. The sedimentation that has accumulated on the river bottom isn't aesthetically pleasing nor does it encourage proliferation of insect species, but caddis are available in quantity and sculpin are here to provide nourishment for the larger trout.

Fly assortments on the Shields can remain fairly simple with adult caddis imitations and attractor dries for use on the surface and caddis nymphs, attractor nymphs, sculpin imitations and Woolly Buggers to be used down near the cobbles.

As previously stated, the Shields wouldn't be rated high on any angler's hit parade, but it is a trout stream that can be easily fished and is available if another option is desired.

SMITH RIVER

Map References 40, 41

Montana is blessed with an abundance of rivers which are rewarding not only from a fishing point of view, but also because of the scenic rewards they offer. For the fisherman who wishes to enjoy an extra slice of cheddar on his angling apple pie, he could hardly ignore an opportunity to fish the Smith River. This tasty stream can be a special treat on one's piscatorial menu and is worthy of thoughtful consideration, but probably not by everyone. This is not a river where you merely pull up and park because, once you do park, you won't see your car again for the next three to seven days. That's the period of time you'll be floating, fishing, camping and relaxing as you work your way sixty miles downstream to the take-out point. Usually one can tailor his float to last from a few hours to a full day; in contrast to that option, the Smith float is one requiring a fair amount of preparation and a definite commitment of time. To experience what this river has to offer you'll have to approach it with considerably more than your fly rod and a candy bar! Once the boat clears the bank and the oars bite the current you'll forego the convenience of civilization to replace it with the caress of near wilderness.

After gathering water from the Castle Mountains and Little Belt Mountains about midway between Bozeman and Great Falls, the South and North Forks of the Smith blend to one channel to form the main river just west of White Sulphur Springs. From this beginning it gathers at least fifteen tributaries on a push to its mouth at the Missouri River near the community of Ulm. The river forms in a meadow environment, slices through a rugged, limestone, canyon section and then pushes once again through a meadow setting during the end of its journey.

Most float trips originate at the Camp Baker fishing access site near the river's confluence with Sheep Creek. Throughout the sixty-plus mile trip to the take-out at the Eden Bridge boat camps have been established along the river by the Forest Service. The first camp is at mile six and the distant, second camp is at mile eighteen, so it's judicious to get a fairly early start on the first day. This suggestion gains vital importance when one realizes that on weekends in June and July the river can sometimes see nearly one hundred launches in an hour. Most of these boats are occupied by pleasure boaters rather than fishermen, but they need a place to rest their heads at night just as much as the anglers do! With this volume of traffic it's easy to imagine an imminent congestion problem. Once into the middle reaches of the river, however, a number of camping sites exist to relieve the overflow situation. The last camp is twelve miles from take out. A volunteer registration system is in effect at Camp Baker, a review of which will give you a good idea of how many boats are on the river on a given day.

At approximately mile six the canyon features start to become evident and by mile twelve you're deep into the canyon itself. At this point you hope you haven't forgotten any important items of equipment. Rain gear, first-aid items, food, sleeping and cooking gear, propane stove and drinking water are essential. Don't forget warm clothing as it's been known to snow here in July. Some areas in this canyon are reminiscent of the Grand Canyon. In addition to the beautiful mixture of rock, grassy clearings and evergreen, you can expect to see some resident wildlife, including deer, raccoons, otter, elk, muskrat, coyote and, in the lower reaches, rattlesnakes. You'll undoubtedly spend two days in the canyon before its ramparts give way to the flatter terrain just a few miles upstream from the take-out.

Under normal, summer water conditions the Smith presents very few problems to the floater who has some experience at the oars. In the interest of safety and passenger well-being, we do offer the following thoughts about which to be mindful before put-in as well as during the float:

1. If you're floating in an inflatable raft (the most popular craft) instead of a canoe (the next most popular craft), be sure to carry a pump and repair kit as some of the shallow riffles have sharp rocks that can bite your boat bottom. There are also spots where barbed wire fencing has been strung across the river to control cattle.

2. For the sake of protecting your gear, make sure it's securely tied to your boat.

3. Under low-water conditions, it may be necessary to pull the boat over the thinly-watered, gravel bars. Also under these conditions, usually late July to late August, don't overload the boat with more than essential equipment.

4. Allow a half day to complete the car shuttle arrangements between Eden Bridge and Camp Baker.

5. If you've not floated the Smith before, it might be sensible to float it at least once with someone familiar with its disposition.

6. Bring plenty of spare tackle because the nearest store is too far away.

Smith River   Lynne Pasquale Photo

If Robert Smith could float the river today, he'd be pleased. Robert Smith was U. S. Secretary of the Navy in 1805 under the administration of Thomas Jefferson. During this period, when the Lewis and Clark expedition was naming each new feature they found on the landscape, Smith's name was chosen to identify this beautiful river. With the exception of an occasional development on its banks, the annual summer irrigation draw-downs and a good number of warm bodies in boats floating on its active surface, the river is much as it was in Smith's day. It hasn't been dammed! Three cheers!

Because there are no dams there are no controls and, without restraints, the river flows as nature intended. Run-off occurs in May and extends into the first two weeks of June. These approximate dates do, of course, presuppose the weather patterns of a normal year. The peak of run-off usually takes place the last week in May and any floating which might be done during this period should be done only by experienced boatmen. The river then is muddy and dangerous. Although the very worst rapids on the river would be rated at no greater than a Class III during high water, there's always the potential of being pinned against a rock wall due to strong, eddy currents. The water in April and then again after run-off will be very clear. From mid-June through mid-July the water is at optimum levels for floating; this is also the period when recreation floaters cover the river en masse, particularly on weekends.

The general character of the river is that of long riffle and pool. The Smith is a delight to wade, with bottom cobbles generally the size of your fist. There are, however, some intermittent deep holes. There are also many boulders in the water in several areas but they only act as good holding lies for the trout. This is definitely a river with plenty of fishable water—and plenty of fish.

The irrigation draw-downs begin in late July and continue into late August. The fish have to adjust by moving into deeper pools to search out the oxygenated water; the boatman has to adjust by lightening his load, pulling his boat over gravel bars and, when a choice must be made, selecting the channel with the deepest water. Water temperatures can reach into the low 70's during mid-day under low water conditions, but thankfully there are springs in the river bed that help keep the temperature from rising to dangerous levels. The water quality is good throughout this entire area and only tends to deteriorate some in the last few miles of the trip where the agricultural environment begins; the banks contain more mud there and the river slows.

If you have any question as to the condition of the river, do yourself a favor and make local inquiry of the Montana Department of Fish, Wildlife and Parks, the Forest Service or any local sports shop that conducts guided trips here. Various regulations have been established to protect the fish of the Smith, so be sure to check the current rules if you are unfamiliar with them. Some areas have been assigned reduced bag limits and others have a slot limit to protect spawning-size fish.

The greatest percentage of trout are rainbows and they'll average about fourteen inches in length. Whitefish are numerous and cutthroat and brook trout not so numerous. Browns are in short supply as you first start down the river but they increase in numbers as you proceed downstream. They'll measure a respectable twelve to eighteen inches. It's not unreasonable to expect to hook a twenty incher during the course of a trip.

The fish here come well to nymphs and April isn't too early to use them. The fish at this time are increasing their metabolic rate and are actively looking for food. This is a good time to use large, stonefly nymphs like the Montana Nymph, Bitch Creek, Yuk Bug, etc. Early in June as the run-off water recedes, the salmonflies emerge and if you're at the right place on the right day you might meet them—or you might float right past them—it's a gamble! At any rate, even though the hatch is good, it's easy to miss when floating. With emergence locations changing and moving upstream each day, they could pass you as you sleep. About the middle of June the caddis appear and will continue to do so through August. Near the beginning of July, morning hatches of Tricorythodes will linger over the water to excite the imagination and casting arm of the dry fly fisherman; then in the afternoon he can switch to caddis imitations. July through August is the most active time for dry fly fishing and if the fish won't come to imitator patterns, attractors work very well. Old standbys such as the Royal Wulff, Royal Trude and Humpy will do nicely. As the weather and water warm, the best results will occur in the morning and evening. Starting about mid-July grasshoppers appear and artificials thrown against the bank will be especially effective, particularly on those frequent, breezy afternoons.

One interesting feature here is the presence of flying ants that appear in late August and continue into September. At times the fish will key onto them and the angler should have something in the box that looks close. Late August is also the time when the browns start to color prior to their spawning run. The Smith contains a large population of sculpin and their imitations can be effective throughout the season, but during September and October they become particularly so. The browns will move up through the canyon these months and the normal fall streamer patterns will work. This is the time of year that offers a good opportunity to hook a big fish. Spin fishermen will also enjoy autumn because irrigating no longer takes place and river levels are higher. Small Mepps or Panther Martins along with hammered brass lures can be quite effective. Weather conditions can start to turn nasty toward the end of October, making a float on the river somewhat less than pleasant, so keep an eye on the forecast when planning a trip during the late fall season.

So there you have it, an overview of one of the more unique rivers in Montana. One last point should be mentioned. Much of the planning and most of the labor of this experience can be removed from your responsibility by local outfitters who make these trips professionally. It might be worthwhile to investigate this possibility.

River Notes

STILLWATER RIVER

Map Reference 42

The Stillwater River is not the slow-moving, peaceful river its name implies. It is instead a boisterous, bully of a river. When you consider that there are certain areas that even expert kayakers won't run during spring run-off, you start to get the idea that the name "stillwater" is a misnomer. There really isn't any still water on this river. It's a mover and must be approached accordingly by the angler; a lot of time can be saved by driving the river to find some water you like, then determining the access situation. It <u>can</u> be floated in certain areas, but we don't recommend that the casual tourist/angler even bother. It can be waded in many reaches with a lot less trouble than handling a boat with all the logistical problems involved. The river contains a thriving population of browns and rainbows that average twelve to thirteen inches. There is also a healthy population of whitefish, so be prepared to catch them throughout the river, particularly in the Absarokee area. It isn't unusual to have a thirty-fish day when the angler does a few things properly and the fish are willing to respond enthusiastically.

The Stillwater begins in the high country of the Beartooths and then flows in a northeasterly direction for about seventy miles through national forest land and finally out across the prairie country of the Yellowstone Valley where it meets the Yellowstone River at the town of Columbus. Approximately forty miles upstream from Columbus the road ends and a hiking trail begins at the Woodbine Access. From the headwaters down to this access the water is really too fast for comfortable fishing except at a wide spot in the river called Sioux Charley Lake. This lake is about 3.5 feet deep, covers about 3.5 acres and is 3.5 miles above Woodbine by trail.

Below Woodbine the river continues to be unfishable for about three miles to the Mouat Mine where it then develops a few characteristics of a traditional trout river and is fishable in some places. Within this reach the fish population makes a transition from the brook trout and cutthroat found upstream to rainbow and browns, with the rainbow predominating.

Below the community of Nye the river slows somewhat but the white water doesn't disappear. Downstream from here, between Beehive and Cliff Swallow Access, the kayaking fraternity conducts a race each year which in itself speaks volumes about the ribald character of the river. Downstream from Cliff Swallow the river braids somewhat, becomes a bit wider, a bit slower and has water diverted for irrigation. Irrigation practices on the Stillwater, although evidenced at times by cloudy return water, are not considered a serious threat to the fishery.

From Absarokee down to the Yellowstone the river is broader, easier to wade, has a bottom comprised of smaller cobbles than above, contains deeper holes, more large fish and more bank rip-rap. Guides occasionally float this portion of the river; sometimes even canoes slide through this section. This lower end of the river experiences a good rainbow migration from the Yellowstone River between mid-March and mid-May. There is also a similar, but smaller, run of brown trout in October and November.

Two tributaries of the Stillwater provide some fishing on a limited basis; the West Fork enters at Nye, and the Rosebud enters at Absarokee. The upper West Fork lies in the forest and offers rainbow and brooks averaging about ten inches. A road follows the stream up for about five miles from Nye and, although the water in this lower section flows through private property, you can ask for permission to fish for the ten to sixteen inch bows and browns that are found here. The Rosebud also flows through private ranch land for about three miles above its confluence with the Stillwater. Here again, the fish, mostly browns, will run between ten and sixteen inches and permission will be required to fish.

All techniques of fly fishing are effective on this river at one time or another. Caddis start to come off in May, followed by a salmonfly hatch in the lower river and smaller stoneflies through June and into July. Caddis continue throughout the summer, with grasshoppers providing good response from fish in August and September. The nymph fisherman is at a great advantage here because the holding water is ideal and its speed gives the fish little time to react. Large, floating attractor flies are also effective in the fast water as are smaller dry flies in the slower, slack-water areas. Streamer fishing isn't considered to be as effective here as it is on many other Montana rivers, however, they are used with some success in the lower reaches where the water is more open and contains smaller cobbles and fewer boulders. Try throwing streamers against the bank in the spring and fall for migrating rainbows and browns. The river is quite easily read, with obvious holding water everywhere—riffles, chutes, cushions around boulders, slicks below boulders and deep runs. Take your time and fish the water thoroughly.

The fly fisherman will feel comfortable with a 6 weight rod, and spin fishermen prefer 6-1/2 to 7-1/2 foot rods for 1/4 ounce lures. Favorites include Mepps, Panther Martins, and Thomas Cyclones.

The Stillwater is a good fishery and receives less pressure than more well-known streams because of its distance from the "fishing centers" to the west, and the fact that it's a mover; many fishermen prefer more "friendly" water.

ST. REGIS RIVER

No Map

Years ago the St. Regis River was considered to be a fairly good fishery, but through time this pretty little stream has experienced more than its share of abuse as progress has pushed forward. From its beginnings near Lookout Pass the stream follows I-90 to its termination into the Clark Fork at the town of St. Regis. Highway construction has taken its toll on the stream, but the contractor did mitigate the effects of the work by placing boulders in the river to create trout holding water as well as allowing the river to flow in its original channel wherever possible. In addition, local and state efforts are being made to improve the fishing.

This is an attractive stream, tumbling through an evergreen valley and winding past willow, larch and cottonwood as it flows from west to east for approximately thirty-five miles. The water is very clear and its character is that of riffle, pool and bend. The deep water in the bends is always a promising place in which to hook a fish of larger-than-average size. Pressure is quite heavy because the access is so good.

The stream is stocked with brook and cutthroat which grow to an average length of eight to twelve inches. There are a few rainbows as well as a good number of whitefish. Casts need not be long—the river measures only thirty to forty feet across—and wading is fairly comfortable on the two- to six-inch cobbles. Small Mepps and Panther Martins do the job for spin fishermen; caddis imitations and attractor dries do well for flycasters. Up-to-date information is available in St. Regis.

SUN RIVER

Map References 43, 44

After skirting the eastern boundary of the Bob Marshall Wilderness area, the North and South Forks of the Sun River meet at the Gibson Reservoir to form the headwaters of the Sun. The river then stretches out through both canyon and farm country east of the Flathead National Forest to ultimately empty into the Missouri River approximately seventy-five miles downstream at the city of Great Falls. The two forks are followed by trails and provide fishing for rainbow, brook and cutthroat in the eight to twelve inch category. The reservoir is very deep, about one quarter of a mile wide by five miles long and offers boat fishing for rainbow and brown from twelve to fifteen inches. Camping facilities are available on the lake's north shore. The dam was built in 1913 to create an irrigation reservoir. The water will fluctuate as much as fifty feet as summer water is pulled out for agricultural use after the impoundment has filled through fall, winter and spring.

The river flows for about two miles through a rocky canyon below the dam before meeting the backed-up water of Diversion Reservoir, another irrigation facility. This is a small, attractive body of water, which is about a mile in length and one-eighth mile in width, looks more like a wide spot in the river than a reservoir. This is a nice place to launch a float tube and cast to rainbows and brook trout between eight and fourteen inches. Throughout this canyon and reservoir area the rock formations and nearby forest present a very attractive setting for fishing, camping or just having a picnic. This upper end of the river does experience severe de-watering at times which makes both fishing and floating an exercise in faith unless you first check water levels with the Forest Service office in Augusta. The Diversion Reservoir supplies water to both Pishkun Reservoir and Willow Creek Reservoir via canals, so it's easy to imagine how the river below could feel the effect of these water disbursements.

From the Diversion Dam to the Missouri, the Sun River (also known locally as the North Fork) flows as freely as possible considering the fact that up to a dozen small diversion dams pull water off for irrigation. Just below the dam, at the Lewis and Clark National Forest boundary, a bumpy, dirt road can be taken down the hillside to the river. This is essentially the upper limit of the rugged Sun River Canyon that extends from this point downstream for twenty miles where it terminates near the crossing of Highway 287. The canyon is

Upper Sun River

a beautiful area of sedimentary rock upthrusts and deep pools of clear water, in many places flowing over ledges of solid bedrock. Within the canyon you experience three narrow gorges where, over millions of years, the water has eroded its way through overthrusts of Madison limestone. The westernmost of these three gorges anchors the Gibson Dam. This short distance of geological wonderment is unique in Montana.

Along the highway toward Augusta the countryside shows arid, rolling hills of range grass and erratic boulders which were deposited by ancient glaciers. The vast moraine west of Augusta is strewn with these irregular rocks and the surface of the ground is covered with small fieldstones giving the impression that this fragile land contains only about one inch of topsoil above deep layers of rock and gravel. Views to the west are spectacular with broad vistas of inclined buttes and ridges, with the Sawtooth Range rising in the distance. At the cemetery on the west end of Augusta, the road becomes blacktop and remains so going north, east or south.

The road east, Highway 21, will follow the Sun River to the community of Simms. You're now passing through farming country where wheat and hay are grown in the flat land next to the river, but where the more distant, low-rising hills to each side of the valley appear uncultivated. The river here is forty to fifty feet in width, is characterized by long riffles and long pools and is bordered by cottonwood and willows. Accesses in this area are few, so rancher permission will be necessary to fish on foot. Floating is done here when water levels permit, but watch for sweepers, log jams and diversion dams. This area really isn't fished often; anglers prefer the water between Simms and Sun River, maybe because of better access.

Between these two communities, the village of Fort Shaw not only provides an access point, but offers a bit of historical interest as well. During the 1860's the U. S. Army built Fort Shaw of local timber and stone plus handmade adobe bricks. The fort was established to protect settlers and miners from possible attacks by Indians and was maintained until 1891. An historical marker is located in the community of Fort Shaw and several of the original military buildings can be seen.

Downstream in the area of Vaughn, Muddy Creek enters the Sun causing considerable turbidity and the end of trout fishing. This becomes an area preferred by ling and northern pike, the latter ranging in size to fifteen pounds. The lower river also sees some spawning migration by brown trout in the fall, but even so, most fishing is done above the community of Sun River.

Browns predominate here, with lesser numbers of rainbow and fair numbers of whitefish. Bait fishermen use the meat of resident suckers for bait. The river does produce hatches of salmonflies in limited numbers, as well as some golden stones, caddis and a few mayflies. None of the hatches is spectacular, but fish are certainly taken on flies, even in the turbid water of summer. Attractor dries and nymphs will work as will Marabou Muddlers and Woolly Buggers and, of course, imitator patterns when the naturals are attracting fish.

By now you're most likely feeling somewhat less than enthusiastic about rushing to the Sun to wet a line and, if so, we can more than sympathize with you. This is physically a rather attractive, easily fished river; unfortunately it takes enough environmental abuse to suppress insect and fish populations to the point where you really need an up-to-the-minute status report to make the trip worth the drive. Local anglers do well here at times, and hook a few fish of truly significant proportions, but they essentially live on the river and can time their trips to maximize their efforts. The overall situation ain't pretty, but that's the way it is!

SWAN RIVER

Map Reference 45

Montana Highway 83 allows you to travel through some of the most densely forested and picturesque terrain in Montana from its south terminus at Clearwater Junction on Highway 200 to its northern end at the community of Bigfork. It also keeps you in touch with water and fishing for its entire ninety-one mile length.

After following the Clearwater River upstream past its chain of lakes for thirty-one miles, you reach Summit Lake which divides the Clearwater drainage from that of the Swan River farther north. Every region, it seems, has that one special location at which to take a photo by which to remember the visit and this lake on the west side of the highway, backdropped with dramatic McDonald Peak, is considered a prime spot for that photo. This doesn't imply that the rest of the valley is unworthy to imprint your film, quite to the contrary. Holland Lake, to the east of the highway, is another much photographed area and is a popular trail head into the Bob Marshall Wilderness, known locally as the "Bob." This wilderness area is sixty miles long, contains hundreds of miles of trails, covers an expanse of over one million acres, is home to many high country lakes and most species of major animal life found in Montana.

Across the valley to the west, the smaller Mission Mountain Wilderness extends for approximately 30 miles, is approximately and 7 miles wide and covers 74,000 acres. Again, wild animals and remote lakes in an undisturbed setting attract many visitors here each year. The jagged peaks in both ranges give testimony to the powerful forces of glaciation that ended with a warming process that began ten thousand years ago and took a period of three thousand years to completely melt the glacial ice.

This entire area is covered with a wide variety of coniferous trees that line the highway, stream banks and lake shores. In the fall the contrasting yellow of the many larch trees presents an added element of appeal to the valley environment. This area receives much more moisture than the more arid regions of the state and has been the target of heavy logging activity; clearcuts on mountain sides are also part of the visual impression you receive. Thankfully, it is a small part. As you proceed farther north along Highway 83 you drop into the Swan River drainage.

The Swan originates at Lindbergh Lake, named in honor of airmail pilot and barnstormer Charles A. Lindbergh, who camped here in 1927 after his famous solo flight across the Atlantic Ocean in his monoplane, "Spirit of St. Louis," on May 20 and 21 of that year. The river continues north for sixty miles with but one interruption, at ten mile-long Swan Lake, before emptying into Flathead Lake at Bigfork. Along the way you'll find periodic pull-outs from the road where you can fish, picnic or take photos. Access to the river, which flows parallel to the highway throughout its entire length, is gained primarily from logging roads leading off the highway. The area has numerous campgrounds that serve anglers, canoeists, hikers and tourists.

In its upper reaches, the river is small and not well suited to floating. As it tumbles downstream, the Swan gathers over fifteen small tributaries, adding enough to its volume to improve floating conditions in its middle reaches. The river is spotted throughout with downed timber, log jams and debris-blocked channels and it's wise for floaters to carry a saw to assist occasionally in opening a pathway for the boat. The use of rafts is not recommended in these upper reaches because of the tight quarters and likelihood of puncture. Canoes are the preferred craft and it would be advisable to obtain some local advice as to prevailing river conditions before launching.

As the river approaches Swan Lake it becomes slower and wider, holding more appeal to both floater and angler. If you float immediately above Swan Lake, passing through the Swan River National Wildlife Refuge to the south end of Swan Lake, you'll have to plan to paddle about a mile across the lake to the nearest take-out point.

A popular float-fishing section lies downstream of the lake between the bridges on the east and west edges of Ferndale, a total distance of about seven miles. The river here broadens and finally slows into the water backed up by the Pacific Power and Light Diversion Dam two miles east of Bigfork.

The best times to fish the Swan are before and after the run-off, which traditionally begins by mid-May, peaks about the first week of June and recedes through late June and into early July. Most of the river fish caught will be small cutthroat with rainbows adding some variety. They average from eight to twelve inches, but there's always the opportunity to hook a big Dolly Varden or northern pike and that possibility draws many anglers to this region.

The "run" of bull trout into the river from Swan Lake takes place annually in June. It seems these fish find a particular area of the river they prefer, not necessarily the same each year, and that's where anglers search for them. As is true elsewhere, large spoons and plugs fished near the river bottom are the most effective lures to attract the bull trout.

One last comment regarding the Swan River region is to again state the need to be alert while fishing here because moose, black bear and grizzlies, do frequent this area. They are normally no problem to humans, but that's no reason to be careless and give them cause them to be.

SWAN LAKE

As a temporary resting place for the Swan River, Swan Lake, which is about one mile wide, impounds the watercourse for approximately ten miles. At one time this region was home to the Trumpeter swan which inspired the name of both the lake and river. Today, the only waterfowl in the area are ducks and geese which are found primarily at the lake's southern end in the Swan River National Wildlife Refuge. The 3,900 acres of this lake are surrounded by trees which grow down to the shoreline. There are a few private residences and resorts nestled along its eastern edge; the lake's west side is densely forested to the foot of the Mission Mountains; and the north and south ends are swampy, making this a lake best fished from a boat.

The entire area to the south of the Swan River inlet represents one of the best places to fish on this lake, as is the region immediately off the inlets of Sixmile and Bug Creeks at approximately mid-lake. Swan Lake offers the fisherman a variety of fish species including rainbow, cutthroat, bull trout, pike, kokanee salmon, bass and perch. Most significant of these are the bass to three pounds and the pike and bull trout, both to fifteen pounds. The bull trout are best caught in the spring after ice-out and in the fall prior to freeze up. Trolling is an effective technique for hooking these substantial fish and using large plugs and spoons near the bottom in the shallows seems most productive. During late spring, lures and bait attached to steel leaders are effective for catching pike at the south end of the lake. The perch, rainbow, cutthroat and salmon, small when compared to the large bass, pike and bull trout, are fished for throughout the season.

CONDON

RESORTS

HOLLAND LAKE LODGE
4 miles east of Hwy. 83 at milepost 35.5, 20 miles north of Seeley Lake, Box 2083
754-2282

> Enjoy family fun in the outdoors at our beautiful lodge on the shores of Holland Lake. Open year round. Gourmet dining in the Lake Room. Pack trips into the Bob Marshall or Mission Wilderness. Conference room available. Call for rates.

SERVICES

MONTANA INFORMATION
Box 229   754-2538

> Distributors of visitor information for families planning a trip to Montana. Our brochures are found throughout the state in many, fine business establishments. Call or write for information about our services.

THOMPSON RIVER

Map Reference 46

The Thompson River rates very highly as a truly attractive mountain trout stream. It's width is a comfortable forty to fifty feet. Its upper reaches flow through private lands and its bottom half runs through the Lolo National Forest. From the point five miles east of Thompson Falls where the paved Thompson River Road starts to follow along the river, the countryside is that of a beautiful, wooded valley. The river is riffle/pool in nature with predominantly small rocks on which to wade, but accentuated occasionally with ten-foot boulders that create deep, dark lairs for the larger fish to occupy. Although the evergreens, grass and bushes come right down to the water's edge, casting isn't a problem.

As you drive along the road and follow the river north toward its source at Lower Thompson Lake, along Highway 2 the blacktop changes to gravel at the Copper King Campground four miles up from Highway 200. Other logging roads intersect this road as you travel upstream, but if you stay next to the river you'll have no problem. The distance from Highway 200 to Highway 2 is approximately forty-five miles.

The upper half of the river meanders more through open meadows while the lower half drops through a relatively narrow canyon. No dams impede the natural flow so there is a run-off, but the water remains very clear after the runoff subsides in June. The river is very wadable, but we suggest felt soles be used because the rocks are quite slick. This is a free-flowing stream unaffected by irrigation demands or pollution. A few cabins have been built in the valley, but for the most part you'll find few creatures stirring here except for the occasional moose, big horn sheep and rare, black bear. The latter have caused no particular problems, but they might investigate your food if its left unattended.

The fish consist primarily of rainbows, with some brook trout inhabiting the upper and middle reaches and brown trout and an occasional bull trout in the lower water. Whitefish are taken throughout the river. Most of the fish will range between ten and fourteen inches, with the occasional trout taken to four pounds.

The Thompson is fortunate to experience a very good hatch of salmonflies in late May, which coincides with the high water of runoff, but it is possible late in the hatch to proceed far enough upstream to avoid the really heavy

Thompson River

water. You can fish the edges with both adult and nymphal imitations and find responsive fish. The hatch begins at the river mouth, progresses quite rapidly upstream and lasts for a total of about two weeks.

Summer fishing is done primarily with caddis and mayfly imitations and, as on most Montana streams, attractor patterns are also effective. Elk Hair Caddis, Adams and Royal Wulff are favorites. Local fly fishermen also fish a good deal of the time with large, stonefly nymphs such as Bitch Creeks and Woolly Worms. These flies, of course, continue to be used into fall, along with streamers, to entice the browns on the lower river.

The Thompson requires no more than a five-weight fly rod throughout the season, and spin fishermen can use six-pound test line comfortably. Favorite lures include Mepps, Panther Martin #1 with brass blade and Thomas Cyclone in smaller sizes. Because of the water clarity, fly fishermen will want to use long leaders and fairly fine tippets.

During the summer the evening hours are the most productive for fishing because the days can be very warm. As the cooler temperatures of fall set in, fishing will also be good through the mid-day hours.

YAAK RIVER

Map Reference 28

If this river were situated but a few miles to the west we'd have to consider it for an Idaho angling guide rather than the one you're reading. It joins the Kootenai only 6-1/2 miles from the Idaho state line. The Yaak River is substantially larger than the several smaller tributaries to the Kootenai and, although it too provides fishing for small brook and cutthroat trout, it also carries a population of rainbow plus some bull trout to ten pounds.

The Yaak originates in Montana a few miles south of Canada and flows down a course of approximately sixty miles to its mouth. It is followed for its full length by Route 508 which, at its northern terminus, intersects the roads paralleling Lake Koocanusa to form a loop back to Libby. While following the Yaak should you see road signs indicating you are on Forest Service Road #92, don't be confused; this logging road has carried that designation for many years.

From Highway 2 you'll proceed north on 508 following the Yaak as it flows through a deep, narrow canyon. This is the stretch in which the large bull trout have taken up residence. The problem for the fisherman here is getting to the river as there are no formal access points except at the campground at Highway 2 and again at the Yaak Falls Campground seven miles upstream. Certainly, there are those hardy folks who do hike down to the river, but they are the exception to the rule. Most fishermen who fish the rough water of the canyon prefer to walk upstream or down from the campgrounds. Regardless of your approach to the river, crowds of anglers are not a problem.

Above the falls the water slows, access is more readily available and the fish are smaller in size. Campgrounds are available and the potential to sight big game is quite good; have your camera within reach. At mile thirty you'll arrive at the small village of Yaak, with its store and a few homes. From here the road continues another forty miles to Lake Koocanusa. It's a good paved road and provides a true back-country drive, but don't be caught with your gas gauge on empty.

YELLOWSTONE RIVER

Map References 47, 48

Most certainly if fishermen were asked to name one trout river located in Montana, the Yellowstone would be the one. It is definitely one of the most popular trout streams in the state and one reason for this is that it's the longest river, about seven hundred miles, in the Continental U. S. not restricted in its journey by the presence of even one dam. It's a free-flowing river from its headwaters in the heart of Yellowstone Park in Wyoming to its mouth at the Missouri River barely across the Montana line in North Dakota.

Within Montana, trout fishing is concentrated along the upper 150 miles of the river from Gardiner down to Laurel, with the greatest concentration of anglers between Gardiner and Livingston.

To do justice to this outstanding water, we'll divide the river into three sections. The top section covers the water from Gardiner down to Carbella, a distance of approximately fifteen miles. The middle reach extends from Carbella to the town of Livingston, a distance of about forty miles and the bottom section includes all the water between Livingston and Laurel, another hundred miles. It is obvious from the mileages indicated that we're looking at a piece of water that holds a large number of fish, and indeed it does. Population studies indicate that within these sections known as the "upper" Yellowstone, it has been established that there are as many as 20,000 fish per mile in certain locations; 5,000 trout and 15,000 whitefish. Conditions in this watercourse are well suited to the production of fish because the headwaters pouring out of Yellowstone Park are clear and unpolluted and the tributary streams tumbling from the Absaroka and Gallatin ranges continually add more water of high quality. Although some of these tributaries are affected by irrigation draw-downs, the river itself experiences little adverse effect from them.

The water quality and fish habitat are actually better now than they were fifty years ago. At that time the river was so adversely influenced by mining waste products and municipal effluent discharged directly into the river that some areas couldn't support insect life meaningful enough to provide a complete food chain. Now, with much higher pollution control standards, the river supports abundant food for the fish. The municipalities along the river, particularly Livingston, are acutely aware of the value of the river and the need to do what's necessary to maintain it as a resource to attract fishermen to the area. Historically the railroad has played a major role in the economic health of Livingston, but its recent withdrawal from the community has increased the economic importance of tourism, of which fishing plays a principal part. Maintaining both quality water and quality fishing assures the significance of the river as a very meaningful asset to the entire region.

The Yellowstone is a big river; in places it measures one hundred yards across. In a normal year its flow rate can vary from about 1,500 c.f.s. to as much as 12,000 c.f.s. near Livingston. It's not a predictable river from either a physical or fishing point of view. Winter ice jams and spring run-off often change the channel configurations, create new channels and tear out rip-rap where banks are susceptible to the forces of ice and water. Almost imperceptible changes in the water level can affect the holding lies of the trout. The totally clear water of one day can become totally opaque the next if an intense rain storm takes place in Yellowstone Park and turns the Lamar and Gardner Rivers to flows of muddy fluid. As the water recedes after run-off, fish holding against the bank one day may be forced to move into deeper water the next. This is a river that requires some degree of familiarity in order to plan fishing trips from one day to the next.

The Yellowstone was once the domain of only two primary fish species, the cutthroat trout and the Mountain Whitefish. More recently these species have been augmented to include the brown and rainbow trout plus forage fish such as sculpin, suckers, carp, and a few shad (locally called goldeneye). The whitefish is the most abundant species throughout the river, with strong populations of cutthroat and browns in the upper reaches and a strong population of rainbow from ten miles above to ten miles below Livingston. Cutthroat again make an appearance below Springdale and browns are fairly evenly distributed throughout this section of the river. By the time the river reaches Laurel, it has slowed, warmed and received a strong infusion of turbid water from the Clarks Fork. At this point the Yellowstone changes from a trout fishery to one supporting more warm-water species. As a means of maintaining the high quality trout fishery between Gardiner and Laurel, the state has imposed restrictive regulations on selected stretches, and we recommend that you review the official state regulations before you start fishing.

The Yellowstone is a great river to float and the beauty of it is that boatmen with relatively little experience are able to handle the river at all times except during the weeks of run-off, when fishing isn't worth the ride anyway. Under normal flows, there is only one section of white water on the river and it includes about fifteen miles of water from Gardiner to the bottom end of Yankee Jim Canyon. Yankee Jim Canyon itself extends for approximately four miles and averages forty to eighty feet in width. The water here is fast, the boulders are large, the holes are deep and it should be avoided by float fishermen. The canyon rapids are rated up to Class III so this is an area best fished from the bank.

A variety of boats will be on the river including the popular fourteen- to sixteen-foot McKenzie drift boats, john boats and rafts. We offer one word of advice concerning the use of a raft. Make sure it has a rowing frame because there are areas on the river where you'll want to put some power into the oars to avoid being pulled into a bend or into a pile of standing waves; the frame will allow you to do so. There are numerous boat launching sites along the river and you can plan to be on the water for as little as an hour or as long as a day. Because the river is big, a boat provides the angler the best means to explore and fish during the course of a day a great deal of water that would not otherwise be accessible. This fact is particularly true in the months from May to August when flows are the strongest of the year.

The general impression one gets from just looking at the water from above is that wading here would be a piece of cake. Not so! The current here is quite strong and can contribute to the invention of new dance steps even before the music starts. Wade with care and use your stream cleats if you have them.

The river flows within a single channel for most of its length, but occasional braiding does take place in some areas. It's generally considered good judgment to stay in the main channel when floating because the side channels are sometimes blocked by fallen trees or by small dams constructed by local ranchers to divert water into irrigation headgates.

Because the river receives water from a vast area, not only within Montana, but also in the high country of Yellowstone Park, and because there are no dams to impede its flow, it feels the effect of snow melt earlier and later than most southwestern Montana rivers. During a normal year the river will start to show some turbidity with rising water levels along about the first week of May. Volume increases steadily until mid-June, when it starts to recede and by mid-July the water level and clarity are optimal and the river is quite fishable. The water level continues to drop through the fall months. The very lowest winter levels exist from November through March and during low snow pack years, the water will sometimes clear in June and be fishable during the salmonfly hatch. Regardless of water level, the fisherman may have his best success by throwing streamers and large rubberleg nymphs up close to the bank, followed by a twitch or pull on the line.

At normal levels the river is fairly flat with long riffles and pools predominating, except in the very upper reaches below Gardiner where plenty of white water smashes its way between large boulders. The water from Gardiner to Corwin Springs is quite easy to read with many pockets, rocks and riffles which define logical holding water. Between Corwin Springs and Yankee Jim Canyon the water slows and flattens somewhat and this area is much more floatable.

An interesting geological feature to watch for about midway between

Gardiner and the canyon is the Devil's Slide, a prominent cliff on the west side of the river composed of several layers of vertically tilted sedimentary rock at the base of Cinnabar Mountain. The "slide" layer is a vivid red color composed of Chugwater mudstone, a formation estimated to be 200 million years old.

Access to Yankee Jim Canyon is considerably easier and less expensive than it was in 1872 when "Yankee Jim" George built a road through the canyon and charged a fee to those wishing to use it. The road was on the main route to Yellowstone Park and Jim finally sold the right of way to the Northern Pacific Railroad.

This entire upper area of the river is an ideal one to fish during the salmonfly and caddis fly hatches. Don't expect a lot of big fish here because most of them will be between ten and fourteen inches, but good numbers of fish can be caught. A fish of eighteen or nineteen inches is considered very good and those to five pounds are exceptional.

Below the canyon the water is relatively swift with plenty of obvious holding water. The valley itself remains narrow downstream to the craggy hillsides at Point of Rocks where it then widens and more agriculture becomes evident in the form of hay and cattle. The water from Point of Rocks to the Mill Creek area is slow and flat, with relatively little character and an abundant population of whitefish. Between Mill Creek and Livingston the river picks up speed and has good access, with cutthroat, browns and an increasing number

Yellowstone River

208

of rainbow. From ten miles above, to ten miles below Livingston the rainbow outnumber browns about two to one.

The entire section of river between Yankee Jim Canyon and Livingston is popular not only because of the potential for excellent fishing, but also because the scenery is spectacular. The stretch from Mill Creek to town is probably the most popular on the river and can take from one-half to a full day to float depending on how many stops are made along the way. This area was named Paradise Valley by the early settlers and they had good reason to so name it! The Absaroka Mountains to the east and the low, rolling grass-covered hills of the Gallatin Range to the west provide a truly dramatic backdrop to a float on the river or a drive along the highway.

Although Paradise Valley is now dotted with ranch homes and out-buildings illustrating the emphasis on agriculture, the valley's early history centered around gold mining. Gold ore was first discovered near Emigrant in the 1860's in a gulch in the Absarokas, which the miners named "Yellowstone City." The present-day natural resource is not what was removed from the earth, but rather the earth itself as it acts as host to the trees and rivers and wild game and lakes and hot springs that attract tourists to this area in large numbers.

By no means does float-fishing the Yellowstone terminate at Livingston. You can continue through town and take out at one of several locations downstream. A word of caution here, however; the abutments of the 9th Street bridge in Livingston are a floating hazard and should be looked at carefully prior to the float so you can choose the proper line when you cruise past them. The river both in and below Livingston remains very good fishing water. This was not always true. During the 1960's, the town discharged its municipal waste into the river and the railroad dumped diesel fuel into it; acts which discouraged local anglers from fishing below town. Both of these transgressions have long since been discontinued, so the water now is clear and the fish population is strong. From town down about seven miles to Highway 89, the river braids around islands and offers not only good fishing but somewhat easier wading than elsewhere. You'll find this a good area in which to fish against the banks. At Highway 89 the river makes its turn to the east at what Lewis and Clark termed "the big bend," and it's in this area that the braiding stops and the river broadens.

It's generally thought that the river below Livingston holds more fish in the sixteen to twenty inch range than the water above town. As the river pushes toward Springdale and on down to Big Timber, the river is lined with cottonwood and the floating fishermen will drift past grazing cattle and numerous hay fields in this ranching country between the Crazy Mountains to the north and the Absarokas to the south. The river is about a hundred yards wide here and the runs and pools are very long. At Springdale you'll notice the reappearance of cutthroat trout. The river is one-quarter to one-half mile from the highway in most places, and foot access is not frequent. As you approach Big Timber the mountains are reduced to bald hills and range grass, with the river and the Burlington Northern Railroad tracks sharing the lower levels of the valley. In the area of Big Timber quite a few islands dot the river along with several gravel bars and the number of brown and rainbow here are about equal. Below Big Timber the fishing remains productive with good numbers and size of trout, along with the added advantage of seeing fewer fishermen on the water. This is deep, wide water and certainly best suited to float fishing. As you progress downstream the water warms and a transition takes place in which the river begins its evolution to a warm water fishery. At Laurel, the turbid water of the Clarks Fork of the Yellowstone enters the main river and from this point downstream the river is no longer considered a trout fishery.

The fishing season on the Yellowstone is open year-round, a situation greatly appreciated by local anglers as well as by fishermen who happen to be nearby when the weather of February, March and April is mild enough to allow casting to trout feeding on adult midges. This time of year is eagerly awaited by anglers who live near the river because it can provide some of the best dry fly fishing of the year. The water is at its lowest level and the trout actively rise to these tiny insects as well as the artificials attached to small diameter leader points. Generally the flies tied to represent midge clusters are more effective than imitations of one individual insect. Many days of winter are too cold and/ or too windy to be on the river, so we don't suggest you take a week of your allotted vacation time to catch the hatch, but if you're in the neighborhood, you might want to check it out. In March there will be a few Baetis on the water in addition to midges, so you should have some small Blue Winged Olives in your fly box along with small Adams and small Grey Bivisibles to imitate the midges.

The caddisfly emergences normally commence about the first week of May, but a special caddis hatch usually comes off in the twenty mile stretch south of Livingston sometime in late April. This is a very dense hatch that lasts for about five days and so many insects blanket the water that they can be scooped up by the handful in quiet backwaters. Often the angler is more successful when using a large, #8 or #10 Irresistible because he can differentiate his artificial from the mass of naturals on the surface. Also streamers sometimes work well at this time because the fish are so totally involved in the feeding frenzy that they'll hit anything representing food. Try to be on the water at about 11:00 a.m. and plan to stay into the afternoon.

The salmonflies usually start to emerge from mid to late June during the high water of the run-off period and the hatch will last for two to three weeks after its start near Livingston. A few insects will come off right in town, but the majority of the hatch starts a few miles south of town. The hatch will progress upstream daily and reach Gardiner about mid-July after having remained strong for the entire distance. In a heavy snow year the river could be too high to fish this hatch, so it's a prudent angler who calls a local tackle shop for a status report before making a special trip to fish the river. Finding the strongest concentration of salmonflies on a day-to-day basis is anything but predictable, and again, local shops will have the most up-to-the-minute information. When you do locate the hatch, throw your artificials very close to the bank, whether using a dry in size #4 to #8, or a nymph in size #2 to #6. As the current pulls the fly away from the bank, pick it up and cast again. Delicate terminal tackle is definitely not the order of the day with this type of fishing, so don't feel that a 1X or 0X tippet is too heavy. It isn't! Because the water most likely will be high and fast, be sure to dress the dry flies well to keep them floating as long as possible. Spin fisherman using lures during the salmonfly hatch should also fish the banks and the best results can be expected by using a lure with a black body.

For most of the year caddisflies and sculpin provide the fish with the majority of their diet. Sculpins thrive in the Yellowstone because of the high water quality, which they require to survive. The caddis start hatching about May 1 and they continue throughout the summer, being particularly active during July. As the salmonfly activity recedes, the caddis, along with small golden stoneflies, start to appear and draw the attention of the fish. Evening is the most productive time for using caddis imitations, Golden Stone patterns and Yellow Humpies. Attractor dries will be most effective through July.

As the water continues to drop during late July, the caddis and mayfly hatches diminish somewhat and hopper fishing comes into its own. Hopper imitations work very well throughout August and into September particularly when they're cast up close to the bank. The highest concentration of these terrestrials extends from about Pray downstream to the Springdale vicinity. Patterns tied with body shades of brown, rather than yellow, seem to be most effective, as do those tied with bullet heads rather than with the standard collar hackle. As for mayflies during August, you can expect to see a few Blue Winged Olives and some Sulphur Duns so watch for them even though most surface fishing will be less productive with caddis and attractors. And don't forget the sculpin patterns in your fly box, as they can be effective throughout the summer when thrown up close to the bank and given some fast tugs as the current pulls the fly out away from the bank. When the high water moves away from the banks after run-off, so do the fish and this a time to start fishing out in the riffles. Use a dry fly somewhat larger than normal in the rougher water so you can better see the strike; don't overlook that water where a riffle dumps into the slower water of a run.

August is the time when wading becomes a viable alternative to floating because of lower water levels and less hydrodynamic effect on knees and thighs. It becomes quickly apparent when wading this river that it can be intimidating. One way to cover the water is to visually break the river into sections and fish each section as if it were a small river. Fish the edges, the rip-rap, the downed timber, below islands, around boulders and at eddies.

Nymph fishing on the Yellowstone is a very effective technique to use at any time of the year. There are good numbers of salmonflies in the river that remain throughout their three year life cycle and black and dark brown stonefly nymphs are a must in sizes ranging from #2 to #12. Large attractor nymphs such as Bitch Creek, Girdle Bug and Yuk Bug are also very effective. Whether large or small, one of the favorite spots for working a nymph is in the riffle corners formed where the river bends and a riffle empties into a pool. Insects accumulate in the quiet water formed here and fish key on the insects. When you spot a riffle corner from a boat, you should pass it by, beach the boat and walk back up to fish it from a downstream position.

The Yellowstone can be capricious and offer a different mood from pool to pool. If one location isn't productive, move to another. With a boat you have the mobility to cover a good deal of water in order to concentrate on those locations where fish are actively working. Fish are rarely in the middle of the river, so concentrate on the banks and don't bother fishing the slack water. It's important here to learn the ways of the river, and an excellent way to do so is to use the services of a guide, at least the first time you fish this water.

One interesting aspect of fishing the Yellowstone is the vagarious nature of the winds that penetrate the region around Livingston. The wind here is a fact of life that must be dealt with, but it doesn't blow continually, nor does it blow uniformly throughout the area. At times it will be windy in town to the extent of discouraging a trip to the river, while at the same time conditions in Paradise Valley will be calm and ideal for fishing. Winds normally come out of the south or southwest, so don't be too quick to write off a windy day before investigating the possibilities nearby. Another thing to remember about the wind when air temperatures are less than mild, is that the wind chill factor will require you dress warmly to remain comfortable. This is particularly true during the cool days of fall.

Autumn brings not only changes in the weather, but in fishing technique as well. This is the time of low water and spawning brown trout. In September insects will still be on the water and fish will be taken on dry flies; nymphs will continue to be effective, but now the main emphasis will be placed on streamer fishing. This is the time when Matukas replace mayflies, when Woolly Buggers and Muddlers search deep runs as they swim down close to the cobbles. The short, accurate, finesse casts used during the summer to thoroughly cover prime holding water are replaced in autumn by fast-sinking lines and eight- to nine-weight rods to throw longer, stronger casts to entice hefty browns to pursue fast moving steamers.

A list of tackle for fishing the Yellowstone might include the following. For the spin fisherman, rods of 6-1/2 to 7-1/2 feet, reels loaded with 6 to 10 pound test line, and lures weighing from 1/4 to 1/2 ounce. Favorite lures include Thomas Cyclone, Panther Martin, Mepps and Kamlooper. The fly fisherman would want to have available a six- or seven-weight rod in addition to an eight or nine weight not only for fall fishing but for those windy days of summer when a more beefy stick is necessary to fight the breeze. Preferred lines include weight-forward tapers in a floater, a sink tip and a fast-sinking, shooting head for the streamers in the fall. Nine-foot leaders are standard, with 3X and 4X tippets in the summer and 0X and 1X in the fall and during the salmonfly hatch.

The Yellowstone is a river for all seasons, and whether you pass through this area in February and happen to find a midge hatch coming off in downtown Livingston, or float the river during salmonfly, hopper or fall spawning periods, you'll find the scenery attractive, the fishing a challenge, and the local anglers knowledgeable and willing to answer your questions.

ARMSTRONG AND NELSON'S SPRING CREEKS

To add contrast and diversity to a fishing trip on the Yellowstone, many anglers enjoy the more intimate atmosphere of the well-known spring creeks eight miles south of Livingston. They provide both challenging conditions and selective trout to fly fishermen who fish on a catch-and-release basis only for fish averaging fifteen inches with a few pushing the five-pound mark. In conversation or in written material the creeks may have been referred to as Armstrong, DePuy's, Nelson's and O'Hair's. If you planned to pack a lunch and drive out to fish one of these four streams, you'd have a problem finding them on a map because only two bodies of water exist here. One is Armstrong Spring Creek which glides along on the west side of, and parallel to, the Yellowstone River and is accessible from Highway 89. The other stream is Nelson's Spring Creek which slides along the east side of, and parallel to, the Yellowstone River and is accessible from Route 540. The term O'Hair refers to the O'Hair Ranch, through which the upper end of Armstrong Spring Creek flows. The term DePuy refers to the DePuy Ranch, through which the lower end of Armstrong Spring Creek flows. The angler's vernacular has applied all three names to this one tiny, but special, stretch of trout stream. Nelson's

Spring Creek is singularly referred to as Nelson's.

While historically they have been ranch creeks and are utilized as such for watering stock and irrigating fields, they have recently taken on another important function as recreation resources. The creeks are physically similar and they are both managed from the trout's point of view. Because of this management policy, fishing pressure is now limited to but a few rods per day and a rod fee must be paid to gain access to either of the creeks. Arrangement to fish can be made directly with the ranch owners or through fly shops in Livingston. It must be noted that the streams are sometimes booked solid, particularly in August, as much as a year in advance. This tells us something of their popularity.

The O'Hair's section of Armstrong contains about 1-1/2 miles of water. Its wide pools and riffles are easy to wade and relatively easy to fish. Of the three sections of water available, this would be the most comfortable for the novice fly fisherman because the riffle water is somewhat more forgiving than the glassy, smooth water elsewhere. This part of the creek holds a predominance of rainbows, most of which will measure twelve to eighteen inches. Very few browns or cutthroat are caught here.

The lower reaches of Armstrong on the DePuy's Ranch flow for approximately three miles. Not only will you find the classic, spring creek characteristics here, but also some water which has been dammed to form ponds and

Nelson's Spring Creek

sloughs providing still-water fishing either afoot or from float tubes. Here again, most fish caught will be rainbows but you will see a few more browns and cutthroat, the latter particularly in June and July when they come in from the Yellowstone to spawn.

Both sections of Armstrong are open to year-round fishing and the two ranches offer reduced fees during the off-season months from fall through spring. As with the Yellowstone, March and April can provide good fishing on the warmer days because the creek water temperature maintains an almost constant fifty-five degrees.

Across the river approximately 1/2 mile from Armstrong, Nelson's Spring Creek flows through the ranch land of the lower Paradise Valley where approximately 3/4 mile of the creek is available to anglers, again on a fee basis with a limited number of rods per day. This water is somewhat more challenging to fish than Armstrong because much of it is table-flat requiring long leaders, gossamer tippets and delicately presented casts. The fish species here include rainbow, brown and cutthroat with the average size being larger than at Armstrong.

Both creeks are formed entirely from natural springs, creating streams of the clearest water. Neither run-off nor rainstorm affects them; they remain clear when the freestone rivers run high and dirty. As in this entire region, the wind is wont to blow, but it pays to check out the valley situation even when it's breezy in town because it could be calm on the creeks. Physically the water volumes remain the same throughout the year because of the uniform flow from the springs, but surface currents change due to growth of aquatic vegetation. As summer progresses the weeds become larger and more dense and slicks, seams and eddies form on the surface which make line control progressively more difficult, particularly in August and September. Bounce casts, slack-line casts and downstream casts become more essential as the weeds capriciously produce complex current patterns.

A few other technical considerations should be mentioned concerning these streams. Wading is relatively easy in most places, but we do suggest that chest waders be worn for ease of mobility. Long casting isn't necessary; quite to the contrary, shorter casts facilitate greater line control, greater accuracy and a drag-free float. A forty foot cast would be a long one here, so fly lines of three weight to five weight are common and appropriate. These fish have inspected many a feathered fraud in their day, so they're not totally unfamiliar with attractive artificials. Sometimes wading the creek is abandoned in favor of the creep, crawl and cast method. Just as the fish have seen a bunch of artificial flies go by they've also seen a bunch of olive and brown feet kick up the gravel in their dining rooms, so staying back on the bank and casting from a crouch can have its rewards. Rising fish, of course, make lovely targets for your casting skills, and when you find a fish large enough to be worthy of your efforts, stick with him tenaciously rather than casting to every riser within range. These fish will come up to your offerings, but they expect the proper pattern presented in a proper fashion. If no fish are showing, try a small nymph thrown just above the lip of a riffle as it pours into a pool below; this is a favorite lie of the trout here. Overcast days are welcomed on these creeks, and if it sputters rain or spits snow, that's all right too. It seems that both insects and fish respond well to dreary days.

Sometimes the fish are coming up to take emergers rather than duns and at times they'll be feeding on a secondary hatch rather than the most obvious one. It's a good idea to carry a net and stomach pump for use on those occasions when the fish are feeding well, but not to your fly. When you do hook one, you can check his stomach contents for a clue to his insect preference. Try to have a good selection of mayfly nymphs, emergers and adults in your fly boxes because several insects in several stages of their life cycle will become the target of trout throughout the course of a day. Caddis and grasshoppers are a minor consideration on these creeks due to the reliable abundance of mayflies in the water. A good selection of artificials would include the following patterns: Blue Winged Olive in sizes #16 to #24, Pale Morning Duns in #16 to #20, Dark Blue Duns in #18 and #20 and small nymphs and emergers in sizes #16 to #20 in shades of olive, black, grey and brown. Midges are effective all year in adult, pupae and larval stages. Scuds and sowbugs work well as do Pheasant Tails and Hare's Ears. Ants will take some fish as will #10 Woolly Buggers.

You can count on the very best dry fly fishing to take place from mid-June through mid-August, and the second best the balance of the year.

GARDINER

A head count of the folks living in Gardiner can vary as much as twenty-five percent between the winter and summer seasons. Even though there are some tourists here during the winter months, the town's population swells during the summer when down parkas have been stored away and short-sleeved shirts are the order of the day. Those residents involved in the local tourist industry are particularly busy in the summer catering to the needs of the thousands of visitors from around the world who come here to enjoy the wonders of Yellowstone National Park and enter or leave the park through the north gate which sits at the edge of town. The "Roosevelt Arch" at the park's north entrance was dedicated by Teddy Roosevelt in 1903, thirty-one years after the establishment of the park. The inscription on the arch states simply

"For the Benefit and Enjoyment of the People."

The town itself was founded in 1880, shortly after regional discoveries of gold, principally at nearby Jardine, five miles to the northeast of town up Bear Gulch. Mining here took place off and on until 1948, a period during which an estimated 2.2 million dollars in gold was extracted. Today Jardine is home to a small group of residents and visitors can make the short but rough drive to view some of the mining relics of the past.

Winter visitors to Gardiner enjoy cross-country skiing, snowmobiling and snowshoeing. A weekend highlight here is the Winter Camera Safari, an activity which concentrates on the photography of game animals prevalent in good numbers here, including big horn sheep, elk, deer, buffalo and a variety of smaller animals. The car-caravan is led by a local ranger-naturalist.

Summer activities include fishing, rafting and kayaking on the Yellowstone River, which bisects the town, plus hiking and backpacking on five hundred miles of trails in the surrounding mountains. Horse pack trips are also popular and several local outfitters are available to conduct such trips. Even rock hounds and gold panners have an opportunity to seek and find throughout the nearby hills and valleys, so if you have a pick and a pan, bring them along.

An auto trip to the south of town will, of course, take you into Yellowstone where a good deal of time can be spent enjoying the myriad of natural splendors it holds. A short trip to the north offers two points of interest worth considering even as a special trip if you're not planning to venture farther into Montana than Gardiner. About a mile north of town a gravel road will take you to a travertine rock quarry where you can observe the extraction of this limestone rock which usually finds itself ultimately secured to the front of a building as ornamental facing. Five miles from town along Highway 89 you'll see the Devil's Slide, a geologic formation located across the river.

Gardiner is a small community but certainly one geared to accommodate the motorist, whether passing through or spending a few days!

**Gardiner Chamber of Comerce: P.O. Box 81, Gardiner, Montana 59030 -
Phone: 848-7681**

LIVINGSTON

As you drive east on I-90 and the highway comes off Bozeman Pass, the terrain approaching Livingston flattens and stretches into grassy plains to the east while to the south the prodigious Absarokas stand as guardians to the soft Paradise Valley below. Random windmills perform in afternoon breezes as cattle graze on fertile ranchland and anglers, looking for clues and admiring its character, covetously regard the transparent water of the Yellowstone River. It's in this environment that one finds many reasons to concur with Livingston's slogan describing itself as "The Heart of Yellowstone Country."

In addition to being known as a hospitable refuge to the world's itinerant trout fishermen, Livingston has also been known through the years as one of Montana's leading centers of railroad activity. The Northern Pacific built here in 1880 and railroading and ranching ushered the town into the twentieth century on steel rails and plowshares. Some railroad functions still exist here, but have been scaled down drastically from the heyday years when over one thousand Livingston residents worked for the railroad. Those years are history now but many buildings in town remain from that period of greatest growth, between 1882 and 1915, and they stand as monuments to an era when special skills and strong dedication provided the means to open the Northwest to profitable development of its resources.

The most imposing structure that remains from the turn of the century is the Livingston Depot Center, an edifice of truly special architecture and sound building practices, which reflects the railroad's dedication to this community. In 1982 the building was donated to the city by the railroad and it has since been refurbished to function as a "satellite" museum to the Buffalo Bill Historical Center in Cody, Wyoming. The Depot Center opened in 1987 with displays of art by many well-known artists, as well as artifacts representing eras in Montana history including the years of the Indians, explorers, miners, settlers, the railroad and of Yellowstone Park. The building is temperature and humidity controlled and the exhibits are designed to withstand vibrations from passing trains. The center is operated by the Livingston Depot Foundation, a non-profit organization supported by contributions. This is a very worthy cause and an interesting site to visit when in Livingston. Another interesting facility is the Park County Museum which specializes in indigenous artifacts. A schoolhouse has been recreated with all appropriate furnishings and, in addition to archeological artifacts and geological relics, early home parapher-nalia is displayed along with items from agriculture, medicine, mining and the railroad. Most of these exhibits are permanent and of great interest to visitors.

The economic lifeblood of Livingston is derived from agriculture, logging, lumber mills and tourism. The town, with a population of 7,500 residents, was founded in 1882, incorporated in 1889 and is now the seat of Park County government. The community was named after Jonathan Livingston, a director of the railroad.

Most visitors arrive here by auto, but commercial airlines fly into both Bozeman and Billings and private aircraft can land seven miles from town at

Mission Field where a paved 5,700 foot strip will accommodate small jets. If you drive or fly in with your golf clubs, you'll be able to use the driving range and clubhouse at the Livingston Golf and Country Club and try to keep the balls out of the water on the nine-hole course adjacent to the Yellowstone River. After golf you and the family can enjoy a swim in the heated municipal pool which is close to Livingston's Sacajawea Park. This is the town's largest park and features tennis courts, playground, lagoon, kids' wading pool and picnic areas. Other neighborhood parks are also available for laying back and relaxing between hatches on the river.

Special events throughout the summer include the Livingston Roundup Rodeo and the Yellowstone River Boat Float, a two-day event conducted annually since 1963, from Livingston down to the community of Laurel. There's a Fine Arts Summerfest featuring "Made-in-Montana" crafts, food, music and drama, plus the Park County Fair and the annual Fiddler's Picnic with, you guessed it, plenty of fine fiddling! Other highlights of the summer include periodic community concerts and, very significantly, the Kid's Trout Derby.

It's pretty obvious that along with its many fishing opportunities, Livingston also has a good number of other activities to enjoy.

Livingston Chamber of Commerce: 1104 W. Park St., Livingston, Montana 59047 - Phone: 222-0850

BIG TIMBER

The town of Big Timber is located at the confluence of two rivers as are many towns throughout the west. The Boulder River meets the Yellowstone about thirty-five miles east of Livingston and it is here in the center of Sweetgrass County, on land where Lewis and Clark, considered to be the first white men to visit here, camped at the "big timbers" and Chief Red Cloud and his band of Sioux Indians hunted, that the town of Big Timber has developed. The Bozeman Trail crossed the Yellowstone River nearby and the gold miners using the trail were often confronted by Sioux warriors who resented their transgression into Indian territory.

Transgression isn't a problem today and the local inhabitants welcome visits by folks who are hitting the trail west or those who plan to stick around for a few days to fish. The town is small but offers plenty of facilities for meals and accommodations. For those travelers wishing to play golf the local nine-hole course in the shadow of the Absaroka-Beartooth Mountains to the south, with views of the Crazy Mountains to the north, offers both the scenery and the usual course-related amenities. Swimming is available at nearby Glasston Lakes, if you enjoy roughing it, but also at the more comfortable, heated pool at City Park where you'll find picnic areas and tennis courts as well.

Sweetgrass County is an agricultural area and as such benefits from the snows collected in surrounding mountains and carried by the rivers in the region. In addition to providing excellent conditions under which to grow beef and lamb, Sweetgrass County offers the tourist a variety of outdoor activities including, of course, fishing in rivers and high country lakes, plus rock hounding, hiking and sightseeing. Two popular locations for the latter on the upper Boulder River include the Natural Bridge and Falls and the ghost town of Independence.

Closer to town the local airport offers a paved, lighted runway of 4,650 feet plus associated storage and maintenance for private aircraft.

Sweet Grass County Chamber of Commerce: Box 1012, Big Timber, Montana 59011

Custer National Forest Office: 2602 First Ave. N., Billings, Montana 59101 Phone: 657-6361

Gallatin National Forest Office: P.O. Box 130, Federal Building, Bozeman, Montana 59715 - Phone: 587-6701

BILLINGS

When people who know something about Montana think of Billings, they probably first envision the state's largest city, one with the services and amenities that larger cities always provide. They probably envision the community as a retail and commerce center as well as a cosmopolitan transition point between the flat prairie and agricultural land to the east and north and the mountainous terrain of the Rockies to the west. A fisherman would have these same thoughts but, in addition, might picture casting to trout in not-too-distant rivers such as the upper Yellowstone, the Stillwater, Boulder and Bighorn. For all of these reasons Billings is a popular location for many conventions and a variety of business meetings throughout the year.

Billings, with a metropolitan population of nearly 120,000, is indeed the state's largest city. The Yellowstone River flows through town providing water to the fertile agricultural surroundings. The economy here is based to a significant degree on agriculture and its allied industries; in addition to cattle and grain crops, the area is known for its production of sugar beets and the major refinery which processes them. Billings is a major transportation center from which a variety of agricultural products is shipped. Retail, energy-related business, tourism and government—Billings is the Yellowstone County seat—round out the most significant economic resources.

The Northern Pacific Railroad has played an important part in the history of Billings. The railroad arrived here in 1882 and its workers reportedly built the town's first building. The president of the line at that time was Fredrick Billings and, not unlike other towns in the west, the infant community was named in his honor. Within five or six months the town boasted two-thousand residents; this surprising growth prompted the nickname "Magic City."

The best way to gain a perspective on the history and heritage of any city is to visit a place that exhibits items that reflect its past. One such place in Billings is the Western Heritage Center where western art is displayed in both permanent and changing exhibits. Historical and cultural events are scheduled as well as educational programs pertinent to the west in general and the Yellowstone Valley in particular. In addition to contemporary exhibits, the Yellowstone County Museum, atop the rimrock north of town, also has displays, dioramas and artifacts reflecting the frontier life of the of cowboys, pioneers and Indians. The Yellowstone Art Center is located in the former Yellowstone County Jail. The center houses a contemporary collection of works in all media by local, regional and national artists. Exhibits change several times a year.

In addition to these facilities, the city is blessed with many city parks, several swimming pools and tennis courts, two public golf courses (one is a par three) and an ice rink. During the summer special events center around rodeos, summer theater and concerts, sports festivals, arts and crafts fairs, the Billings Symphony Orchestra and Chorale, repertory theater and childrens' theater.

Outdoor attractions are located a short distance from Billings. The Pictograph Cave State Monument, also referred to as the "Indian Caves," is about seven miles to the southeast. Images of figures and animals which were painted in red, white and black by aboriginal people who lived here approximately four- to five-thousand years ago are found on rock walls in caves in the area. A drive along the Black Otter Trail which follows the edge of the rimrock north of town will lead to Boothill Cemetery at the east end of the city, as well as the grave of Indian scout Yellowstone Kelly and the bronze statue of the Range Rider of the Yellowstone. There is a particular spot on the rimrocks, the exact location of which is unknown, called the Sacrifice Cliffs. It was here that some Crow Indians, while on the backs of their blindfolded horses, made suicidal leaps from the cliffs to avoid the possibility of dying a slow death from smallpox and/or because they wished to join their friends and families who had already died of the disease. Another natural feature of interest is Pompey's Pillar, a huge limestone rock located about a half hour east of town along the Yellowstone River. This rock on which William Clark inscribed his name in 1806 is the only physical evidence known to show he passed through this area.

For big-city culture or a convenient convention, Billings is a popular destination.

Billings Chamber of Commerce: 200 N. 34th St. - Box 2519, Billings, Montana 59103 - Phone: 245-4111

Bureau of Land Management: P.O. Box 36800, Billings, Montana 59107

River Notes

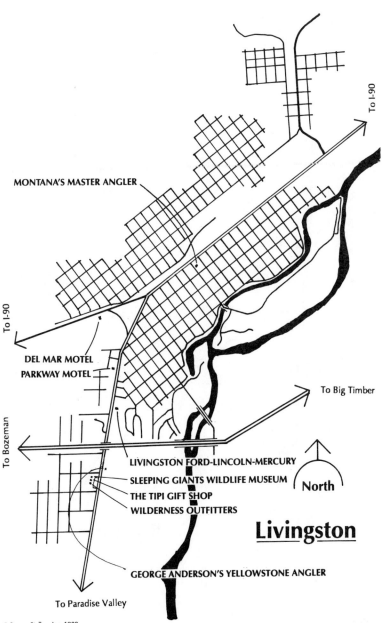

MONTANA'S MASTER ANGLER

To I-90

To I-90

DEL MAR MOTEL
PARKWAY MOTEL

To Bozeman

To Big Timber

LIVINGSTON FORD-LINCOLN-MERCURY
SLEEPING GIANTS WILDLIFE MUSEUM
THE TIPI GIFT SHOP
WILDERNESS OUTFITTERS

North

Livingston

GEORGE ANDERSON'S YELLOWSTONE ANGLER

To Paradise Valley

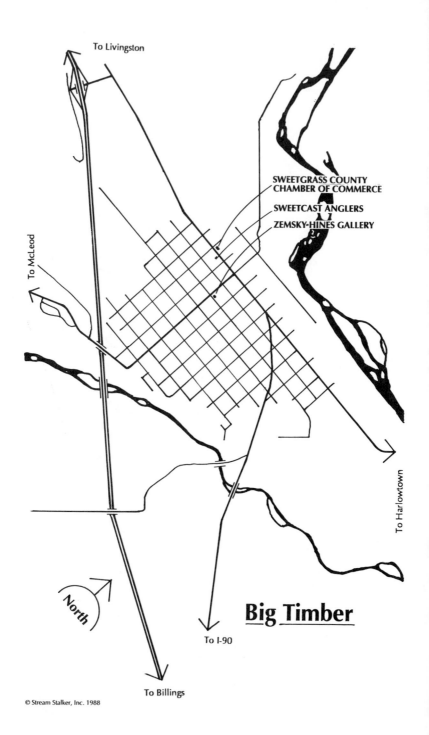

To Livingston

SWEETGRASS COUNTY
CHAMBER OF COMMERCE

SWEETCAST ANGLERS
ZEMSKY-HINES GALLERY

To McLeod

To Harlowtown

North

Big Timber

To I-90

To Billings

© Stream Stalker, Inc. 1988

EMIGRANT

GUEST RANCHES

POINT OF ROCKS GUEST RANCH
19 miles north of Yellowstone Park on Hwy. 89, at the Point of Rocks fishing access, Rt. 1, Box 680,   848-7278 or 333-4361
> A 5,700 acre guest ranch, bordering four and one-half miles of the famous Yellowstone River, catering to serious fly fishermen and their families. Heated swimming pool, horseback riding. Write or call for our brochure and references.

PRAY

RESORTS

CHICO HOT SPRINGS LODGE
At Chico Hot Springs, Box 127   333-4933
> This unique resort has swimming, horseback riding, fishing, hunting, gourmet dining, pack trips and a full service hotel. Every angler should bring the family to visit and enjoy this special place.

LIVINGSTON

FISHING SHOPS

GEORGE ANDERSON'S YELLOWSTONE ANGLER
Highway 89 south, Box 660   222-7130
> Visit George Anderson and his staff for friendly advice, quality flies and tackle, and experienced guides. We specialize in the spring creeks, and the Yellowstone and Bighorn Rivers. Open all year.

MONTANA'S MASTER ANGLER
124 N. Main St., Box 1320   222-2273
> Full service fly shop, with the most complete fishing information center in the area. We have a complete selection of flies, tackle and fishing finery for the angler.

GUIDES / OUTFITTERS

MONTANA'S MASTER ANGLER
124 N. Main St., Box 1320   222-2273
> The fisherman's headquarters for angling adventures across Montana and around the world. Offering float and wade trips on all major rivers in the area, plus fishing trips to Yellowstone National Park and many area lakes. We also offer day trips to Armstrong's, DePuy's and Nelson's Spring Creeks.

SPORTING GOODS

WILDERNESS OUTFITTERS
Hwy. 89, south, Rt. 62, Box 3110, at the Sleeping Giant Trade Center   222-6933
> Livingston's all-round sporting goods store. This unique shop has everything you need for the outdoors and your fishing trip. We specialize in serving the lure fisherman and have the largest and best selection of lures in the state.

GUEST RANCHES

YELLOWSTONE VALLEY GUEST RANCH
14 Miles south of Livingston on Hwy. 89, Rt. 38, Box 2202   333-4787
>Anglers Paradise. Ten beautiful cabins, overlooking one mile of the fantastic Yellowstone River and the Absaroka and Beartooth mountain ranges. Nightly or weekly rates. Continental breakfast included and kitchen facilities available. Reservations suggested.

MOTELS

DEL MAR MOTEL
I-90 Business Loop west, Box 636   222-3120
>Thirty-two units, some with kitchens and queen size beds. Quiet location, color cable TV, phones in all rooms. Winter plug-ins, heated pool, playground. All major credit cards accepted.

PARKWAY MOTEL
1124 W. Park St., 4 blocks north of I-90, exit 333
>Welcome fishermen! We give you a discount! We have 27 quiet units, some of which have kitchenettes. Outdoor heated pool. Five minutes away from downtown Livingston or great fishing on the Yellowstone River. Fifty-six miles to Yellowstone National Park.

CAR RENTAL

LIVINGSTON FORD-LINCOLN-MERCURY
1415 W. Park St., 2 blocks north of I-90, exit 333
>We have daily and weekly car rentals, including all models, 4 WD vans and sedans. We also have shuttle delivery to the Bozeman and Livingston airports. Give us a call and we'll get you to the river fast and at a very reasonable cost. Please reserve in advance.

GIFT SHOPS

THE TIPI GIFT SHOP
Hwy. 89 south, Rt. 2, Box 3110E, at the Sleeping Giant Trade Center   222-8575
>Original Sioux art, including paintings, beadwork, jewelry, authentic hand crafted arts and crafts, shields, bows, arrow and other Indian artifacts. We also have examples or original Indian petroglyphs from the west.

MUSEUMS

SLEEPING GIANTS WILDLIFE MUSEUM
Hwy. 89, south, Rt. 62, Box 3110-C   222-8719
>magnificent displays of North American big game. Record class animals in dioramas depicting natural situations. Spectacular buffalo jump and white elk displays. Also visit the Roche Jaune Galerie of Western Art next door, featuring outstanding bronze sculptures by Burl Jones. Stop by to se us when you're heading for Yellowstone park. We're on the way!

BIG TIMBER

FISHING SHOPS

SWEETCAST ANGLERS
Main St. and Highway 10 west, Box 582   932-4469

Float trips! Quality fishing tackle. Loomis rods, Hardy and SA reels. Raft rental (with rowing frames), shuttle service, guide service and casting instruction. Three great rivers, the Yellowstone, Boulder and Stillwater to choose from.

SERVICES

SWEETGRASS COUNTY CHAMBER OF COMMERCE
15 No. Hart, Box 1012   932-5131

Big Timber! Motels, restaurants and campgrounds. Guide services, public golf course, guest ranches, deer and elk hunting. The Yellowstone and Boulder Rivers offer some of the best trout fishing in southern Montana. Yellowstone cutthroat trout hatchery, waterslide, paved air strip. Home of the Montana Cowboy Poetry Gathering and the World Championship Pack Horse Race. Rodeos, horse shows and cutting contests. You are always welcome.

ART GALLERIES

ZEMSKY HINES GALLERY
108 E. 3rd St., Box 1043   932-5228

A broad spectrum of original paintings and prints. Browsers are always welcome!

PART II:
YELLOWSTONE
NATIONAL PARK

INTRODUCTION

We have, over the years, made many fishing trips into Yellowstone National Park; we have waded its rivers, driven its roads and viewed its scenery and wildlife. We still enjoy doing so and will always feel it offers a special reward to all who visit this great-granddaddy of national parks. We always expect, but, contradictorily, never really think it possible that the park can retain its pristine, wild, seemingly untouched environment year after year. Its landscape of more than two million acres appears to be soberly cared for, its wildlife judiciously managed, and its millions of visitors respectfully welcomed. Park personnel are gracious to the very end when summer activities are terminated on October 31.

Yellowstone became our nation's first national park on March 1, 1872 through enactment by the Congress of the U. S.; the approval was signed by then President, Ulysses S. Grant. This act became effective before Wyoming officially became a state and was accomplished because of several expeditions conducted in the area in 1860 and 1870. The engineers and scientists on these trips realized the unusual value of the area and had the foresight to want it preserved for all people to enjoy. This concentration of hydrothermal activity, canyons, wildlife, rivers, lakes, mountains and trout fishing is unique in the world.

The Gallatin Mountains in the north and the Absaroka Mountains in the east of the park were formed almost seventy million years ago during the Laramide Revolution. The plateau region in the center and southwest sections of the park was formed approximately 600,000 years ago as the Earth's surface violently collapsed into what is now one of the world's largest calderas. Subsequent volcanic eruptions eventually filled this depression, but the heat remains beneath the Earth's surface and today, it is estimated that ten thousand thermal features still exist here.

The "steam" one sees throughout these thermal plateaus is really just tiny water droplets condensed from steam. Our perception of them is significantly altered depending on weather conditions; on cold and humid days the plumes we see are enhanced, while on warm and dry days they are diminished. The water that we see bubbling from many of these features is actually surface water from rain and snow that has found its way into the Earth's crust and has sunk up to ten thousand feet below the surface.

In the mountains of the high country in the park we see glacial cirques and moraines that have resulted from at least three ages of glaciation extending back as far as 300,000 years and ending only 8,500 years ago. These glaciers came and went depending upon air temperature and snowfall. If the air temperature didn't allow all of the year's snowfall to melt, the snow depth increased, compacted to ice and eventually its own weight caused it to move downhill. Geologists now determine the distance traveled by these glaciers by finding rocks, indigenous to the "mother formation," downhill in another area some miles away. The giant boulder (estimated at more than 500 tons) near Inspiration Point was transported at least fifteen miles by glacial movement.

The two hydrothermal features of most interest to visitors are Old Faithful Geyser and Mammoth Hot Springs. The former is actually a geyser, the term having been derived from the Icelandic word "geysir," meaning to gush or rage. Old Faithful gushes, or erupts, from eighteen to twenty times daily. Each eruption lasts from 2 to 5 minutes, throwing 5,000 to 8,000 gallons of water an average of 130 feet into the air. Most of this water then drains into the Firehole River.

Mammoth Hot Springs does not gush forth as a geyser, but rather flows at a steady rate in a quantity of about five hundred gallons a minute. During the course of a day the water transports to the surface an estimated two tons of travertine, a form of calcium carbonate (limestone). This discharge makes Mammoth an unusual area because most of the mineral discharges throughout the park contain sinter (with silica as its major component) rather than travertine. This terraced structure is truly a natural wonder; it's always worth the time to stop and have a look. Lodging, dining and general store are nearby.

No matter where you are in the park, you can usually spot wildlife of one type or another. Biologists have recorded over sixty species of mammals, two hundred different birds and several cold-water fish species, including whitefish and grayling. All of these creatures are interesting to see and photograph, but it's important to realize they are wild and deserve to remain unmolested. As for the elk, moose, buffalo and bear, keep a safe distance away from them. Although they may allow you to approach fairly near, they can charge unexpectedly and cause serious injury.

The principal waterfalls in the park are on Tower Creek and the Lewis, Gibbon and Yellowstone Rivers. The greatest attraction to the tourist, however, is the Lower Falls and Grand Canyon of the Yellowstone River. The canyon itself varies in depth from 1,000 to 1,500 feet and extends for approximately 20 miles in length. The falls drop 308 feet (almost twice the height of Niagara Falls) as the clear water of the river rushes over the brink of rhyolite lava. Although the normal color of this rhyolite is grey or brown, chemical and physical alterations have taken place within the canyon over the

centuries to change these somber colors to the yellow shades seen now. These colors are credited for the inspiration in naming the park.

Although roads are relatively few considering the size of the park, they were laid out to good advantage for gaining access to all of the most interesting features available. Five entrance roads give access from all four directions. In addition, auto travel throughout the park is well facilitated by two internal road loops which form a "figure eight" in the center of the park. Each loop is worthy of a day spent sightseeing; we suggest you allow yourself enough time to unhurriedly enjoy all the natural wonders the park contains. As a complement to the overall orderly maintenance of the park, individual areas and features are well signed along all roads. A word of caution to those who are traveling the park for the first time—don't stop suddenly in the middle of the highway to take a photograph when you sight an animal within camera range. It's a natural thing to do since you don't want to miss that "shot of a lifetime," but an accident could easily occur with a car behind you or, at the least, traffic could be delayed for other tourists. If you must stop your car, pull it up to a safe pullout and walk back to take the photo. The animals here move very slowly and will usually give you time to shoot their picture.

In addition to the "driving and looking" method of enjoying the park, visitors may also wish to become more involved with the activities available such as boating, fishing or hiking. Special regulations have enhanced the quality of the angling in the park and access to the water is extremely simple. Many roads follow a beautiful trout stream and one needs only the proper tackle and a no-fee permit to enjoy the fishing. Boating is enjoyed on Lewis Lake and Yellowstone Lake where launching facilities are available. Permits are required and some waters, such as Shoshone Lake and parts of Yellowstone Lake, are limited to powerless boats only (similar to canoes or other small craft). Inquire about permits at park entrances.

For persons who enjoy leaving the roads and hiking into the back country, the park has over one thousand miles of trails available. There is a variety of hikes possible, from a few hours to a few days, and serious hikers may wish to obtain trail information prior to their trip. There are organized hikes and walks to several of the more interesting features of the park conducted by park rangers who provide the visitor with a greater understanding of the park's total ecology.

Camping is available throughout Yellowstone in campgrounds within easy access of the road. Some areas accommodate both tent camping and recreational vehicle parking, while others are limited to RV's only. These sites are under the jurisdiction of park rangers and regulations are posted with rules for safe camping. Of particular importance is the storage of food, as it can attract bears into camp if not properly cared for.

In our opinion, the 3,472 square mile Yellowstone National Park is a treasure of incalculable worth. It offers its guests recreation, relaxation, education and a concentration of natural wonders found no where else in the world. It is one of few areas in the United States where man's minimal alteration of nature's design has afforded him the opportunity to study and appreciate a most dynamic and rapidly changing natural environment.

Camping

Campground	Location	Number of Sites	Comments
Bridge Bay	3 miles south of Lake Village near Fishing Bridge	438	Marina, boat launch, laundry nearby
Canyon	0.5 miles east of Canyon Jct.	280	No tents, laundry nearby
Fishing Bridge	1 mile east of bridge	308	No tents, near lake, laundry
Fishing Bridge RV Park	At Junction	358	Near lake
Grant Village	2 miles south of West Thumb Jct.	438	Visitor Center, Laundry, near lake
Indian Creek	7.5 miles south of Mammoth	78	
Lewis Lake	At Lewis Lake	100	Boat Launch facility
Madison Jct.	0.5 miles west of the junction	292	
Mammoth	0.5 miles north of the junction	87	Visitor Center
Norris	1 mile north of Norris Junction	116	Visitor Center
Pebble Creek	7 miles south of northeast entrance	36	
Slough Creek	10 miles northeast of Tower Falls Jct.	30	Located on Slough Creek.
Tower Falls	3 miles southeast of Tower Jct.	37	Good fishing from campground

PARK FISHING

You can stand in a Yellowstone National Park river in August with your head bowed against the wind-driven snow as you attempt to throw a fly upstream, or you can enjoy a picnic along that same river in October while welcoming the heat of the mid-day sun. You may wish to wear heavy socks against the chill of a headwater creek or wear no socks at all in a geothermally-influenced reach of a sister stream. The afternoon wind may rush across the open meadows of Biscuit Basin or be partially subdued by the lodgepole pines hugging the banks of the Lewis River. Yellowstone is a region of contrasts, a place of beauty, the birthplace of rivers, the graveyard of geysers.

For the angler, Yellowstone offers diverse challenge and opportunity, from the sometimes easy-to-catch cutthroats of the Yellowstone River to the often difficult-to-catch rainbows of the Firehole River. In some circumstances the fly fisherman will want to gently cast his little three-weight fly rod, while in other situations a seven-weight is none too heavy. In many waters of the park fly fishing is by far the most effective method of hooking fish, however, many areas are also fished with spin tackle. The estimated 100,000 anglers who fish here each summer are required to obtain a no-fee fishing permit and should read the regulations thoroughly before making their first cast. The quality of the angling experience is high due to the strong and thoughtful management practices employed and special restrictions which apply to many waters. With the exception of one short section of the Gardner River, no bait fishing is allowed in the park and much of the better water is designated "catch-and-release."

The weather in the park can be capricious, so anglers should be outfitted with the proper equipment to face it: lightweight shirt, sun screen and polarized sunglasses for the intense sun; raincoat, wool sweater and lined windbreaker for the cold rain or snow.

We suppose that fly fishermen never really feel they have in their fishing vests every fly that they might possibly need for a given time and place. Possibly the vest hasn't yet been produced that would accommodate the number of patterns needed to completely satisfy our imagined requirements. To bring some degree of order and practicality to a fly selection for the short-term visiting angler, we would suggest the following list which should meet the majority of needs throughout the season on the four Park drainages of the

Snake, Madison, Gallatin and Yellowstone Rivers:

DRY FLIES
Adams
Lt. Cahill
Pale Morning Dun
Quill Gordon
Elk Hair Caddis
Hair Wing Variant
Royal, and Grey Wulff
Yellow, and Red Humpy
Stonefly patterns
Midges

WET FLIES AND NYMPHS
Hare's Ear Nymph
Renegade
Various Caddis
Midge Larvae
Woolly Worm - Black, Brown, Olive
Various Stoneflies - Black, Brown, Golden
Yuk Bug

STREAMERS
Muddler Minnow
Spruce Fly
Sculpin imitations
Woolly Bugger

TERRESTRIALS
Various Hopper patterns
Ants - Black, Rusty

The authors have enjoyed fishing the rivers and lakes of Yellowstone National Park for many years; we hope our readers will have the same opportunity. The park offers many worthwhile diversions to angler and family alike and an allocation of time to both fishing and sightseeing will be very rewarding.

BECHLER RIVER

Map Reference 49

For those preferring to approach fishing opportunities by hiking rather than driving to the water, this river offers just such an opportunity. The Bechler provides approximately twenty miles of fishing before it empties into the Falls River. It's located in the southwest corner of the Park and access is from the end of the road coming from Ashton, Idaho. A walk of five miles puts the angler at Bechler Meadows where Boundary Creek enters the river; at the upper end of the Meadows is the confluence of Ouzel Creek and the Bechler. The reach between these two tributaries offers good fishing for rainbow and cutthroat. The river is deep and clear and the undercut banks and runs hold fish in the ten to fifteen inch range, with a few larger ones safely tucked into protected areas along the way.

Fall is recommended for fishing here because the early-season angler sees high water, has wet hiking in the meadows and is bombarded by a lot of mosquitoes. Standard fly patterns are used, with small, dark nymphs and attractor dry flies being the most popular.

FIREHOLE RIVER

Map Reference 51

If ever a river could be described with a profusion of adjectives, the Firehole would be the one! The sightseer has his favorite descriptions; the angler has an even wider range of approbations, not to mention a few defamations when fishing has been difficult; and the earth scientist has his special terminologies in cases where geothermal or earthquake activity affects the water and its sub-aquatic environment. These latter factors usually aren't a consideration on most trout streams of the world, but the ever-changing influences on the Firehole make this a truly unique river.

In a swampy area on the Madison Plateau about four miles to the west of Shoshone Lake is tiny Madison Lake, the birthplace of the Firehole River. The headwaters of the river, as well as the reaches continuing downstream to Old Faithful Geyser, are rarely seen by visitors to the park. There are no trails in the area below the lake, and only downstream near the Grand Loop Road do visitors have the opportunity to see this immature trout stream. Only after it passes through Upper Geyser Basin and into Biscuit Basin does the stream take

Firehole River in Upper Geyser Basin

on the appearance of a trout fishery; from this point downstream anglers from all over the country wade its geyser-fed waters with the intent to deceive wary fish into striking delicate artificials. This section of river contains about one mile of winding water with deep runs, weed beds and undercut banks. This reach is considered excellent dry fly water. The capricious surface currents require constant attention to the floating imitation lest it be drawn off natural course, alerting the trout below that something is not quite right. The angler's skills are put to the test here and faint mutterings and mumblings have been noticed coming from the mouths of more than one frustrated fisherman as he tries to accumulate all the subtleties of effective angling into at least one rewarding cast. In this area of the upper river the volume of water is enhanced considerably by the addition of flows from the Little Firehole River and Iron Springs Creek. These streams run at a colder temperature and fish can be found resting in their cooler currents during the hottest months of the year when temperatures in the Firehole can reach as high as eighty degrees.

In this portion of the river—from the faster flows found near the Morning Glory Pool, down to the Midway Geyser Basin—small mayflies and caddisflies are found in abundance making this a delightful area of concentration for the dry fly advocate. At the upper end of Midway Geyser Basin is the well known Muleshoe Bend, a half-mile section of river considered to be one of the best on the river for hooking larger trout. Above this point the river seems to carry more brown and brook trout, but from Muleshoe Bend downstream the

Firehole River above the Cascades

river is predominantly a rainbow fishery. At the parking area overlooking the bend, the angler can view the river and any surface activity from its resident trout, fifty feet below.

Ten miles downstream from the Old Faithful turnoff, in the Lower Geyser Basin, you can turn off the Grand Loop Road onto the Fountain Flats Freight Road to the Goose Lake Meadows and the riffle water above. Before the road comes to a dead end it takes you to some interesting water near which the banks can be soft and swampy, so be careful of your footing. At the lower end of this Geyser Basin the cooler waters of tributary streams such as Sentinel Creek, Fairy Creek and Nez Perce Creek offer refuge to the trout during the hot days of August. To fool them under these conditions, however, is no small challenge.

Below the Lower Basin and above the Firehole Cascades, Firehole Falls and Firehole Canyon provide about three miles of varied water referred to as the "Broads." The water in the canyon is fast, sometimes deep, and contains considerable pocket water. There are browns, rainbows and whitefish in this water and the insect population includes larger stoneflies not found in the meadow water upstream. Although considered good in the early season, this portion of the river is considered best in the fall because it receives some of the spawning brown trout that have migrated up the Madison and then into the Firehole as far as the falls.

The Firehole holds a fascination for all who cast over its waters. From newcomer to old-timer, its selective trout, warm currents, tiny insects, lava bottom, silt-filled depressions, trailing weed beds, buffalo and elk grazing nearby, springs and fumeroles and geysers emitting billows of water vapor, plus the "fishy" appearance of the crystal clear water and grassy banks brings us back time after time to this area which is seemingly unchanged by the millions of tourists who enjoy the park each year.

The fisherman should be prepared to throw small flies on small tippets to shy fish. Popular patterns include Quill Gordon, Adams, Light Hendrickson, Light Cahill, Midge, Pale Morning Dun, Blue Quill and Blue Dun in sizes from #16 down to #22. Larger patterns include Hoppers, Muddlers, a variety of nymphs, and, in the fall, streamers in the lower reaches. The river is rich in insects and vegetation due to the calcium bicarbonate released from thermal activity in the area; this abundance of insect life makes the trout suspicious of artificial offerings. Size is important, and the dry fly fisherman should expect to use few floating patterns larger than size #16.

Although some areas of the river are protected by the lodgepole pines, the wind can be a factor that sometimes determines where you fish on the river. Many days are overcast in the park, but don't let that discourage you from fishing; such days can be very productive!

GALLATIN RIVER

Map Reference 49

As you drive north from the town of West Yellowstone, you'll travel outside the boundary of Yellowstone Park. After proceeding a distance of eleven miles, you enter the park once again and, after twenty-four miles, you cross the Gallatin River. After seven more miles, the road leaves Yellowstone and enters the Gallatin National Forest in Montana. Numerous, high-country tributaries have fed the river to this point; from here downstream to its confluence with the Missouri River, the Gallatin becomes one of Montana's most viable trout streams.

The character of the river which has a width of twenty-five to fifty feet in the park, is that of riffle and run. It's an easily-accessed, delightful river to fish, although the insects are scarce and of small size. The gravel bottom is easy to wade and hip boots will suffice in most of the stream.

Most of the fish are rainbows and cutthroats, from ten to thirteen inches in length, that share the river with a few browns and many whitefish. The mayflies and caddisflies are generally of small size and the fly fisherman will do well to fish small Adams, Humpies, Elkhair and Goddard Caddis, and Wulff patterns. Hoppers also work well in this meadow environment, as do Hare's Ear Nymphs, Muskrats and wet Renegades.

GARDNER RIVER

Map Reference 53

As a general rule, rivers tend to flow primarily in one direction; the Firehole flows from south to north, the Madison from east to west, and the Gibbon from northeast to southwest. The Gardner, however, starts out flowing to the south, makes a sharp, 180-degree turn to the left and finally flows directly north to complete its journey to the Yellowstone River.

This river heads approximately four miles south of the park's northern border near Electric Peak, west of Mammoth. It flows south through Gardners Hole gathering water from Fawn, Panther, Indian and Obsidian Creeks on the way to Sevenmile Bridge, after which it turns abruptly to the north. About halfway to Mammoth, the river flows past Bunsen Peak, over Osprey Falls, and continues its journey past Mammoth to join the Yellowstone River at Gardiner, Montana.

The upper reaches of the river are accessed from trails to the west of Mammoth; two of the most popular are Sportsman Lake Trail and Fawn Pass Trail. The Howard Eaton Trail provides access closer to the road. Farther downstream, access is available from the Bunsen Peak Road, on which traffic moves one-way north to south. From Mammoth north to Gardiner, the road parallels the river, affording easy access.

For purposes of discussing the fishing available in the Gardner, we'll divide the river into two sections, one above Osprey Falls, and one below. The upper section consists primarily of small brook trout and is considered a good area for family fishing. Children can use bait here and the average fish will be about ten inches long. To fish the upper reaches, particularly on water away from the trails, we suggest that you have proper maps to confirm your location.

In this part of the river caddisflies are more prevalent than mayflies, but both caddis and mayfly imitations work well here as do attractor patterns such as Royal Wulff and Royal Humpy. During late July and through August one should definitely have a supply of grasshopper imitations on hand.

The lower river below the falls takes on a different physical character and harbors different insect types. Large stoneflies inhabit the river here and imitations of the larvae can work well throughout the season. Adult floating imitations are used when the adults come off in late June and early July. The water here contains boulders and pockets and nymph fishing with an assortment of brown and grey nymph patterns can prove successful. The fish are larger than in the upper river and, therefore, this easily-accessed area receives more pressure from serious anglers. Fall is the best time to be here as browns from the Yellowstone migrate up the river to spawn and are fished for with large nymphs and streamer patterns. Some portions of this area may be closed during this time of year to protect these spawning fish, so be sure to read the regulations pertaining to this water.

River Notes

GIBBON RIVER

Map Reference 51

This pretty, little river, while not particularly known for producing large fish, is one that has a great variety of character throughout its approximately thirty-eight miles of flow from its headwaters at Grebe Lake near Canyon, to its union with the Firehole River at Madison Junction. Throughout its length the Gibbon averages approximately twenty-five feet in width. It first comes into view to vehicle passengers as it passes under the Norris-Canyon road bridge at the head of Virginia Meadows; it then glides over the Virginia Cascade, through another canyon, and into view once more at the head of the Norris Meadows at Norris Junction. It then turns southwest past the Norris Geyser Basin, to be nourished by the outflow water of these geysers, and flows on to become a mature trout stream at Elk Park and the larger Gibbon Meadows. The river in these two areas offers a variety of water moods including undercut banks, shallow riffles and runs, short reaches of glassy, smooth water and deep pools. Throughout the river to this point the angler can expect to hook small brown and brook trout in the ten-inch class plus rainbows, cutthroats, a few grayling and some whitefish. These meadows, with the attractive sight of lodgepole forests in the distance, are also likely areas in which to spot and photograph elk as they often frequent these grasslands to feed.

From Gibbon Meadows to its confluence with the Firehole, the Gibbon picks up speed due to increased elevation drop; it tumbles over beautiful Gibbon Falls, provides riffle water in the canyon below the falls and completes its journey in the meadow flats above Madison Junction. Whereas brook trout predominate in the upper reaches of this river, rainbow and brown trout are more prevalent below Gibbon Falls, with good runs of brown trout coming into the Gibbon from the Madison during the fall spawning run. This area is also protected under special regulations stipulating fly fishing only throughout the season.

Because of stream size and water clarity, small leader tippets are strongly recommended, with size 5X and 6X being most common. A variety of small mayfly and caddisfly imitations is popular including Adams, Lt. Cahill, Elk Hair Caddis, and Goddard Caddis in sizes #14 through #18. As is true on many meadow streams, grasshopper imitations work well during August, as do Humpies, Royal Wulffs and the Trude in sizes #14 through #18.

Gibbon River

LAMAR RIVER

Map Reference 50

The humble beginnings of the Lamar River originate at an elevation of over nine thousand feet in the Hoodoo Basin of the Absaroka Mountains between Lamar Mountain and Parker Peak. The river tumbles swiftly westward, then in a more northwesterly direction, picking up two notable tributaries, Cache Creek and Soda Butte Creek. It then enters the upper end of the Lamar Valley and runs parallel to the Tower-Cooke City road. From its confluence with Soda Butte Creek to its confluence with the Yellowstone River about two miles below Tower Junction, the river's pace slows somewhat as it flows through the meadow terrain of the valley and the canyon of its lower reaches. At this point it has traveled approximately forty-five miles and dropped approximately three thousand feet in elevation.

Below its confluence with Slough Creek and above its confluence with Soda Butte Creek, the river is accessible only by foot. Access to the lower portion of the river is relatively difficult as no defined trail exists, but above Soda Butte Creek the angler can follow the Lamar River Trail. There are places along the Lamar where care should be taken when walking to, or along, the river because of marshy areas that make walking quite difficult. One particular place to watch for is across from the Lamar Ranger Station near the Lamar's confluence with Rose Creek.

Because of the steep gradient in the upper section of the river, it isn't popular with most fishermen. The lower reaches, on the other hand, are considered quite good with high catch rates per angler. The water in the canyon area is marked with large boulders, has a faster pace than in the valley, is home to a greater number of large insects and its deeper holes are home to larger fish than in the slower water upstream.

The fish population in the Lamar consists of approximately seventy percent cutthroat and thirty percent rainbow and hybrid crosses between the two. The fish will average about thirteen inches in length throughout the lower sections with smaller fish populating the upper reaches. Portions of the Lamar are designated "catch-and release," so be sure to check the regulations before fishing.

Although rated quite high as a fishery, the Lamar does have a tendency to become dirty after rain showers, so timing can play an important part in successful fishing results. Disappointing catches are common during rainy periods. Also, the run-off on this river lasts quite a long time and, after a winter with a deep snow pack, the water can be high well into July. If you do wish to fish the area when the Lamar is dirty, success and clear water can usually be found on either of its two fine tributaries, Cache Creek and Soda Butte Creek, with fish averaging about ten inches in length. A hiking trail follows along Cache Creek, while the highway follows Soda Butte Creek. Of course, Slough Creek is a tributary of the Lamar and is also a fine river.

The Lamar Valley exposes the angler not only to the wind, but also to the fish, so we suggest you keep your casts and your profile as low as possible when the situation calls for it. The fish hold more in the deeper water and other areas of protective cover. Because of the different character of the river in its various sections, a variety of fly patterns can be used with success.

In the lower river, large stoneflies are common and black and golden stonefly nymphs in sizes #4 to #8 should be tried. The adults come off near the confluence of the Lamar and the Yellowstone in late June and early July. Woolly Worms and size #8 Hare's Ear nymphs also work well in this section of the river. Throughout the length of the Lamar, grasshopper patterns work well in August, while standard dry patterns during the summer include Humpies, grey and brown Elk Hair Caddis, Royal Wulff and Adams. Common wet patterns include brown and tan Damselfly and Dragonfly nymphs, Zug Bugs and Gold Ribbed Hare's Ear nymphs. Throughout the upper reaches, small dries work well in patterns such as Quill Gordon, Blue Dun, Blue Quill, Pale Morning Dun, Blue Winged Olive, Light Cahill and Hendrickson—all in sizes #14 to #18.

LEWIS RIVER

Map Reference 51

The Lewis River begins and ends within the boundaries of Yellowstone Park. Although only sixteen miles long, it needs to be divided into four sections for discussion as a trout river. From its beginnings at the outlet of Shoshone Lake to its termination at the Snake River just above the south entrance to the park, this river offers a broad range of physical variety as well as angling diversity.

Its upper reaches include the area between Shoshone Lake and Lewis Lake, commonly referred to as either the Shoshone Channel, the Lewis Channel or the Lewis-Shoshone Channel. This reach consists of four miles of slow-moving water with a capricious nature during the summer, but a more consistent temperament during the fall. Access is only by foot or by boat; you can hike to the water from the trail head located approximately 0.5 miles above Lewis Lake off the South Entrance Road or paddle to it from Lewis Lake with a motorless craft. With angling success rated as only fair during most of the season, the heartbeats of anglers quicken during the fall as the number of browns, and the potential for success, increases dramatically in the upper two miles of the channel as these fish enter the river from the lakes to spawn. The upper two miles are considered better than the lower two because it's believed that more fish drop down from Shoshone Lake than move up from Lewis Lake. No matter what the proportionate migration pattern might be, the fisherman willing to spend the time to get there is usually well rewarded for his effort. Standard flies including attractor patterns such as Trudes, Royal Wulffs and Royal Humpies are used during the summer months. Fall sees a change to streamers such as Marabou Muddlers, Woolly Buggers, Light and Dark Spruce Flies and Sculpin imitations. Don't be shy as to size here as a #2 can be very effective. These browns like them big!

The second section of river to consider is situated about two hundred yards from the South Entrance Road between Lewis Lake and Lewis Falls. The best access to this stretch is from the south end of Lewis Lake. If you drive as far as possible into the campground here you'll be near the lake. You can then hike along the beach for less than half a mile until you reach the outlet. Again, fall is the most rewarding time to fish this stretch of water as browns drop out of the lake into the riffles and pools that characterize the stream here. These trout are fished successfully with the same fly patterns used in the channel mentioned in the previous paragraph. The summer months produce fish of smaller size but the surroundings are beautiful and the fishing is delightful with small caddis and mayfly patterns being most productive. Dries work well in the evenings and, because of the character of the water, nymphs can be very effective at any time.

Small water craft of all types are used on Lewis Lake itself. Because motors are allowed on the lake, many anglers prefer to troll with the hope of hooking either brown trout or the lake trout that inhabit this water. Storms appear quickly over the lake and boaters are cautioned to keep an eye to the weather and head to shore if the wind kicks up. If a boat isn't used, the angler can wade along the east shore and cast to cruising fish. With a launching facility just off the road, access is easy and the fishing pressure is relatively heavy, especially in the summer when the campground adjacent to the lake attracts large numbers of tourists. As with other sections of the Lewis River, the fall of the year is the preferred time to be here.

The third area for consideration is that section from Lewis Falls downstream to the Lewis River Canyon. This is generally meadow-type water, averaging about seventy-five feet in width, with abundant insect populations, but with relatively small fish. Much of the water has open banks so a stealthy approach with long fine leaders is the rule. During the summer use caddis and mayfly imitations as well as hoppers along the banks. The silty bottom here is also home to dragonfly and damselfly larvae. During the fall, streamers can be effective when occasional large browns come out from under favorite banks to find spawning gravel.

The fourth section of river, between the top of the Lewis River Canyon and its confluence with the Snake River, is considered too inaccessible to be discussed here. The walls of the canyon are very steep and unsafe and therefore not recommended as an approach to the river.

MADISON RIVER
Map Reference 51

Let's take a drive down the Madison River—a stretch of water long on reputation with fly fishermen throughout the country, yet short in length. Our drive will cover a distance of only fourteen miles. We'll start at the base of National Park Meadows at Madison Junction where the cool waters of the Gibbon River from the east and the warm waters of the Firehole River from the south join chemistries to start the Madison's journey of 150 miles to Three Forks, Montana where it joins the Gallatin and Jefferson Rivers to create the Missouri River.

At Madison Junction the parking area and campground provide ample opportunity for anglers to approach the river with no more than a short walk. The riffles, deep runs, undercut banks and weed growth provide plenty of cover for the trout which here, as well as throughout the rest of the river, consist primarily of browns and rainbows with adequate numbers of whitefish to provide action for fishermen using nymphs. The weedy reaches are best fished with dry flies and, because the season is concentrated in the summer and fall months and the water temperature is uncommonly warm, insects are on the water throughout the season.

As you proceed downstream from the Junction, the river is on your left and you'll notice a number of parking areas used by anglers for access to inviting stretches of river; between the Junction and West Yellowstone there are no fewer than thirty such pullouts. At 4.5 miles you'll notice a stretch of river filled with large boulders; this is deep water with many weeds and interesting surface currents. It is home to good numbers of trout and its water has trickled over the tops of many waders as fishermen have tried to inch ever closer to seductive areas on which to float their artificials with a drag-free drift. This run of about a quarter mile in length is named the Nine Mile Hole because of its location nine miles from West Yellowstone.

For the next two miles, until you cross the bridge above the Seven Mile Hole, the approach to the river is very swampy and unstable. You can unexpectedly sink to the top of your boots, get stuck in the muck, and generally find yourself in a frustrating and potentially dangerous situation. We suggest staying out of this area altogether.

For a half mile below the bridge, the Seven Mile Hole provides interesting water to the angler while offering the fish numerous places to rest among the weeds, channels and debris of the river bed. Throughout this stretch and on down to an area called the Long Riffle, the angler should be attentive when wading to avoid slipping into deeper water from the many little hillocks of sand in the river bed. The three miles of riffle water below this point provides little cover for larger fish so the angler can expect to catch smaller trout and whitefish.

The river now pulls away from the and the next vehicle access is from a side road to the north off the highway at a point 0.6 miles from the West Entrance to the park. This road leads to the river in an area known to all habitues of the Madison as "The Barns Holes," so called because this was the location in a bygone era where the Union Pacific Railroad housed the coaches and horses used to transport tourists from West Yellowstone into the park on sightseeing excursions. Driving directly to the river on this road, the angler parks at "Barns No. 1." If other anglers are fishing the obvious run in front of you, you'll notice they start at the head of the run and inch their way to the tail, the technique commonly used when steelhead fishing. The same technique is used at "Barns No. 2." About a quarter mile downstream the road ends and foot traffic provides the access to "Barns No. 3" and the water below. Just above the No. 1 hole is the well-known Cable Car Run, popular to all who fish here.

The riverside below the Barns Holes, known as Beaver Meadows, becomes soft and marshy and caution is advised while walking the banks here. Beaver runs and vent holes offer unexpected surprises when anglers are watching for fish rather than their footing. The river through these meadows splits into several channels and offers plenty of water to fish.

The last designated water within the park is called Baker's Hole, a large, deep, impressive piece of water in a bend of the river near the west boundary of the park. It's accessible by walking from above or by driving on Highway 191 north of West Yellowstone. The total length of river not directly accessible by vehicle in this lower section is approximately four miles; needless to say, it receives less fishing pressure than the twelve miles running next to the highway.

The variety of fly patterns used on the Madison adds to the interest and intrigue of the river. An abundance of insect life inhabits the river from the tiniest mayflies to the largest stoneflies. In very general terms, the upper river will be best fished with smaller artificials imitating mayflies and caddis; while the lower reaches, from the Barns Holes to the park boundary, can often be fished best with larger patterns, such as stonefly nymphs, dragonfly and damselfly nymphs, and streamers. Streamers are used mostly late in the season when spawning brown trout enter the river from Hebgen Lake. Hoppers are excellent throughout August and tiny Tricorythodes dressings are effective in the fall. The Madison is truly a river where many artificials in the fly box can be used with success, but this doesn't imply that the catching of fish is easy; quite to the contrary, it can prove to be extremely challenging. The water is totally clear, natural insects abound, surface currents beg to tug the fly line and drag the fly, and fisherman access to most of the river's length has given the fish ample opportunity to learn the difference between an elk and an angler!

Beautiful sunny weather isn't a prerequisite to successful fishing on this river by any means; some of our finest days have been spent under dreary grey skies, shedding inescapable drops of rain or flakes of snow from our coats, while chilled hands alternated between warming in pockets and holding the rod, as water dripped from hat brims and whisker-bristled chins. Fortunately under these conditions, one's feet stay relatively warm in the thermally-heated currents of the river.

Most of the fishing in the park section of the Madison can be comfortably accomplished using no heavier than a six-weight rod, a floating line and leader tippets down to 5X, although when using tiny dry flies over very shy fish on calm sunny days, 6X and 7X are not unusual. Nymph fishermen may wish to use a sink-tip line but we prefer using weighted flies and leaders and a well greased floating line. Equipment and good advice is abundant in West Yellowstone at many fine tackle shops. It's apparent when traveling through town that this community knows what fishing is all about and is willing to help make your experience here a good one. Guides and outfitters can be hired for wade or float fishing; local guides fish not only the park, but surrounding areas as well. They know when and where the chances for successful fishing take place throughout the year and are experienced in the techniques required to fool fish under all stream conditions.

Although our friends George Kelly and Jim Danskin have been chased across the river by grizzly bears, these frightening experiences took place many years ago and such events are extremely rare today. Sightings of wildlife are common however, and it isn't unusual to see geese, ducks, trumpeter swans, deer and elk feeding at the river. Fall is the best time of year to spot elk and their bugling will fill the valley and excite one's senses as they graze at the river's edge. Seagulls are common over the water, ravens perch in trees along the river and an osprey will occasionally be spotted flying overhead. Fishing on the Madison is truly a memorable experience whether or not the fish cooperate.

SHOSHONE LAKE

Map Reference 51

Shoshone Lake is six miles long, making it the second largest lake in the park after Yellowstone Lake. Only the dedicated fisherman casts into this body of water because access is by either hiking a minimum of 2.5 miles or rowing or paddling a boat upstream for approximately 4 miles.

The 80,000 surface acres of Shoshone Lake are situated at an elevation of 7,800 feet in the southwestern section of the park. Hiking access trail heads are located just north of Lewis Lake off the South Entrance Road, in DeLacey Park off the Grand Loop Road west of West Thumb, and in the Old Faithful area along the Howard Eaton Trail to the south over Grants Pass. This latter trail is the long way to the lake at approximately eight miles; the DeLacey Trail is the shortest.

Waterway access is via the Lewis River Channel between Lewis Lake and Shoshone. This is a small-craft route, where only paddles or oars may be used; motor-driven craft are not allowed in the channel or on Shoshone Lake itself. The further into the season one makes this trip, the lower the water level becomes and the greater the probability that a portage will be necessary in some areas.

Although brook trout in small numbers inhabit the lake, fishermen mostly pursue browns and mackinaw. They have their best success in early and late season when the bigger fish cruise near the shoreline and along the rock shelves out from shore. The south shore seems to be the most popular. Because of the access, Shoshone receives relatively little fishing pressure throughout the season, but the channel between Shoshone Lake and Lewis Lake sees increased numbers of fishermen in the fall when spawning browns occupy the channel. Should you wish to camp in this area, a permit is required.

Although standard fly patterns are common here, the most success seems to be gained by use of a variety of streamer flies, with Muddlers, Woolly Buggers and Spruce Flies being most popular.

SLOUGH CREEK

Map Reference 50

After originating in the Beartooth Mountains, Slough Creek winds its way through the Absaroka Range to enter Yellowstone National Park from the north. During its sixteen mile flow through the park, this gentle river makes its way about seventy percent of the time through meadow terrain and the balance through rocky canyons. Access is almost entirely achieved by foot because the road goes only to the campground, while the river flows from above the campground with no road access, and continues the same way. The lower river travels approximately three miles to its confluence with the Lamar River and in this reach the angler has approximately two miles of easy access from the road. The last mile the river runs through a rugged canyon. The more desirable and popular water is above the campground, reachable after a two mile walk to the first and second meadow areas.

To access the meadows, it's best to pick up the trail head located halfway

Slough Creek

between the highway and the campground and then follow the old Slough Creek Wagon Trail. If you start out along the river at the campground, the trail will take you through a canyon with difficult passage. The first meadow is about a forty-five minute walk; waders aren't really necessary, but a net is recommended for landing the fish from the stream bank. For those wishing to fish farther upstream, a hike up to the second meadow will take approximately three additional hours; this travel time cuts considerably into the available fishing hours if the angler plans to accomplish the total trip in only one day.

Experienced fishermen feel that the fish above the campground are more easily caught, probably due to less pressure, but that the fish below the campground are of a somewhat larger size, possibly due to slightly warmer water and a greater variety of available insect life. If you choose to fish above the campground, you'll find the first mile or so of trail is rather steep, so take your time and enjoy the scenery. Visitors from lower elevations should take care not to overdo it!

Slough Creek has been designated a "catch-and-release" fishery. It has a high rating as a cutthroat stream, with some rainbows also available. An average fish is about fourteen inches. To fool these wary fish the angler should consider using leaders down to 5X and 6X, with 7X used on tiny flies. Caddis are the predominant insect here, with Brachycentrus, Rhyacophila and Hydropsyche in abundance. Soft hackle patterns in orange, yellow and green are favorite wet flies as is the Gold Ribbed Hare's Ear Nymph, all of these in size #14 and #16. A variety of dry patterns work well including Elk Hair Caddis, Humpy, Hair Wing Variant, Renegade, Blue Dun, Blue Winged Olive, Adams and Lt. Cahill, all in sizes #14 to #18. Midges come off the creek, as do mayflies, dragonflies and damselflies so the nymphs of these insects should also be tried.

During August the grasshopper imitations can be the premier fly patterns, fished up along the grassy banks. A variety of sizes and colors should be tried, but #6 and #8 seem to work best.

Along with the variety of aquatic and terrestrial insects enjoyed by the trout, the angler will be enjoyed by the mosquitoes if repellent isn't part of the tackle used here. Mosquitoes are numerous, so protect yourself! Along with sightings of mosquitoes, the angler may see more interesting creatures along the river including elk, moose, marmots, ducks, geese, loons and, on rare occasions, bear.

SNAKE RIVER AND FALLS RIVER

Map References 51, 49

Most of the major rivers and streams in the park that provide interest to the angler are easily accessible by vehicle. In many areas the stream and road share the same valley floor and, as a result, the fisherman is allowed an almost instantaneous transition from "driving" the river to fishing it! The popular Madison, Gibbon, Firehole, Gallatin and Yellowstone Rivers all fall into this category. The Snake and Falls Rivers, however, are two streams that require that the angler do some hiking, as they are followed only by foot trails.

The Snake originates in the southeast section of the park directly south of Yellowstone Lake, adjacent to the park boundary. It flows to the northwest for about ten miles before it turns southwest to exit the park near the south entrance, about sixty miles north of Jackson. Access to the river is along the South Boundary Trail.

The Falls River begins in the southwest corner of the park south of Pitchstone Plateau. It travels approximately forty miles before it leaves the park as it crosses the South Boundary Trail, which provides the primary access to the river, and continues into Idaho. The river derives its name from the fact that its swift currents traverse relatively steep terrain that produces several cascades and waterfalls.

The predominant fish species in both of these rivers is the cutthroat and the average size of approximately ten to twelve inches, is rated somewhat below park standards for other rivers. Rainbow will also be taken in the Falls River and rainbow, brown and brook trout will be found in the Snake.

These are considered back-country streams and if you're not planning to camp, you should allow time to return to your vehicle before darkness sets in. The mosquito population exceeds the trout population here, so don't forget the repellent! Fly patterns include the standards, with nymphs somewhat more popular on the Falls than on the Snake.

YELLOWSTONE LAKE

Map Reference 52

Resting at 7,733 feet in elevation, beautiful Yellowstone Lake covers an area of approximately 150 square miles. Its depths of almost three hundred feet are home to the largest fishery for pure-strain cutthroat trout in the world. Fishermen catch these fish in the size range of from ten to twenty inches, with the average being fifteen to eighteen inches.

Fishing from boats as well as wading the shoreline is effective here with both methods being more productive the farther one goes from the boat-launching areas, which include Bridge Bay, Fishing Bridge, Grant Village and Lake Village. Motors are prohibited in some areas and life vests should be in each boat because of severe storms that come up unexpectedly and imperil small craft. Boating regulations are available and should be followed when on the lake.

For fishermen without boats, the shoreline can offer good fishing and many anglers wade out as far as possible to cast to fish that cruise near shore. Both spin and fly fishermen find this technique to be effective. Seasons here are established to protect the spawning runs of cutthroat in both the lake and the inlet streams, so regulations should be understood before fishing. Mid-June is the usual opening of the lake and mid-July is the normal opening for fishing in the feeder streams.

YELLOWSTONE RIVER

Map Reference 53

As the park through which it flows was named for the yellow rhyolite lava rock in the canyon through which it tumbles, the Yellowstone River was also appropriately named. This river begins at the southern boundary of the park, flows through its largest lake, surges over great falls and through two canyons and finally exits the park at its northern boundary. It is the park's longest river system and its largest. The major canyon it carved through the earth's surface was designated "Grand" in an attempt to properly describe the magnificence it displays. As with other wonders of nature, we often reflect on the emotional impact it must have had on those first explorers who, without advance knowledge or preconception, came upon its wondrous sights unexpectedly and realized that their eyes were the very first to absorb the vista before them. When we now look upon the Grand Canyon of the Yellowstone we know we're not the first to view it, but the impact is no less exhilarating This river should definitely be experienced by all who visit here, fisherman and sightseer alike.

For purposes of description we'll start at the headwaters where the river evolves in the marshy, meadow country southeast of Yellowstone Lake on the park border. It flows through this valley at the eastern edge of the Two Ocean Plateau for approximately fifteen miles before entering the southeast arm of Yellowstone Lake. This area of the park is known as the Thorofare Region and the river is followed for its length by the Thorofare Trail which also hugs the eastern shore of Yellowstone Lake. This remote region is seen by very few visitors as the trail itself is long and difficult; anglers with boats usually fish only the inlet area to the arm itself, rarely taking the trouble to walk up along the river. The stream here is small, but does contain cutthroat trout to eighteen inches.

Although the river enters Yellowstone Lake as a relatively small stream, it exits as a substantial river—one of the largest trout rivers in the country. The first mile of water below the lake is a spawning area for trout and therefore is closed to all fishing; the next six miles downstream, from the angler's perspective, is the most popular water on the river. This area of catch-and-release fishing is home to the native Yellowstone Cutthroat Trout, the only species found in this portion of the river. The area is carefully managed to protect the fish population and the regulations are designed to enhance the fishing experience for all who enjoy these waters. Fish of sixteen to eighteen inches are common, with some beautiful specimens exceeding twenty inches. This open area extends down to Sulphur Cauldron and consists of a variety of water types; some can be waded and some cannot. This is heavy water running over loose gravel in many places, so fishermen are forewarned to wade with care and not take reckless chances in order to reach attractive, but potentially dangerous, areas of the river.

One of the more popular locations on this section of river is Buffalo Ford, a picnic area offering excellent access to a delightful quarter-mile section of the river containing gentle runs, brisk riffles and deep holes dropping from rock ledges. Access is most easily gained from the highway side of the river here. The Howard Eaton Trail does, however, extend along the eastern bank of the river; access to the trail is from Fishing Bridge.

The next six-mile section between Sulphur Cauldron and the confluence of Alum Creek and the Yellowstone is closed to all fishing. This area is in the beautiful Hayden Valley, with its open meadows, rolling hillsides and abundant wildlife. It's very likely that travelers in this area will see several species of waterfowl on the river and, at the same time, sight numerous buffalo and elk grazing in the valley by the river or in the meadows to the west of the road.

From Alum Creek down to Chittenden Bridge the river is again open to fishing, but due to its swift currents, it is not a popular section of river with the angler. From Chittenden Bridge downstream to Inspiration Point the river is closed to all fishing. This is the area of the upper Grand Canyon with its magnificent Upper and Lower Falls, Artist Point and the settlement of Canyon Village. Below Inspiration Point the river is open to fishing. The Grand Canyon itself is becoming very popular with fishermen who are willing to make the 1,500 foot descent to the river. The area is truly spectacular and the fish are among the largest in the entire river system. Accesses are available out of Canyon Village on the Seven Mile Hole Trail as well as on the Howard Eaton Trail coming upstream from the Tower area.

The next region of interest to the angler is in the vicinity of Tower Junction downstream into the Black Canyon of the Yellowstone. The fishing here can be compared favorably with that of the Grand Canyon, but the advantage of this reach is that the hike into the river is much less strenuous. This portion of the river is big and brawling, with fast currents and a boulder-strewn river bed. Wading here is difficult and most fishermen work it from the bank. We find rainbow, whitefish and some brook trout here, in addition to the predominant cutthroat. The insect population also varies somewhat, with large stoneflies in abundance along with good populations of caddis and mayflies. In addition to standard nymph and dry fly patterns, the angler will want to fish large black and golden stonefly nymphs near the bottom. We'd suggest a six- or seven-weight fly rod here as this is big water and some of the time you'll be casting either sink-tip lines or using weighted flies and leaders. Because of the hiking distances required, one's attention should probably center first around the hike and secondly around the fishing. The trails require from half an hour up to two hours just to reach the river, so allow plenty of time to get in, do your fishing and return to your car before dark. Be prepared for inclement weather and take proper maps and compass to avoid becoming lost!

There are several accesses to the lower portions of the river. The Barronette Bridge Trail is just off a side road which turns north immediately east of the river bridge on the Northeast Entrance Road near Tower Junction. This trail follows the Lamar River to the east for about a mile, crosses the Lamar, then swings back to the west along the Yellowstone. This one is some distance from the river, so some off-trail hiking will have to be done to gain access to the river. West of Tower Junction the Garnet Hill Trail heads north toward the river which is about four miles away. There is a bridge across the river here and the trail continues northwest along the north side of the river. Approximately seven miles east of Mammoth, the Blacktail Trail heads north from the road at Blacktail Pond. This access also requires a hike of about four miles to the river. A foot bridge crosses the river and intercepts the Yellowstone River Trail on the north side. This trail can then be taken downstream past Crevice Lake, Knowles Falls, Rattlesnake Butte and finally into the town of Gardiner, Montana at the North Entrance of the park. Below Gardiner, the river is paralleled by the highway, access is easy and fishing pressure is therefore increased considerably.

For any of the trips mentioned here, be sure to allow yourself plenty of time to enjoy the hike, enjoy the fishing and return to your starting point in comfort and safety. Carry as little as possible, but by all means carry the necessities of food, drink, clothing and fishing tackle.

That's the Yellowstone River—approximately seventy miles of beautiful water, spectacular countryside and rewarding trout fishing! We always feel grateful to those who manage the park and the fishing as this is unquestionably a unique and magnificent part of our country, and its preservation as a natural environment available to millions of visitors each year is an important and valuable national heritage.

To Yellowstone National Park

Silver Gate

Cooke City

BIG BEAR LODGE

To Red Lodge

North

© Stream Stalker, Inc. 1988

COOKE CITY

LODGING

BIG BEAR LODGE
6 miles east of the northeast entrance to Yellowstone National Park, on Hwy. 212, near Cooke City, Box 1052   838-2267

Fly fishing headquarters for Yellowstone National Park. Log cabin lodging, home cooked gourmet meals, expert guide service, tackle shop and saddle horses. Guided fly fishing expeditions into Yellowstone Park's splendid northeast corner.

PART III: ISLAND PARK, IDAHO

HENRY'S FORK RIVER

Map Reference 26

Idaho's Henry's Fork of the Snake River, also known by its more formal name, the North Fork of the Snake, hardly requires an introduction. To the angling community it's as well known as is Babe Ruth to the baseball devotee. It originates in that corner of Idaho that butts against Yellowstone Park on the east and the Centennial Valley of Montana to the north. We include this tiny area of Idaho in this Montana book because the waters here have traditionally been an intrinsic part of the angling experience for those who fish in southwestern Montana. Usually when anglers make West Yellowstone their fishing vacation headquarters they fish not only Montana, but venture toward Yellowstone Park in Wyoming, and Island Park in Idaho. We would be remiss not to include both areas in this volume.

If you enjoy fishing fairly heavy water in a canyon environment, you'll like the Henry's Fork. If you delight in picking out a rising trout in a spring creek

Henry's Fork in the Box Canyon

256

and spending considerable concentrated time in the attempt to seduce him, you'll like the Henry's Fork. If you'd like to do the above on fairly big water, with plenty of casting room, you'll love the Henry's Fork. It does offer a great variety of challenges to anglers and anglers from across the country flock here at times to test their skills and often their patience.

The Henry's Fork has its origin at Big Springs. This surge of 50-degree water comes from the ground at a rate of 92,000 gallons per minute, year in and year out. No fishing is allowed here, but very large rainbow and browns hold in its transparent water and they are beautiful to see.

In addition to Big Springs, the Henry's Lake Outlet also contributes water to this river. From the Outlet mouth the river flows into Island Park Reservoir, below which the Buffalo River makes its contribution into the "Fork," and from there it continues south through the Box Canyon, Harriman State Park and finally empties into the main part of the Snake River below Rexburg, Idaho. In this review we'll cover the area from the river's source to Mesa Falls.

Within this distance there are three distinct areas with different water types. Traditionally the writings about this river have been concentrated on only one area, giving the general impression that the watercourse is made up entirely of a wide, slow-moving body of water with little surface character and displaying an abundance of tiny mayflies on the water. This image is accurate but for only one of the three sections involved. There is fishing, of course,

Henry's Fork River at Last Chance

257

above Island Park Reservoir, but most anglers gravitate to the water below the Reservoir. The water that flows from the dam at Island Park soon enters the area known as the Box Canyon where the water is fast and therefore belies the "spring creek" image of the river. The spring-creek image is best described by the stretch of water below the canyon in the meadow reaches between the community of Last Chance and Riverside. Below Riverside the water once again picks up speed and loses the spring-creek personality.

The three mile stretch of the Box Canyon, referred to as "the Box" by those who frequent it, is usually floated, but it can be waded at times when outflow from the dam is at lower discharge rates. This generally occurs before and after the summer months when irrigation demands are made by downstream potato and wheat farmers. The water in the Box does put a push on your waders at all times and in most places the river cannot be forded. The Box offers the best opportunity on the river for taking large trout and some truly substantial fish have been caught here. Even a three or four pound fish in that swift current will test your skill and equipment. Floaters will often put in just below the dam at the launching ramp there and float down to Last Chance. Foot access is available throughout the canyon via offshoot roads to the river. Not far below the confluence of the Buffalo River, facilities for overnight camping are available at the Box Canyon Campground. One thing to remember while floating the Box is that it is illegal to fish from a boat. You must beach the boat and wade the river.

Between the canyon and Last Chance, the terrain changes to a much wider valley, showing only occasional boulders and displaying more sagebrush and grass along the river, which now is much slower and moving in a wide channel. This transition is gradual, but we now begin to experience the spring-creek nature of the river, which has an average depth of about three feet and a width of one hundred yards. There are about seven miles of river in this section including Harriman State Park or what is referred to locally as "the Ranch." The ranch was formerly owned by the Harriman family and was kept open to public fishing through the kindness of the owners. It has recently been sold and is now under the control of Idaho's state park system.

This portion of river has all the characteristics of a classic spring creek, a flat, weedy bed covered with small gravel which makes for easy wading, even when the water is at wader top. Many anglers prefer to float this section of river in order to cover a lot of water and avoid the necessity of walking fairly long distances to find fish. Floaters prefer using McKenzie-type boats or the lower-profile boats such as prams or rafts which are more maneuverable and easily transported in and out of the river. Belly boats are more often seen on the river as their use grows in popularity. This section of river within the state park boundaries is limited to fly fishing only with a single, barbless hook; a recommended outfit would be a five-weight rod with a floating line. Although

Henry's Fork River in Harriman State Park

the river iş wide, its currents are tricky and short casts are the rule to provide the all important line control necessary to avoid drag on the fly. Long leaders, fine tippets and controlled line drift are important on this water. There are many fish between fifteen and twenty inches here but the majority of catches are of fish from ten to twelve inches. The "granddaddys" do not succumb to temptation as easily as many of us would wish and novice anglers often have to settle for the more realistic satisfaction of catching the more numerous "grandsons."

Below the "Ranch" the river flows flat for several miles before again picking up speed near Riverside where the gradient increases. From Riverside to the Lookout Butte area, the floater is confronted with white water rated to Class II rapids. There is a boat ramp at Lookout Butte and it should be used by all floaters since between this point and the Upper Mesa Falls, the river is considered to be unfloatable. These spectacular falls of 105 feet and 65 feet respectively, are well worth visiting, but you wouldn't want to boat over them! This lower section above the falls is accented with boulders, lava rocks, log jams and the surrounding evergreen forest. This is water best fished with stouter tackle than used above. We'd recommend using a size six- to eight-weight outfit. Spin fishing is allowed here, as it is in the Box Canyon, and favorite lures include smaller sizes of Mepps, Panther Martin and Triple

Teaser. Rapalas are also popular and account for some of the larger fish being hooked.

Throughout the Henry's Fork drainage, special regulations have been assigned to specific reaches to help optimize the quality of the fishing experience. It behooves the angler to read the regulations applicable to the area he intends to fish as some of the river is open to fishing only during the summer and fall. Some reaches are assigned special method restrictions and slot limits.

It is estimated that up to ninety percent of the trout population are rainbows throughout this entire section of the river, from Island Park Reservoir down to Mesa Falls. Anglers also hook a few cutthroat and a good number of whitefish. In the Box Canyon and the lower reaches, sculpin are common and provide good forage for the trout. Insects, however, provide the bulk of food for the fish here, and they reside in this river in enormous numbers. A handful of standard patterns really isn't adequate to fish the river properly, so we're listing those which usually produce well throughout the season.

In the Box as well as the lower river you'll do well at any time with nymphs and streamers. Large rubberleg patterns, Bitch Creeks, Yuk Bugs, Brown Hackle Peacocks, Prince and Zug Bug from size #2 through #8 are all excellent patterns and fish well, depending on conditions. Streamers include Woolly Buggers, Light and Dark Spruce and several different patterns of the Muddler Minnows. These patterns should be part of a standard selection for these two areas of the river. The greatest variety of insect life occurs on the Ranch section and the following synopsis is directed to, but not limited to, that area. This rather comprehensive listing is available because anglers have been compelled to study the trout's aquatic insect diet in order to hook him on a more regular basis. Many anglers keep records from year to year relative to emergence data of the various insects and are constantly experimenting with new artificial fly patterns. The development of these new patterns by anglers such as Rene Harrop and Mike Lawson are almost always imaginative and successful and they eventually become standards on this river.

In March the Iron Blue Quills appear in size #16 and 18 and olive-bodied dries and emergers are used to imitate them. In April and May expect to see the Black Quill and use imitations such as Mahogany Duns and Dark Quill Gordons in #14 to match them. About May 20 the well-known Salmonfly hatch will start below the ranch and progress upstream to arrive at the Box about June 10. If you're on the river between the first and fifteenth of June, you should find the hatch somewhere on the river. These large, three-year old insects are imitated with several standard stonefly patterns in size #4 and #6 for the adults and #2 and #4 for the nymphs.

From late May through July there are excellent hatches of caddisflies on the river in a variety of species with several color and size variations. For the most part fishing these patterns is more effective during the late afternoon and evening hours, whereas mayfly activity is concentrated more in the mid-day hours. Pale Morning Duns hatch from June through August, usually during mid-morning, with spinners on the water in early morning. Imitations in size #16 to #20 will be effective.

The best known, and certainly most enthusiastically attended, hatch of the year is the Western Green Drake. Its emergence varies according to weather and water conditions, but it is traditionally expected around June 22. These large, #10 and #12 mayflies will show for about two weeks. They come off in late morning and are more numerous in water of medium-fast speed. It's during this hatch that the river undergoes its greatest angler invasion of the year. Fly rod enthusiasts from across the country enjoy the fishing, the renewal of acquaintanceships and general comraderie along the river bank. In late June the golden stoneflies start to emerge and they continue to do so into the first part of August.

In early July the large, #10 Brown Drakes begin to emerge just as the Green Drakes are subsiding. At times both duns and spinners are on the water simultaneously during the evening hours. Blue Winged Olives in size #14 to #16 as well as #20 to #22 are standard patterns during July. Look for these duns primarily in the afternoon, with spinners on the water during morning and evening hours.

In August the larger caddisflies tend to give way to a small, dark species in size #16. From late August into September the Tricorythodes make their appearance and anglers can have great success with both the dun and spinner forms in size #20 and #22 .

As September heralds the beginning of autumn, Blue Winged Olives will again appear on the river in tiny size #20 and #22, along with #16 and #18 Mahogany Duns coming off about mid-morning. In addition you can expect to see Callibaetis in size #16. Adams and Speckled Spinner patterns work well for imitating these insects.

There are times throughout the season when hatch-matching becomes totally perplexing and anglers will shift strategy and use ant and beetle patterns. Attractor flies can also work well at times with Royal Wulff, Royal Trude and Wright's Royal being popular patterns to try.

For specific information on day-to-day fishing strategy we strongly suggest you contact the local shops that specialize in being up to date about conditions on the river. We've attempted here to discuss the river sections fished most often by those visiting anglers who include this area of Idaho in their Montana trip. Other angling opportunities are available in the area and the local shops can give you information about them.

The fraternity of concerned anglers throughout the U. S. grows daily as the popularity of sport fishing increases and, sadly, the water available in which to enjoy the sport, decreases. No matter how prime a river appears to the casual "vacation" angler, such vacation destinations can and many times do have their problems; sometimes they are created by natural causes, sometimes by anglers. Unfortunately, more often than not, the latter is the case. Nonetheless, concerned anglers from Idaho and other states throughout the nation, have formed an organization to monitor the various influences affecting the Henry's Fork and to address problems, old and new, with vision and enthusiasm not only to prevent degradation of the river and its riparian environment, but to improve conditions in general. The organization is the Henry's Fork Foundation, Inc. Specifically, the Foundation has instigated many fishery projects including studies on proposed hydro-power projects that could severely affect the river, the design of improved access facilities for fishermen and the installation of several miles of solar powered electric fencing to prevent bank deterioration due to cattle grazing. The goals, efforts and results of this organization are important and we wish to make their cause known, as they can use any mental and financial contributions that come their way. For information regarding this worthwhile organization, write the Henry's Fork Foundation, Inc., P.O. Box 61, Island Park, Idaho 83429.

River Notes

ISLAND PARK RESERVOIR AND HENRY'S LAKE

Map Reference 26

Most of us would have difficulty imagining a community with a population of fewer than five hundred residents, yet having a main street that extends for a total length of thirty-three miles. Nevertheless, these incongruous figures do describe Island Park, Idaho. The description, however, applies to neither an island nor a park, but rather to an extensive resort area that lies at approximately seven thousand feet in elevation and is located along the highway. Rather than the tightly-knit community of homes and stores that characterize most communities, this one takes all the space it needs! Within this area you'll find many miles of good water to fish and enough stores to serve your vacation needs. Not only does the legendary Henry's Fork of the Snake River flow through here, there are two reservoirs of no small importance that provide still water fishing opportunities for many anglers. We'll discuss both Island Park Reservoir and Henry's Lake here.

Island Park Reservoir is the southernmost and largest of the two. It is about ten miles long and two miles wide and is nourished by water from several feeder streams, the most notable of which is the Henry's Fork River entering from the northeast. The reservoir is a popular family recreation area with camping, boating and water sports attracting folks who enjoy other activities along with their fishing. Fishermen also have good reason to use this water because the fish are plentiful and their size is respectable. Rainbows make up the majority of the population, with cutthroat and brook trout coming in a distant second and third. There's also a good population of kokanee salmon and a healthy number of chubs offering forage to the larger trout.

This impoundment was established as an irrigation project. The reservoir fills during the spring run-off and water is released during summer months to the agricultural areas downstream. The effect of these draw-downs on the reservoir can be dramatic; extremely low water levels occur during low-water years and this, of course, changes the fishing grounds substantially.

Most of the fishing here is done from boats and there are five launching ramps to accommodate them. Four of the ramps are located on the eastern arms of the reservoir and one is on the south shore at West End Campground. Camping is also available at several areas on the eastern arms. Some shore wading is effective and many anglers use float tubes. One popular area to fish is the west end. Boaters float the mouths of the feeder streams and the fingers are accessible and provide good fishing to the angler afoot. Another popular area is Trude Bay which contains a large spring that seeps into the reservoir. Many fish here are taken while trolling and some are taken fly fishing. Good summer hatches of Callibaetis bring trout to the surface creating good dry fly fishing in addition to the more frequently used techniques of casting nymphs and streamers.

Regulations governing fishermen on the reservoir present an interesting problem in that it's difficult to keep a limit of fish. The regulation states that an angler may keep six fish, but only two may be longer than sixteen inches. If you wish to keep all six fish allowed, you'll have a problem because most fish are larger than sixteen inches.

The other important body of water in the region is Henry's Lake which, for the past fifty years, has received innumerable well-deserved accolades for the quantity and quality of fish here. This lake is only open five-months out of the year, opening in May and closing in October. It is surrounded by grass, sage and a few willows. The lake is shallow with a maximum depth of twenty feet and an average depth of eight feet, but when summer weeds bloom, the fisherman has much less water in which to cast his fly or lure. Nine tributary streams and seven major springs in the lake bed continuously pump pure water into it.

This body of water is considered one of the best in the country for its production of large numbers of large fish. The population consists of cutthroats, cutthroat/rainbow hybrids and brook trout. There are no pure rainbow strains or browns here. The hybrids thrive in this environment and many in the fifteen-pound class have been caught. The brook trout average four to five pounds. The regulations allow fishing only between 5:00 a.m. and 9:00 p.m. and the limit has been set at two fish per day.

Most of the fly fishing here requires the use of a full Type II sinking or intermediate line. Flies used are primarily wet, with scuds, damsels, dragons, mays, caddis and leeches all producing well. Of all these, the local imitations of the scud are probably used with the greatest frequency. The lake is basically rectangular in shape and wading is a poor option, so most fishing is done from boats and float tubes. There is heavy weed growth throughout the lake and anglers seek out the open areas between the weed patches. Hooking a fish here is not difficult but once it is hooked the weeds come into play and landing the fish is not so easy.

Popular areas for fly fishing include the shore south of the county boat dock on the west shore, the southwest corner at Hope Creek, south of the fish hatchery along the east shore and at the lake's outlet. Fly patterns include Woolly Buggers, Henry's Lake Leech, Henry's Renegade, Henry's Lake Shrimp, Prince Nymph and damselfly nymphs in June when the naturals emerge. Occasionally dry fly fishing is effective, usually near the outlet, using

Callibaetis imitations. Spin fishermen do well with the Rocky Mountain Spinfly Lure and the Flatfish. Two public boat ramps and camping sites are available on the lake as are stores and lodging.

The Henry's Lake Foundation was formed by a group of concerned anglers in 1981 in an attempt to preserve the outstanding fishing in this lake. Thousands of dollars have been raised and donated to projects such as predation studies, fish screen installations, hybrid trout production and riparian habitat restoration. Information on membership and current projects is available at the lake.

River Notes

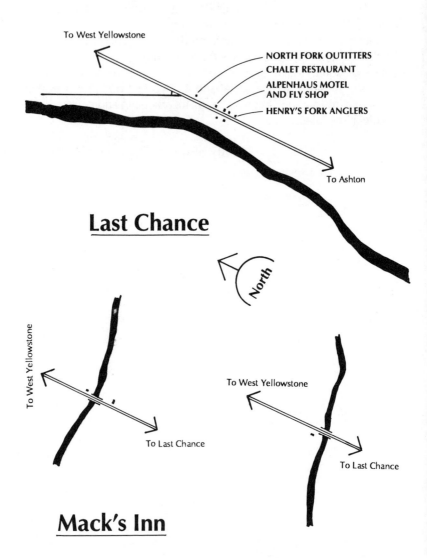

To West Yellowstone

NORTH FORK OUTITTERS
CHALET RESTAURANT
ALPENHAUS MOTEL
AND FLY SHOP
HENRY'S FORK ANGLERS

To Ashton

Last Chance

North

To West Yellowstone

To Last Chance

Mack's Inn

To West Yellowstone

To Last Chance

Island Park

LAST CHANCE

GUIDES / OUTFITTERS

HENRY'S FORK ANGLERS
Last Chance, (mailing address HC 66, Box 38A, Ashton ID 83420)   (208) 558-7525
summer, (208) 624-3590 winter
> Float trips, wade trips, individual instruction and fly fishing schools. We serve the Madison and Henry's Fork Rivers, as well as the popular streams in Yellowstone National Park. Full service tackle shop, mail order catalog. Accommodations arranged.

NORTH FORK OUTFITTERS
Last Chance, (mailing address HC 66, Box 31, Ashton ID 83420)   558-7388
> Your complete angling headquarters for the Henry's Fork, Henry's Lake, Yellowstone National Park and nearby Montana rivers. Float trips, guide services and top lines of equipment and clothing for all anglers.

CAMPGROUND / RV PARK

VALLEY VIEW GROCERY, INC.
Hwy. 20 at Henry's Lake, (mailing address HC 66, Box 26, Mack's Inn ID 83433)   (208) 558-7443
> With the campground, we have full hook-ups, barbecue pits and full shower facilities. We also have one cabin. We have complete laundry facilities and an RV section. At the store, we have a complete fishing department, including hunting and fishing licenses, a hand crafted gift shop, beer, wine, groceries, gas and propane.

LODGING

ALPENHAUS MOTEL AND FLY SHOP
Last Chance, (mailing address HC 66, Box 40, Ashton ID 83420) (208) 558-9951
> Complete fly shop, motel and guide service with experienced, licensed guides serving the Henry's Fork and Yellowstone National Park. Open all year. Motel has clean, comfortable, reasonably priced units. Fly tying bench available in the motel lounge.

STALEY SPRINGS LODGE
West shore of Henry's Lake, (mailing address Star Route, Box 102, Island Park, ID 83429)
(208) 558-7471
> Located on the west shore of Henry's Lake where trophy trout are common. Housekeeping cabins, restaurant, bar, boat rental, store and tackle shop, plus lakeside RV park with complete hookups.

RESTAURANTS

CHALET RESTAURANT
On the banks of the Henry's Fork at Last Chance, (mailing address HC 66, Box 46, Ashton ID 83420)   (208) 558-9953
> For many years, the favorite meeting and dining spot in Last Chance for the visiting and local anglers. The best breakfast in town. Hot scones, homemade pies, sack lunches to go. We cooka' da food, you eat!

Acknowledgements

One of the most vital aspects of conducting research for a book of this type is gathering information from individuals who have intimate knowledge, frequent contact and prolonged experience with the waters about which we write. Throughout our intensive, and extensive, travels in Montana we were extremely fortunate to talk with fishermen who not only possessed these qualities, but were genuinely interested in sharing their unique store of knowledge so that others might benefit from it. If time restrictions weren't a factor, we could still be conducting interviews, for Montana has no shortage of fishermen with skills, insights and opinions from which we could all profit.

Fortunately none of the individuals listed below was in the least bit reticent concerning their favorite sport and for the time and wisdom they shared with us, we once more extend our heartfelt appreciation along with an offer to reciprocate if ever we can.

Bill Abbot—Hamilton—Near the Bitterroot River in a first floor room of his City Center Motel.

Al Anderson—Jefferson Valley—In the lower level of his Canoeing House with a panoramic view overlooking a wide bend on the lower Jefferson River.

John Bailey—Livingston—Taking time from C.E.O. duties at Dan Bailey's Fly Shop, his thoughtful reflections of a life on the Yellowstone River, expression of current conditions and hope for the future of Montana trout fishing were special words to these authors.

Doug Brewer—Missoula—Whose enthusiasm for the Blackfoot made us wish we were fishing it rather than just talking about it.

Bob Butler—Twin Bridges—In the comfortable "lounge" section of his downtown fly shop next to one of the bridges.

Chris Cauble—Livingston—With a complete and precise monolog of local angling lore from the office sanctum of George Anderson's Yellowstone Angler Tackle Shop.

Dick Crain—Thompson Falls—On a cloudy morning over breakfast in a local eatery.

Jim Danskin—West Yellowstone—In the living room of his handsome log home at Baker's Hole.

Craig Fellin—Wise River—In his cozy fishing lodge next to the river while enjoying Peggy's coffee and trying to spot a moose in the backyard.

Steve Gary—Libby—While watching the logging trucks pass his fishin' Hole Tackle Shop window and his customers head for the river.

Tom Glorvigen—Three Forks—Sitting in the warm, fall sunshine on the deck of his home at his KOA Campground overlooking the broad vista of the Missouri Headwater country.

Ron Gras—West Yellowstone—In his spacious tackle shop, the Sportsmen's Outpost, during the fall "quiet time" in an otherwise busy town.

Fritz Groenke—Bigfork—While soaking up the sun in the community park next to the Swan River spillway.

Monty Hankinson—Dillon—On a bright afternoon when he wasn't guiding and we would rather have been fishing the Beaverhead.

Rick Hauer—Flathead Lake—In his laboratory at the University of Montana Research and Education Biological Station at Yellow Bay.

Jack Hutchison—Sheridan—On a beautiful fall afternoon in his fly shop when he had a rare day off.

Ron Johnson—Seeley Lake—Via a very comprehensive and thoughtful letter about the fishery surrounding his home town.

Mike Lawson—Last Chance, Idaho—In the back room of his Henry's Fork Anglers fly shop on the east bank of Idaho's famous Henry's Fork River.

Greg Lilly—Bozeman—Between customers and "trick-or-treaters" in his River's Edge fly shop.

Frank Little—On the phone one cold, winter day as he reflected on how it is now and how it was back in the 1930's. Them days are gone forever!

Frank Marcotte—Hamilton—Only twenty feet from the Bitterroot's banks enjoying a wine and cheese lunch at Anglers Roost.

Glen Overton—Libby—A thorough rundown of Kootenai fishing over three cups of coffee and one stick of Wonderwax.

Rick Pasquale—Great Falls—In his comfortable Fly Fisher's Retreat tackle shop under the watchful eye of Max, Rick's handsome and faithful Doberman.

Steve Pauli—Big Timber—As he tied buggy-looking stonefly nymphs in his tidy Sweetcast Angler tackle shop, surrounded by the small forest of peacock quills on his bench.

Terry Ross—Formerly of Fort Smith—In the living room of the author's Colorado home, as he expressed ebullient recollections of his experience as a professional guide on the Bighorn in years past and his anticipation of continued visits there in the future.

Bill Sansom and J. L. Alexander—St. Regis—In J.L's kitchen as he recalled the past and Bill portrayed the present on the Clark Fork.

Rick Smith—Polson—A telephone call on a January day with this serious student of angling and writer of piscatorial prose.

Bob Snyder—Lewistown—While sitting within a hundred feet of 250,000 trout at the Big Spring Trout Hatchery.

Burdick Stone—Silver Star—On the front porch of his lovely, log home next to the Jefferson River that he's fished for half a century.

Tim Tollett—Dillon—As he built a bow string in his Frontier Angler's tackle shop and expressed high praise for the Beaverhead.

Paul Updike—Townsend—While he sorted slides in his photo studio and fly shop near Canyon Ferry Lake.

Suzanne Vernon—Seeley Lake—In the front office of Seeley Lake's weekly newspaper, the "Pathfinder."

Bob Walker—Ennis—With Theo and Leah at their beautiful T-Lazy-B Guest Ranch in the shady hollow next to Jack Creek.

Warren Wiley—Missoula—Under the hanging waders in the north wing of his Streamside Anglers Shop in town, yet near the banks of the Clark Fork River.

Montana Information Sources

Montana Campground Association
P.O. Box 215
West Glacier, Montana 59936

Montana Chamber of Commerce
P.O. Box 1730
Helena, Montana 59624 - Phone: 442-2405

Montana Department of Fish, Wildlife and Parks
1420 E. 6th Ave.
Helena, Montana 59620 - Phone: 444-2535

Montana Historical Society
225 N. Roberts
Helena, Montana 59620 - Phone: 449-3770

Montana Outfitters & Guides Association
P.O. Box 631
Hot Springs, Montana 59845

Travel Montana, Dept. of Commerce
1424 9th Ave.
Helena, Montana 59620 - Phone: 444-2654

Bureau of Land Management
P.O. Box 36800
Billings, Montana 59107 - Phone: 657-6564

U. S. Forest Service
P.O. Box 7669
Missoula, Montana 59807 - Phone: 329-3511

Beaverhead National Forest
P.O. Box 1258
Dillon, Montana 59725 - Phone: 683-3900

Bitterroot National Forest
316 N. Third St.
Hamilton, Montana 59840 - Phone: 363-3131

Custer National Forest
P.O. Box 2556
Billings, Montana 59103 - Phone: 245-4111

Deerlodge National Forest
P.O. Box 400
Butte, Montana 59703 - Phone: 496-3400

Flathead National Forest
P.O. Box 147
Kalispell, Montana 59901 - Phone: 755-5401

Gallatin National Forest
P.O. Box 130
Bozeman, Montana 59715 - Phone: 587-6701

Helena National Forest
Drawer 10014, Federal Office Bldg.
Helena, Montana 59626 - Phone: 449-5201

Kootenai National Forest
Rt. 3, Box 700
Libby, Montana 59923 - Phone: 293-6211

Lewis & Clark National Forest
P.O. Box 871
Great Falls, Montana 59403 - Phone: 727-0901

Lolo National Forest
Bldg. 24, Fort Missoula
Missoula, Montana 59801 - Phone: 329-3750

Bibliography

Alt, David and Hyndman, Donald W., *Roadside Geology of Montana*, Mountain Press Publishing Company, 1986.

Burk, Dale A., *Montana Fishing*, Stoneydale Press, 1983.

Filler, A. W., *Northwest Montana Traveler's Guide*, A. W. Filler Publishing Co., 1985.

Fisher, Hank, *The Floater's Guide to Montana*, Falcon Press Publishing Co., Inc., 1979.

Fothergill, Chuck and Sterling, Bob, *The Wyoming Angling Guide*, Stream Stalker Publishing Co., 1986.

Konizeski, Dick, *The Montanan's Fishing Guide, Vol. I*, Mountain Press Publishing Co., 1986.

Konizeski, Dick, *The Montanan's Fishing Guide, Vol. II*, Mountain Press Publishing Co., 1982.

Marcuson, Pat, *The Beartooth Fishing Guide*, Falcon Press Publishing Co., Inc., 1985.

Sample, Mike, *The Angler's Guide to Montana*, Falcon Press Publishing Co., Inc., 1984.

Stevens, Robert T., Jr. and Story Block Advertising, Inc., *The Northface of Yellowstone National Park*, Robert T. Stevens and Story Block Advertising, Inc., 1983.

Turbak, Gary, *The Traveler's Guide to Montana*, Falcon Press Publishing Co., Inc., 1983.

Van West, Carroll, *A Traveler's Companion to Montana History*, Montana Historical Society Press, 1986.

Index

Wolf Creek Bridge, 162
Woodbine Access, 192
Wraith Hill, 84

Y
Yaak Falls Campground, 204
Yaak, Mt., 204
Yaak River, 127, 204
Yaak River Falls, 132, 204
Yankee Jim Canyon, 206, 207, 208, 209
Yellow Bay, 94
Yellowstone County, 221
Yellowstone Lake, 227, 250, 251, 252
Yellowstone National Park, 3, 12, 105, 113, 138, 147, 148, 151, 152, 153, 154, 205, 206, 207, 208, 216, 218, 223, 254, 256
Yellowstone River, 4, 5, 27, 71, 72, 174, 186, 192, 193, 205, 213, 215, 217, 218, 219, 220, 221, 222, 225, 229, 230, 236, 237, 240, 241, 250, 252, 254
Yellowstone River Trail, 254
Yellowtail Dam, 39, 40, 49
York, Mt., 161
Young's Creek, 100

TREAT YOURSELF—OR A FRIEND—TO THE
ROCKY MOUNTAIN "ANGLING GUIDE" TRILOGY

The Rocky Mountain area is the most popular trout fishing destination in the country and when anglers think of Rocky Mountain fishing, they think of Colorado, Wyoming and Montana. When they want the most comprehensive information available concerning these states, they reach for the Stream Stalker®ANGLING GUIDES.

If the information in this book enhances your enjoyment of fishing and traveling in Montana, you'll enjoy *The Wyoming Angling Guide* and *The Colorado Angling Guide*. These volumes also encompass the major streams and rivers of each respective state. Should they already be in your library, use this handy form to order the Trilogy or single copies as gifts for fishing friends. We'll gladly send signed volumes at your request—either individual copies or as the Trilogy; be sure to so designate on the order form.

Please allow a six week lead-time if you're ordering for special occasions such as birthdays, Christmas or Father's Day.

Send to: (Please print or type)

Name _____

Shipping Address _____

City _____ State _____ Zip _____

_____ Check or M.O. Enclosed _____ MasterCard _____ Visa

Card Account Number _____ Exp Date _____

Signature _____

Qty _____ Colorado Angling Guide @ $27.95 $ _____
     _____ Wyoming Angling Guide @ $27.95 $ _____
     _____ Montana Angling Guide @ $29.95 $ _____
     _____ Trilogy (1 of each state) @ $83.00 $ _____
              Shipping & Handling $ 5.00
              Colo. Residents add 3% tax $ _____

                              TOTAL DUE $ _____

STREAM STALKER®, INC., PO Box 238, Woody Creek, Colorado 81656
(303) 923-4552

PART IV:
River Maps

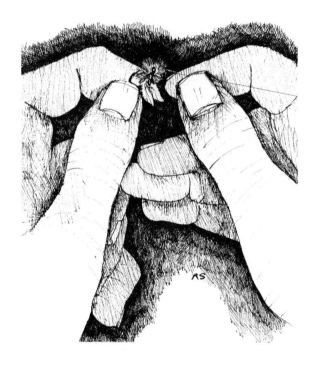

Maps

Use these maps to help you find fishing accesses, camping areas, boat accesses and get a good idea of the length of your float trip, where you are and where you want to be!

Roads are schematic, but rivers and lakes are as accurately portrayed as scale permits. The scale of all the river maps is one-half inch equals one mile, or about the distance between the terminals of the semi-circle on the north arrows.

Legend

Interstate, or controlled access highway	
Paved arterial highway	
Improved, maintained secondary road	
Unimproved, two track, 4 WD road	
Hiking trail	
Developed camping facilities with potable water	▲
Undeveloped camping facilities, no water	△
Developed fishing access with boat ramp	BEAVERHEAD
Fishing access, no boat ramp	
Major community, full services	
Small community, settlement or developed area, limited services	
Geographical features	

288

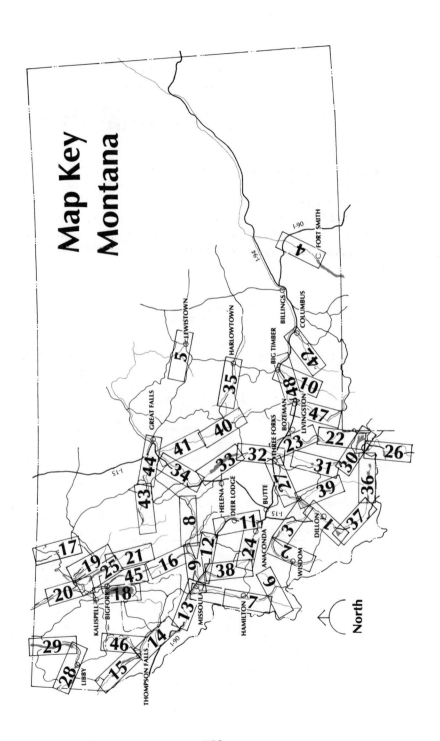

Map Key
Montana

North

Map Key
Yellowstone National Park

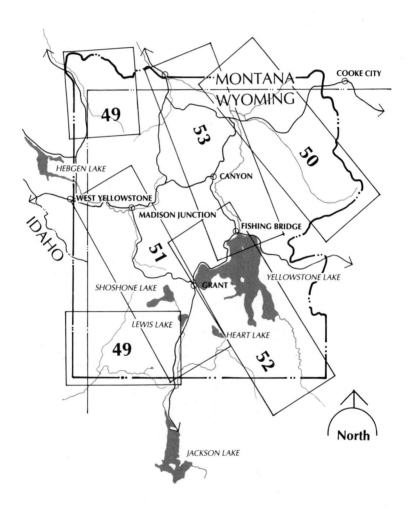

Montana Mileage Chart

From \ To	Big Timber	Billings	Bozeman	Butte	Cooke City	Deer Lodge	Dillon	East Glacier	Eureka	Gardiner	Great Falls	Hamilton	Hardin	Helena	Kalispell	Lewistown	Libby	Livingston	Missoula	Polson	Thompson Falls	Three Forks	Townsend	Virginia City	West Glacier	West Yellowstone
Anaconda	170	251	109	27	244	26	78	267	276	188	171	127	297	82	212	262	293	135	103	169	203	80	106	98	234	177
Big Timber		81	61	143	144	183	173	313	410	88	172	291	127	150	346	101	435	35	262	328	362	91	118	128	368	142
Billings			142	224	125	264	254	360	484	169	172	372	46	224	420	128	509	116	339	405	439	192	209	128	415	217
Bozeman				82	135	122	112	282	355	79	177	230	188	95	291	162	380	26	201	267	301	165	63	67	313	89
Butte					217	40	65	251	290	161	153	148	270	64	226	235	309	108	119	185	219	53	93	71	248	150
Cooke City						257	234	417	490	56	279	365	171	230	426		515	109	336	402	436	165	198	177	448	92
Deer Lodge							91	241	250	201	145	126	310	56	186	244	269	148	79	145	179	93	88	111	208	190
Dillon								307	341	191	209	163	300	120	277	265	360	138	170	236	270	219	83	109	299	142
East Glacier									131	361	141	239	406	187	87	246	176	308	192	126	195	253	219	308	55	362
Eureka										434	272	226	530	260	64	377	69	381	179	113	159	326	292	361	76	435
Gardiner											223	309	215	174	370	189	459	53	280	346	380	109	142	139	392	54
Great Falls												216	265	89	228	105	317	170	169	235	269	155	121	210	196	264
Hamilton													418	162	162	321	237	256	47	113	147	201	194	219	184	298
Hardin														270	466	168	555	162	385	451	485	218	238	255	461	263
Helena															196	188	285	121	115	181	215		32	121	218	175
Kalispell																333	89	317	115	49	108	262	228	297	32	371
Lewistown																	422	136	274	340	374	190	156	229	301	243
Libby																		406	190	138	90	351	317	380	121	459
Livingston																			227	293	327	56	89	93	339	107
Missoula																				66	100	172	147	190	137	269
Polson																					91	238	213	256	71	335
Thompson Falls																						272	247	290	140	369
Three Forks																							34	62	284	110
Townsend																								90	250	143
Virginia City																									319	85
West Glacier																										393